Whoever You *Thought* You Were…You're A Jew!

by Ken Biegeleisen

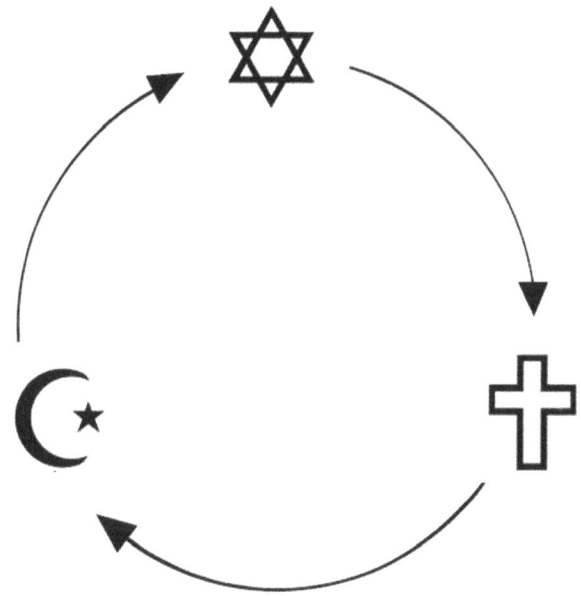

A blueprint for world peace…under God

www.Ark-Of-Salvation.org

Copyright © 2007 by Ken Biegeleisen

www.Ark-Of-Salvation.org

All rights reserved. No part of this book may be reproduced or transmitted in any form or by any means, electronic or mechanical, including photocopying, recording or by any information storage and retrieval system, without the written permission of the author.

If you understand the meanings of these two Bible passages, you don't have to read this book:

"...whosoever shall do the will of my Father which is in heaven, the same is my brother, and sister, and mother.
                                                                Matthew 12:50

"...in the last days it shall come to pass, that the mountain of the house of the LORD shall be established in the top of the mountains, ... and people shall flow unto it. And many nations shall come, and say, Come, and let us go up to the mountain of the LORD,...<u>all people will walk every one in the name of his god</u>, and we will walk in the name of the LORD, our God, forever and ever."
                                                                (Micah 4:1-5).

Pronunciation Note

In various places throughout this book you will find instances of the letter "h" with a dot underneath it:

$$\d{h}$$

This is a common means of indicating the Hebrew-Arabic guttural sound. It is a harsh sound, which may be likened to the clearing of the throat. This sound is not found in the English language, and there is therefore no English letter to represent it.

Contents

Summary and Conclusions 1

1 The Beginning 7

2 The Covenant...With Whom Was It Made? 11

3 The Father of Oriental Religion Was God... 20

4 Where is "David" Now? 66

5 Yeshua Moshiaḥ (Jesus Christ) 73

6 Islam. Part I. History of the Covenant Between God and Man 117

7 Islam. Part II. The Christian Councils 123

8 Islam. Part III. Life of Muḥammad 134

9 Islam. Part IV. Jihad. 146

10 The Question of Race 167

11 What is the Relationship between "Enlightenment" and "God"? 187

12 A Symbolic Representation of the World's Religions 204

13 The *New* 'New World Order' 211

14 Epilogue: The Ark and the Third Temple 234

Appendix 1 —Is Ishmael *really* a "wild ass"? 245

Appendix 2 —The Covenant between God and Abraham:
   With *whom* was it made? 252

About the book, and about the author 261

Index 263

Summary and Conclusions

The LORD has already revealed the solutions to all problems based upon religious, ethnic and racial hatred. All praise to the LORD.

Of course, the ultimate solution to every problem — though not likely to be seen anytime soon — is the coming of a Deliverer. This Deliverer is known to Jews and Christians as *Messiah*, although he is also expected by many other religions, and called by many other names. Messiah is he who has the God-given power to show God to the people. His works are all good, and his authority is complete.

But Messiah is not here now. In the meantime, the moral vacuum in society is being rapidly filled by a world-wide banking dictatorship, often referred to as the "New World Order". Although its advocates try to persuade us that it will be a "paradise", the truth is diametrically opposite: Within this "New World Order" over 95% of people will be wretched serfs in the global equivalent of some horrid medieval-style feudal manor. Why? Because the amount of money in the world keeps increasing, but the number of hands holding that money keeps *decreasing*. If this process is not curbed — *and soon* — it will go forward to completion, and then it will be irreversible.

The minute the door slams on our freedom, we, the children of Adam and Eve, will be suddenly and rudely awakened from our 6,000-year moral slumber, but it will be too late. In desperation we will rebel, and war will break out, as envisioned by countless science fiction writers over the past century. The nature of the war is that a vast impoverished army of peasants — *i.e.,* **you** — poorly armed or unarmed entirely, will fight against a tiny ruling class which has the advantages of unlimited funding and ultra-deadly high-tech weaponry. This war — if you allow things to go that far — will *never end,* but will spread across the universe, as space travel slowly and painfully advances, spreading our mental illness beyond the stars.

This is not what *will* happen; only what *might* happen. We have the power to stop it, because the LORD, in His mercy, has given us a solution. It is revealed, in concise form, in a rarely-quoted verse from the Book of Micah in the Hebrew Bible:

Summary and Conclusions

"...in the last days it shall come to pass, that the mountain of the house of the LORD shall be established in the top of the mountains, ... and people shall flow unto it. And many nations shall come, and say, Come, and let us go up to the mountain of the LORD,...<u>*all people will walk every one in the name of his god*</u>, and we will walk in the name of the LORD, our God, forever and ever."

(Micah 4:1-5).

"Mountain of the LORD", insofar as it refers to a place, can only mean Jerusalem. Note that it says "all people", not just some. And it says all will walk in the name of *"his god"*, not in the name of the God of Israel.

Nevertheless, since it is the Hebrew Bible alone which provides the basis for this outpouring of religious tolerance and unity, it is therefore the Jewish religion which, in some way, must provide the framework within which Micah's prophecy is fulfilled. This gives rise to the title of the present book, "Whoever You *Thought* You Were...You're A Jew!". As used here, however, the word "Jew" is a reference to something larger and more encompassing than the title might suggest. Furthermore, the purpose of this book is not to turn everyone into a "Jew" in the usual sense of the word, but rather to make people better members of the religions they already belong to.

Similar conclusions can be reached from the following passage in the New Testament, where Yeshua, called Jesus in the English language, said...

> **"...<u>*whosoever*</u> shall do the will of my Father which is in heaven, the same is my brother, and sister, and mother.**
>
> Matthew 12:50

...demonstrating that salvation is not for a special group, but for "whosoever...", and that the criterion for salvation is not a particular church membership, or even a particular form of worship, but only that the *will* of our Father in heaven be done. This means that certain acts of thought and deed must be carried out.

Note that there is no mention in the passage as to *which* religion shall promote these acts, or what body of teachings shall be used to encourage that the acts be done. Jesus' brotherhood may, therefore, include members of religions such as Buddhism, which makes no mention of God at all. Is a person nominally "Buddhist", but who *does* the Will of our Father, not better than a person nominally "Christian" who *rebels* against that Will?

In order to see the relationships between different religions, it is necessary to stand outside all of them, because attachment to any one of them breeds contempt for all the others. Although not by choice, I do so stand outside all of them. Therefore, I have nothing to lose from speaking the truth.

The truth about Judaism, Christianity and Islam is illustrated diagrammatically by the symbol on the cover of this book:

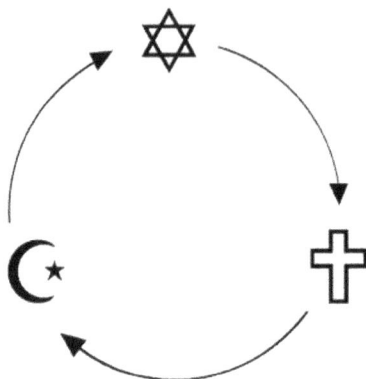

The logic of this ordering of religious icons, and of the directions in which the arrows point, is revealed in Chapter 12. For now, it is sufficient to state that all three of the religions depicted in this symbol are incomplete, and no one of them could exist without the other two.

Not all the world's great religions can be fit into the above symbol. Yet the truth about the others (mainly the "Oriental" religions; Buddhism, Taoism, Jainism, etc.), is that they can be proven to have arisen from acts of the very same God who established Judaism, Christianity and Islam. Although this can be directly demonstrated from the Bible, the most compelling proof — which is in fact *so* compelling as to be incontrovertible — is an indirect proof; namely a *mathematical* proof, strange though that may seem. This proof is given in Chapter 3, to which the interested reader can turn immediately if the proposition seems startling.

I also said at the outset that the LORD has provided us with the solution to all problems which arise from racial hatred. The truth is that the solution involves no more than an unbiased reading of world history, much of which is not taught in western schools. Such a reading reveals the answer: God raises up civilizations without regard to race. Could it possibly be that simple? Yes, it is that simple. That fact that "black" culture vastly surpassed "white" culture for many centuries is not really news, but perhaps the telling

Summary and Conclusions

of the story by me, a "white" man, will make the history more accessible to people who don't know about it, or who have heard of it, but just can't believe it.

These various principles, taken together, lead to the conclusion that a religious organization I refer to as a "Council of Priests" can be formed, and that it can provide an effective remedy, or counterbalance to the world's great disease: the almost unshakeable faith most people have in the power of money to "save".

The Council of Priests has a structure and an authority which is ultimately derived from the Bible. It alone will have the moral strength and the wherewithal to stand up to the power of global banking, by means of its own focusing and concentrating of the collective *spiritual* power of all the churches created by our God. The Council of Priests is the logical outcome of the principles contained in this book, and is described close to the end (Chapter 13, "The **New** 'New World Order' ").

Once this is all accomplished, the pathway is cleared for the greatest spiritual act in modern history: the proclamation of the nation of Greater Israel, spoken of repeatedly in the Torah, and extending from the Nile to the Euphrates. This includes the return of the Ark of the Covenant to Jerusalem, and the construction of the Third Temple. Impossible? Not at all. As I said at the outset, God has provided. All praise to God.

Once you have read this book, you will be faced with a rather stark choice: either to believe what it says and proposes, or — since there are no alternative proposals I know of — to spinelessly acquiesce to the New World Order and its "god" of Gold; to hope and pray that you will be among the 5% who have the money, and not the 95% impoverished, who will face only perpetual Hell-on-Earth. This latter possibility is illustrated in Figure 1.

The better way, the "**New** 'New World Order' ", under the God of Abraham, is described in the 14 chapters which follow.

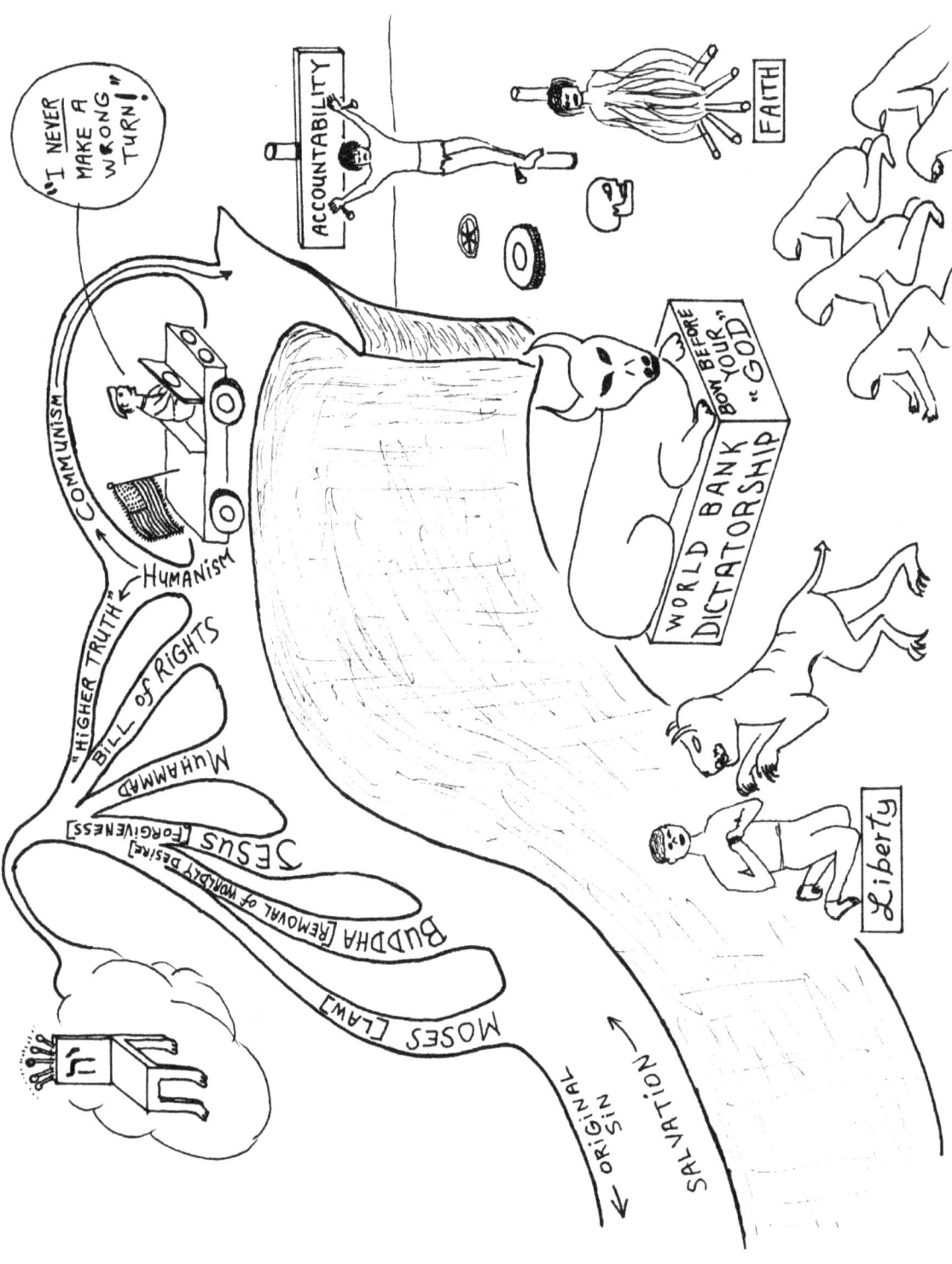

Figure 1. The New World Order

Summary and Conclusions

This almost inexcusably amateurish drawing, by the author himself, is justified only in that it takes advantage of the old adage, "one picture is worth a thousand words", to concisely illustrate the current moral state of the world. The picture portrays an arrogant, over-confident soldier in a jeep, informing us that he "never makes a wrong turn". Really? Then why is he heading, full-speed, toward a dangerous cliff?

The pathway he is on begins with Original Sin (to the left of the drawing) and is *supposed* to end with Salvation, which is portrayed as the throne of the King, God. Many paths to God are shown (in the order of their historical appearance), but our overly-confident soldier has bypassed all of them.

Although the religions depicted by the paths shown may have numerous followers, in some cases a billion or more, the fact remains that we live in a world with over *6 billion* people. This means that each religion shown represents only a small minority of the worlds total population, and that the vast majority of people, like the soldier in the drawing, have *rejected* each and every one of them.

We have even bypassed secular humanist pathways to salvation, the existence of which are acknowledged in the drawing. The American "Bill of Rights" is a document of almost religious intensity, but an examination of the events of the latter 20th century reveals that its formerly-sacred rights now exist on paper only. Likewise, the pathway of "Higher Truth", as exemplified by the teachings of philosophers such as Socrates or Confucius — pathways which make little or no mention of God — may nevertheless also lead eventually to His throne, if pursued to their logical conclusions. Alas, however, even they have been bypassed.

Communism, and any other form of Marxist-socialist thought, is portrayed here as a false path, leading only back to the main road.

If all these pathways to Salvation are decisively rejected, the only thing that remains will be the spiritual underworld of the drawing: the 'New World Order' global banking dictatorship. When our driver finally plunges over the cliff, from which there is no return, he will find himself in a place where all are compelled to bow to a Golden Calf. Anyone who speaks of liberty, faith, or accountability will be treated as shown. The only "liberty" which will exist will be the "freedom" to pay tribute. The only accountability will be *your* accountability to your bank Lords, in return for which, however, they will acknowledge *no* accountability to you. And the only faith remaining will be a firm belief that things will never get better. In other words, the 'New World Order', as currently construed by its advocates, will be Hell-on-earth.

Chapter 1

The Beginning

Thus said the LORD:

> **" 'Behold, the man is become as one of us, to know good and evil'...therefore the LORD God sent him forth from the garden of Eden...and He placed at the east of the garden of Eden Cherubims, and a flaming sword which turned every way, to keep the way of the tree of life."**
> **(Genesis 3:22-24).**

This passage, which the foolish dismiss lightly as being a "legend" of no consequence, is actually laden with meaning at more levels than can even be comprehended by the human mind.

For our current purpose, which is to try to understand what God's plan is for the world we live in today, it is sufficient to understand that we brought upon ourselves the wrath of God, whereby we were removed from a place where everything was provided fully-formed, and put into a place where nothing is provided at all, except as raw material.

Everything we want done, we must do ourselves, or—God forbid—get slaves to do for us.

It is explicitly understood by the majority of orthodox sects of Judaism, Christianity, Islam and Buddhism that we are all descended from people who have *fallen* spiritually, and that we are born with a legacy of guilt. Incredibly, none of us needs to be taught what guilt is. We all know when we're wrong.

That's because the primordial form of guilt is rebellion against God, and we all share it. The various forms of guilt we experience in this world are reflections and permutations of the guilt we experienced in the beginning, which we have known of all along. But we haven't yet benefited from the knowledge.

The non-believer, of course, rejects every part of this, and proudly proclaims that man is born "pure", an accident of "nature" resulting from random collisions of chemicals in some primordial soup. According to this false and dangerous view, we shall, in the very near future, know "everything" and become "gods" ourselves.

The evidence usually presented for this is of an apparently "scientific" variety. Nowadays, for example, physicists say that everything is made of "quarks", and that all the quarks have been identified. Therefore, we shall soon know "everything". There will be no further need to talk of, believe in, or pay homage to any "god".

Of course, only a century ago, the same thing was said upon the discovery of the *atom*, which was—almost without delay—smashed into so many pieces you'd think scientists would have learned something from that. They didn't.

If there's nothing wrong with you, then you don't need any help. If the world is perfect, then there's no need to change anything. If science can distinguish between good and evil from the chemicals thereof, then you don't need either churches, bibles, or laws. But do you believe any of these things?

I hope not.

Most of us understand that we are in spiritual peril all the time, and that we need help. How did it start? Other than the Bible, that silly book of "legends", we have no clue. It's been said that most people lead "lives of quiet desperation". In your hour of desperation, the "Big Bang" will not raise you up.

So what does the Bible tell us? It tells us that an evil power, described as a "serpent", counseled us to rebel against God. What was the form of the rebellion? God advised against eating from a certain tree, called the "Tree of Knowledge of Good and Evil". Why? Because it imparted to us knowledge that we were not able to cope with, and because it caused us to die. The serpent pointed out that we would *not* die, which was a half-truth. The fruit of this tree does not, in fact, kill quickly like poison. But it kills. Our deaths are a slow, agonizing process.

This was an "easy sell" for the serpent. All he had to do was to show Eve the fruit of the tree, which she had quite evidently ignored previously:

> **And when [Eve] saw that the tree was good for food, and that it was a delight to the eyes, and that the tree was to be desired to make one wise, she took of the fruit thereof, and did eat; and she gave also unto her husband with her, and he did eat.**
>
> **And the eyes of them both were opened, and they knew that they were naked...**
>
> **(Genesis 3:6-7)**

This passage is certainly known to Jews and Christians, but it is not discussed much.

Nevertheless, the message of this passage has become the bedrock of the "Eastern" religions—Buddhism, Hinduism, Jainism and Taoism. Taking Buddhism as the prototype, we may note that Buddhism does not speak of any God. But it speaks of an entity called "Enlightenment", whose description is curiously similar to the Western description of God. Enlightenment is described as being: unique, supreme, infinite, eternal, good, and nearly impossible to reach.

How does one attain Enlightenment? By removal of worldly desire. "Worldly desire" means an excessive and unnecessary craving for things such as those mentioned above in the quote from Genesis 3:6-7: good food, pretty sights, and practical knowledge. Buddha taught that mankind was *seduced* by worldly desire a long time ago, and is now in its clutches. He never addressed the question of where, when or how this happened, and he cautioned his followers to refrain from speculating about it, warning them that if they did so, they would waste their lives, and die of old age before they figured out any of the answers.

So Buddhism is a process for the removal of excessive or unnecessary desire for worldly objects of distraction such as food, beauty, and practical knowledge. Now look again at our Biblical passage, and see whether or not you can discern therein the Buddhist concept of the fall from grace:

> **And when [Eve] saw that the tree was *good for food,* and that it was a *delight to the eyes,* and that the tree was to be *desired to make one wise,* she took of the fruit thereof, and did eat; and she gave also unto her husband with her, and he did eat.**
>
> **And the eyes of them both were opened, and they knew that they were naked...**
>
> **(Genesis 3:6-7)**

It seems that Adam and Eve's fall did not result from a direct rebellion against God for its own sake, but rather from a weakness of will, wherein we allowed ourselves to be seduced by the lure of worldly pleasures, all of which are, in the final analysis, nothing more than mirages.

So our separation from the one enduring reality, God, came about because of our yielding to a desire for the transient. In our Western religions, we strive mightily to re-establish our connection with God the creator, and think very little about removing our desire for the physical world. In the East, we strive mightily to remove our desire for the physical world, but think very little about our relationship with the creator thereof.

In the End Times, or Messianic days to come, we of the West will admit that we have indeed succumbed to the lure of worldly desire, and begin to take steps to control that desire. We of the East will recognize that there was indeed a Creator, and begin to make an effort to learn something of His nature.

Therefore, the Buddhists (and Hindus and Jains and Taoists) will indeed come to Jerusalem, but, as we saw previously, they will come in the name of *their* God. No one is "right" or "wrong" here. God is simply too large to be encompassed by the belief system of any one church, or even by the collective beliefs of all 9 churches we shall shortly begin to make mention of.

Chapter 2

The Covenant...
With Whom Was It Made?

God said to Abraham:

> "Get thee out of thy country, and from thy kindred, and from thy father's house, unto a land that I will show thee. And I will make of thee a great nation, and I will bless thee, and make thy name great; and thou shalt be a blessing. And I will bless them that bless thee, and curse him that curseth thee: and in thee shall <u>all the families of the earth</u> be blessed."
> (Genesis 12:1)

So what's our problem? It says God's blessing will be upon "*all* the families of the earth". Why all the wars?

The problem is that God said he would make Abraham a "great nation", and we disagree about who this "great nation" is. Each of us claims that the "great nation" is *ourselves,* and then we proceed to do our best to exterminate everyone else.

All right. Let's suppose, for the sake of argument, that it really *matters* who the "great nation" is. Of course, in reality, it doesn't. But let's pretend. So? Who's this "great nation"?

The answer is: The "great nation is the one which entered into God's Covenant". Do we know who that is? Not exactly, but we have some data in our possession. Let's look at it.

The Covenant defined

It is made clear in the Bible that God was pleased with Abraham, and that this, broadly speaking, was because Abraham believed in God, and acted accordingly. God does not care what you loudly proclaim from the lecture podium, or what answers you give silently in a written examination. He cares what you *do.* He put Abraham to the test, and Abraham *did* all the right things.

Nevertheless, the Covenant between God and Abraham was more specific than that. Here's how the Bible defines the Covenant. God said:

> "And I will establish my Covenant between me and thee and thy seed after thee in their generations for an everlasting Covenant, to be a God unto thee, and to thy seed after thee.
>
> And I will give unto thee, and to thy seed after thee, the land wherein thou art a stranger, all the land of Canaan, for an everlasting possession; and I will be their God...
>
> ...This is my Covenant, which ye shall keep, between me and you and thy seed after thee; Every man child among you shall be circumcised.
>
> And ye shall circumcise the flesh of your foreskin; and it shall be a token of the Covenant betwixt me and you...
>
> ...and my Covenant shall be in your flesh for an everlasting Covenant."
> **(Genesis 17:7-13)**

Note that there is a territorial inheritance here—the land of Canaan—roughly equivalent to the modern state of Israel. There is, at this very moment, a 4,000 year-old land war going on over this disputed territory. The war will not end until we come to an agreement as to precisely with *whom* this Covenant was made. Therefore, whether we like it or not, we must find an answer to this question.

The passage states that circumcision is both a "token" of the Covenant, and also *the Covenant itself*. After receiving this message from God, Abraham, without delay, circumcised himself, his son Ishmael, and the men of his household.

Abraham was 90 years old when he was circumcised, and his first-born son, Ishmael, was 13. Nine years later, Abraham's second son, Isaac, was born. Isaac was circumcised at the age of 8 days.

Jews, to this day, consider Isaac to be the one, and *only* one, through whom God's Covenant has come down to us in our day. In remembrance of Isaac, Jews still circumcise their sons on the 8th day.

Some Christians, embracing a doctrine known as "replacement theory", claim that God *cancelled* his Covenant with the Jews because of their wicked ways. They say the Covenant now resides exclusively with *them*, yet they don't circumcise their sons. Their "official" position is that belief in Christ is the "equivalent" of circumcision.

Muslims agree that Allah cancelled his Covenant with the Jews, but they also regard both Jews *and* Christians as "infidels". Furthermore, they believe *Ishmael* to be the one—and *only* one—through whom Allah's Covenant has come down to us in our day. Muslims, in remembrance of Ishmael, circumcise their sons at the age of 13 (ouch!)[1].

It is quite evident that the story of Abraham and his two favorite sons, Ishmael and Isaac (yes, he had others), needs to be read and understood, if the world today is to be understood.

So here's the story. Abraham married his half-sister Sarah, but she was barren. In those days, property was inherited only by male offspring, and a woman who was childless stood to receive no inheritance. Therefore Sarah decided to try to get "builded up"[2] by giving Abraham her maid, the Egyptian woman Hagar, as a second wife.

Since Hagar was Sarah's "property", Hagar's children would also be Sarah's property. Sarah would thereby be "builded up". This, at any rate, was the "letter of the law" of that day.

But when Hagar conceived and gave birth to Ishmael, she evidently began to rebel against her role as Sarah's servant, and she began to act as an equal. Sarah complained bitterly about this to Abraham, who advised her to do as she saw fit. Without going into detail, the Bible reports that Sarah treated Hagar "harshly"; so much so that she fled.

In Genesis 16:7 we read that "the angel of the LORD found her by a fountain of water in the wilderness, by the fountain in the way to Shur", which was located in the vicinity of Egypt. In other words, Hagar, the Egyptian, having been expelled from the tent of Abraham, was heading home.

What the angel said to her in the wilderness is the most maliciously mis-translated passage in the Bible. To understand this we need to consider some important facts about the Hebrew language.

Hebrew consonants and vowels

Hebrew originally had *no vowels*, only consonants. The written language was therefore merely a form of shorthand—only a clue as to what the speaker actually said.

---

[1] Acquiring precise information about Muslim circumcision is difficult. The Qur'an makes no mention of it, and the practice is far from universal in Islam. Although Ishmael was circumcised at age 13, it seems that nowadays, the procedure, when performed at all, is done at various ages ranging from 13 down to infancy.

[2] These are Sarah's actual words in the Hebrew Bible (Genesis 16:2). In the King James English Bible, the words which actually mean "builded up" are translated, correctly in principle only, as "have children".

The system worked better than one might imagine. Most of the time—like 95% or more—the correct meaning could be deduced from the context. But, in such a system, problems will inevitably arise.

Allow me to illustrate in English. If English had only consonants, then you couldn't tell whether a person ate "grains" or "greens", since, in writing, they would both be the same: "GRNS". Or consider this: a "bit", a "bet", a "bat" and a "boat" would all look exactly the same in print: "BT".

How odd, that God gave us the Bible in such an ambiguous language as Hebrew, where we can't be 100% sure what the text actually says in difficult passages.

Or maybe it isn't so odd. Maybe He wants us to exercise judgment. Maybe He's testing us. *You'll now get a chance to participate in this test.*

Vowels were added to the Hebrew language during the early Christian era, by a group of Rabbis called the *Masoretes*. The vowels which they added, and which are used to this day, consisted of dots and dashes attached to the letters of the Hebrew alphabet, which, as we have said, were (and still are) *all consonants*. How can we know that the Masoretic vowels were correct? We can't! We're supposed to take their word for it.

Myth of the "wild ass"[3]

In the case of the following passage from Genesis, the one I described above as "the most maliciously mis-translated in the Bible", you can take *my* word for it that the Masoretes erred, or worse. Here's how it reads in English:

> **"And [the angel of the LORD] said 'Hagar, Sarai's[4] maid, whence camest thou? And whither wilt thou go?' And she said, 'I flee from the face of my mistress Sarai'.**
>
> **And the angel of the LORD said unto her, 'Return to thy mistress, and submit thyself under her hands'.**
>
> **And the angel of the LORD said unto her, 'I will multiply thy seed exceedingly, that it shall not be numbered for multitude'.**

---

[3] The grammatical arguments concerning the myth of the "wild ass" cannot be fully laid out without resorting to Hebrew. These arguments may be read in their entirety in Appendix I.

[4] "Sarai" was Sarah's original name; at about this time God changed it to "Sarah", which means "Princess".

> **And the angel of the LORD said unto her, 'Behold, thou are with child, and shalt bear a son, and shalt call his name Ishmael[5]; because the LORD hath heard thy affliction'.**
>
> **'And he will be a wild ass of a man; his hand will be against every man, and every man's hand against him...'"**
>
> (Genesis 16:8-12)

What's wrong with this passage? Is there not a disturbingly *disjunctive* quality to it? What sort of God would send all these words of comfort to a suffering woman and her son, and then top them off with **"and he will be a *wild ass of a man*...."**? Does that sound "comforting" to you?

If we look at the Hebrew which is interpreted "wild ass", we find a three-letter word whose spelling corresponds closely to the English spelling "PRH". Remember that at the time these words were written, Hebrew had *no vowels.* So how do we translate it? That is, *what vowels should we add?* The Masoretes decided to vowel it as follows: "PEREH", which indeed means "wild ass".

But it could just as well have been voweled "POREH", which means "fruitful". Which vowels fit the context best? You decide.

There's more. The phrase "his hand will be *against* every man, and every man's hand *against* him" is the most **un**likely possible interpretation of the Hebrew. According to the basic rules of Hebrew grammar, the correct reading is "his hand will be *with* every man, and every man's hand will be *with* him."

This gives us a completely new translation of the above passage from Genesis 16:

> "And the angel of the LORD said unto her, 'I will multiply thy seed exceedingly, that it shall not be numbered for multitude'...
>
> ...'And he will be a <u>fruitful</u> man; his hand will be <u>with</u> every man, and every man's hand <u>with</u> him...' "

You, dear reader, have every right in the world to accept the translation you believe to be correct, because there is *no way to know what the original vowels were*. Consider yourself to be in a court of law. You are the jury, and the facts have been placed before you. It is now in your power to render a decision, and a judgment. Which version seems to you to make the most sense? Is it

"I will multiply thy seed exceedingly.....and he will be a fruitful man...:"

Or is it the Masoretic version:

---

[5] The name "Ishmael" is derived from the Hebrew verb "shamah", which means "to hear", and from the ancient Semitic name for God, "El". It means "God will hear".

"I will multiply thy seed exceedingly....and he will be a *wild ass...*"

Which makes the most sense? Which fits best into the context of the passage? Clearly the first. It's logical and consistent. Moreover, it honors Ishmael, the founder of Islam, and therefore promotes peace in Israel. The second version is disjointed and illogical. It is an insult to the founder of Islam, and therefore promotes war.

In fact, the "wild ass" translation is nothing more than a bad joke. Is this what the world needs now?

Does it matter?

The Jewish child, at an early and psychologically defenseless age, is introduced to Ishmael—and therefore to Islam—by the reading of this passage. Let us reason together: If every Muslim belongs to a religion whose founder was a "wild ass", then how can there be peace in the Middle East, unless all such "animals" are driven out of the Holy Land?

This is, therefore, no laughing matter, or a matter to be brushed aside lightly.

Note also that some Christians[6], whose hatred of Islam exceeds even their hatred of Jews, have blindly accepted the Masoretic "wild ass" translation, because it gives them an excuse to hate and kill. How much longer do we have to put up with this?

With Whom Was the Covenant Made?[7]

With whom was the Covenant made? There's a fast answer to this question: The Covenant was made with Abraham and his seed. Remember Genesis Chapter 17, where God said:

---

[6] I have already been faulted for making this comment. It is true that the last century has seen a marked diminution of Christian antisemitism, and a corresponding increase in love for the Jewish people. I'm not sure, however, that this has extended to Islam, and I have not, as of the time of this writing, met a single Jew or Christian — *not one* — who does not believe that Ishmael is a "wild ass".

[7] A complete Hebrew-English discussion of the fine points of grammar in the biblical definition of the Covenant between God and man may be found in Appendix 2 at the end of this book. I have attempted to make the discussion accessible to non-Hebrew readers by transliterating the Hebrew into English characters.

> "And I will establish my Covenant between me and thee and thy seed after thee in their generations for an everlasting Covenant, to be a God unto thee, and to thy seed after thee.
>
> And I will give unto thee, and to thy seed after thee, the land wherein thou art a stranger, all the land of Canaan, for an everlasting possession; and I will be their God..."

It certainly would appear to be the case that *all* offspring of Abraham are included in this Covenant. But people arrogantly disagree about this—as if God might care what they think.

When Abraham was 100 years old, and Sarah was 90, she finally conceived, as had been prophesied earlier by the LORD. In accordance with this prophecy, they named the child *Isaac,* and circumcised him on the 8th day of his life.

Which son would be heir to the Covenant? Isaac or Ishmael?

Jews say "Isaac". Why? Partly because Isaac is perceived by Jews as having been 100% "Jewish", but Ishmael only "half-Jewish", having been the son of an Egyptian mother.

But more importantly, the Bible—at least when read in English translation—appears to contain text which lends support to the Jewish/Christian belief that the Covenant was made *exclusively* with Isaac. In the days before his birth, at which time Abraham had only one son, Ishmael, God said to Abraham:

> "As for Sarai thy wife....I will bless her, and give thee a son also of her: yea, I will bless her, and she shall be a mother of nations: kings of people shall be of her".
>
> (Genesis 17:15-16)

Then Abraham said to God:

> "O that Ishmael might live before thee!"

...to which God responded:

> "Sarah thy wife shall bear thee a son indeed; and thou shalt call his name Isaac: and I will establish my Covenant with him for an everlasting Covenant, and with his seed after him.
>
> And as for Ishmael, I have heard thee: Behold, I have blessed him, and will make him fruitful, and will multiply him exceedingly; twelve princes shall he beget, and I will make him a great nation.
>
> **BUT** my Covenant will I establish with Isaac, which Sarah shall bear unto thee at this set time in the next year."
>
> (Genesis 17:19-21)

The Covenant...With Whom Was It Made?

You've got to admit that there's a certain ambiguity here. After all, just a few lines above we saw that God said of Sarah, referring to her son-to-be, Isaac, that **"she [would] be a mother of nations: kings of people [would] be of her"**. Now we see that God says pretty much the same thing of Hagar, through Ishmael: **"Twelve princes shall he beget, and I will make him a great nation"**. It sure sounds like Isaac and Ishmael are getting the same deal.

Yet there's a sense of exclusivity in the language used here to describe the Covenant with Isaac. We must take care, however, because the apparent sense may arise from a misunderstanding of the text. When God says of Isaac, **"I will establish my Covenant with him for an everlasting Covenant"**—which God *never specifically says* about Ishmael—one must keep in mind that up to that time, the Covenant could only have existed for *Ishmael*, since Isaac hadn't yet been born. Therefore, this statement: **"I will establish my Covenant with [Isaac] for an everlasting Covenant"**, which Jews (*and* Christians) would like to think of as an *exclusive* Covenant, may have merely been a *reminder* that the Covenant had indeed *already been made* with Ishmael as the natural right of the first-born, and that it should not be assumed, simply because Isaac was second-born, that he did not *share* in it.

The difficulties increase, however, when we read the statement **"BUT my Covenant will I establish with *Isaac*, which Sarah shall bear unto thee at this set time in the next year"**. This appears to be compelling evidence of an *exclusive* Covenant between God and Isaac, but again we've got to be careful about the language. The apparent exclusivity arises from the word "BUT". This is read, by Jews (and Christians), *as if* it said **"But...my Covenant will I establish with *Isaac*, and NOT with Ishmael"**. However, it doesn't say that! In fact, the word "BUT" is not even present in the Hebrew text!

In the place where we seek the word "but", we find only a *prefix:* a single Hebrew letter, **"vav"**, the 6th letter of the Hebrew alphabet.

Please pay attention, because you're going to see that the outcome of a 4,000 year-old war may be hanging on the meaning of a single letter!

When used as a prefix, the letter **vav,** read **"va-"**, usually means **"and"**, although there are other possible meanings. According to modern Hebrew dictionaries, the other meanings include: "also", "then", "yet" and..."but".

The phrase translated **"*But* my Covenant..."**, can therefore be read a number of different ways, depending on how you choose to translate the prefix **"va-"**. The leading alternatives are:

> "*And* (or *also*) My Covenant will I establish with Isaac..."
> "*But* My Covenant will I establish with Isaac..."

Either of these readings would be a grammatically valid interpretation of this verse.

The first of them employs the more common reading of the prefix "va-", giving **"*And* My Covenant I will establish with Isaac..."** (or **"*Also* My Covenant I will establish with Isaac..."**). This implies that there is *already* a Covenant established with Ishmael, and now an *additional* one shall be established with Isaac. The Biblical text might in this instance be translated:

> "...And as for Ishmael, I have heard thee: Behold, I have blessed him, and will make him fruitful, and will multiply him exceedingly; twelve princes shall he beget, and I will make him a great nation.
>
> <u>ALSO</u> my Covenant will I establish with Isaac, which Sarah shall bear unto thee at this set time in the next year."

The implication here is that fruitfulness, multiplication and greatness, which are promised to Ishmael because of his acceptance of the Covenant, shall now *also* be given to Isaac.

The second reading, **"*But* My Covenant will I establish with Isaac..."**, implies an exclusive Covenant with Isaac only. This is the reading which appears in virtually every printed Bible today.

But which reading is correct? We can't say from the grammar. Either of the above readings is a valid interpretation of the Hebrew.

From the context, however, it seems incontrovertible that God made a Covenant with *all* the descendants of Abraham. This certainly includes Ishmael. Therefore, his spiritual descendants, the Muslims, will not be thrust out of Israel, now or ever.

At the same time, it must be pointed out that nothing whatsoever in the text even remotely suggests that there is any lack of a Covenant between God and Isaac, the spiritual forerunner of today's Jews. Therefore, neither will Jews be thrust out of Israel anymore, now or ever.

If you have followed the above arguments then you know now that the trouble in Israel today does not arise from the Bible. By way of preview, I'll tell you that it doesn't arise from the Qur'an either. As we shall see, it arises from love of money, the false "god" given to the world by the devil; a tool employed successfully by him for over 4,000 years and still going strong.

Chapter 3

The Father of Oriental Religion was God

A Rigorous Mathematical Proof

The Bible says that in the End Times, the House of David will rise up again. That sounds just fine to most Jews. Others, however, might rightly ask : "What does this mean for Christians, or for Muslims?"

And, even more so, one might ask: "What about the peoples of the East: Buddhists, Hindus, Taoists, and others?" What is *their* place in this prophecy? Are they simply excluded from all consideration?

In this chapter we will show that God was the Creator of all the Eastern religions, although their external appearances may conceal that fact.

In order to show this, we must first orient ourselves with respect to history as a whole, by putting the major events of **Western** religious history on a time line (the **Eastern** religions have no such time line, since—as we shall shortly see—they all began more or less simultaneously):

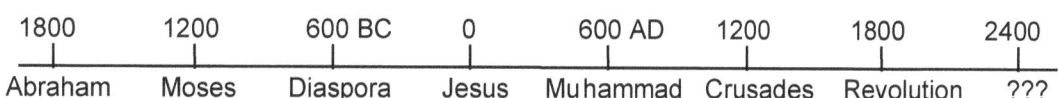

Note that every 600 years[8], an event of tremendous religious significance occurs. We start with Abraham, who is considered to be the founder[9] of religion, at least in its current form, by all three monotheistic faiths (Judaism, Christianity and Islam).

---

[8] These dates are, of course, approximate, and the subjects of academic dispute. Few historians, however, would place any of them more than a century from the dates given here. The Diaspora took place in two stages; the Northern Kingdom was invaded a little before 600 BC, and the Southern Kingdom a little after.

[9] By calling Abraham "the founder", we do not mean to diminish the importance of earlier prophets, especially Noah. No modern religion, however, considers the Noahite Law to be the root of its current system of beliefs and practices.

Six hundred years later, Moses received the Law from God on Mount Sinai. The three faiths all recognize Moses as the primordial lawgiver, and as the founder of the ancient nation of Israel.

Six hundred years after that came the Diaspora. Ancient Israel was decimated, and millions of Jews were scattered abroad to the ends of the earth. This Diaspora altered the course of history in every continent in the "known" world, and possibly even in the Americas.

Six hundred years after the Diaspora came Yeshua (Jesus).

Six hundred years after Yeshua came Muḥammad.

Six hundred years after Muḥammad came the period of the Crusades, which, in addition to the massive social upheaval, also generated the towering religious commentaries which have remained the backbone of modern Jewish and Islamic thought, down to the present day.

What about 1800? What happened then? The significant event which took place at that time (1775, to be exact) was the American Revolution, the beginning of the overthrow of the world's monarchies. But was this a "religious event"? You decide.

Although non-readers of the Bible may not know it, ancient Israel had no king at first. God was its King. Israel's rejection of God as King, and the demands of the people for the establishment of a secular monarchy, are described in the First Book of Samuel, Chapter 8. Although the prophet Samuel strictly warned Israel that it was making a mistake in demanding a king, the people were quite insistent, and could not be reasoned with.

The tradition of rule by human monarch, established in ancient Israel 3,000 years ago, was carried forward into every Christian and Muslim nation until the modern era.

If you are still not convinced that 1775 was a religiously-significant year, then please bear in mind also that previous to that time, Kings were generally considered to rule by "divine right". But in the American Revolution, a Western nation—for the first time since the days of the prophet Samuel—rose up and proclaimed that it had **no King but God**.

How important was this? It is self-evident that most other nations in the world today have followed in America's footsteps. Unfortunately, we have utterly failed to accept the responsibilities which go along with self-rule, and we find today that the world is on the verge of surrendering itself to an ugly, brutal and godless dictatorship—the "New World Order". This nightmare is unfolding day-by-day, before our horrified and "helpless" eyes.

Therefore, whether or not 1800 is really religiously significant or not depends upon whether or not we *mature* into **one world under God**, or *degenerate* into **one ugly godless world under money**. The choice is ours.

Be careful. There's no turning back.

As to what's going to happen in the year 2400, I won't even venture a guess.

Brief history of Israel

The rise of Oriental religion was inextricably linked with the downfall of the ancient state of Israel, in 600 BC. In order to see this, it will be necessary to review the history of the Jewish people.

In the beginning, before Adam and Eve ate from the Tree of Knowledge of Good and Evil, there *was* no "religion". God was present, and we knew Him personally. Because we disobeyed Him, and fell from grace, we have taken upon ourselves the unbelievable task of finding the way back.

Religion has been our main tool in this regard. But somehow, we have always found it easier to attack the religions of others than to devote ourselves single-mindedly to God.

From the day that Adam and Eve ate from that tree, man has been a great disappointment to God. After centuries of watching people fall into evil ways over and over again, God saw fit to establish His *Covenant* with Abraham, who is generally regarded as the first Jew (and the first Muslim as well).

About 1800 BC, God brought Abraham up out of Ur, Iraq, into the Promised Land of Israel. God chose Abraham to be the messenger who would remind mankind that there was **One** God, and that He did not reside in stone idols. But even Abraham himself was not perfect. For example, both he and Sarah laughed when God told them they would have a son in their old age, and God was not pleased (Genesis, Chapters 17, 18).

Abraham's great grandchildren, the sons of Jacob, were the Patriarchs of the 12 Tribes of Israel. These men were therefore towering figures in world history. But among them, there was not much honor to be found. For example, certain of them became jealous of their younger brother Joseph, and so they decided to murder him. Fortunately, two of them, Reuben and Judah (the latter being the progenitor of the line of David), persuaded the others that they should "only" sell Joseph as a slave, to a passing caravan. Joseph's life was therefore spared, but he was carried down to Egypt where he suffered for years, first as a slave, then as a prisoner, having been falsely accused of a crime he did not commit. (Genesis, Chapter 37 *ff*).

Many years later, there was a famine in Israel. The brothers were sent by their father, Jacob, down to Egypt to obtain food. There, they were most embarrassed to find that Joseph had risen up from slavery to become Governor of the country! But Joseph accepted them graciously. After the "misunderstandings" of the past were patched up, the family relocated permanently to Egypt. This was the seed of the Jewish nation, numbering in total 70 souls at that time[10].

Israel remained in Egypt for about four centuries. At first they prospered exceedingly, growing to a nation of several million people. Later, however, the Egyptians turned against them, and their fortunes began to decline. In time, they were reduced to slavery. And why not, since their sojourn began with the wish that their brother be a slave? How fitting that they should suffer that same punishment themselves!

God sent Moses to redeem the Jewish people, and to begin to fulfill the territorial Covenant He had established with Abraham. But when God called Moses, he did nothing but complain, to the point that the "anger of the Lord was kindled" (Exodus Chapter 4).

Nevertheless, Moses led Israel out of Egypt in what must be the most remarkable exodus in world history. Anyone who hasn't done so ought to begin thinking about the sheer mechanical difficulty of leading millions of people into the wilderness—a veritable sea of hostility, within which they were received as enemies wherever they went.

It was truly miraculous. But what did the Israelites do when they were finally delivered from slavery into freedom? They complained. Bitterly and incessantly. They complained as if they were spoiled children of the rich. The wrath of God was again kindled, and He made them wander 40 years in the wilderness.

Moses had to go *twice* up to the summit of Mount Sinai to receive the 10 Commandments and the other parts of the Jewish Law. These were carved into two tablets of stone, which he eventually put into a gold-plated box called the Ark of the Covenant.

The first time Moses came down from the Mount, he found the Children of Israel worshipping an idol, a golden calf. Only 40 days had passed, but they had forgotten all the wonders that they had been shown, and all the vows that they had made. They had reverted to primitive idolatry! The wrath of the Lord was again kindled (Exodus Chapter 19 *ff*, and Chapter 32).

---

[10] The Bible makes specific mention of these 70 souls; there were undoubtedly a goodly number of slaves and/or servants who went along. About these, however, the Bible is silent.

When, after 40 years in the wilderness, nearly all those who had offended God were dead, God brought the Children of Israel into the Promised Land. But not Moses. Moses had sinned against God, by failing to glorify Him (in a manner which is not precisely specified in the Bible; see Deuteronomy 32:48-52). Moses would be permitted to *see* the Promised Land, but not to enter into it.

So even Moses, whom Jews, Christians, and Muslims alike venerate almost to the point of worship, was not worthy in the eyes of God. Are any of us better?

Establishment of the Davidic Line of Kings

Once in the Promised Land, the behavior of the Jewish people improved, at least temporarily. They were ruled for many years by "Judges" such as Samson. These were leaders who seem to have arisen spontaneously, according to the needs of the moment. Their deeds and exploits are found in the Bible in the Book of Judges.

Israel, under the Judges, progressed in a rather halting manner, conquering and subduing some, but not all of the pagan peoples whom God had conditionally promised to remove from the Holy Land. God's condition, of course, was that Israel keep His Covenant. This they did, but only half-heartedly.

God's command has always been to go straight—to look "neither to the right, nor to the left" (Deuteronomy 5:32). Israel certainly did *not* do that. The Children of Israel looked to the right *and* the left, and they looked back also. But the net direction of their movement was forward, and again God forgave them for their sins.

The last Judge of Israel was Samuel. When his sons were caught accepting bribes, and thus became unsuitable to judge in his stead (I Samuel 8:3) the elders of the nation came to Samuel clamoring for him to anoint a King. This we made mention of earlier.

God was not pleased, explaining to Samuel (I Samuel 8:7) that the demand for a King amounted to a rejection of Him. But God did not forbid the Jews to have a King, He only warned of the consequences of such a thing.

So Samuel sought out, and found a suitable candidate for King. The LORD showed him Saul; scion of a powerful family of the tribe of Benjamin; taller and better-looking than anyone else in Israel. This was surely a man who would please the people, and satisfy their demand for a powerful-looking monarch. But alas, in the end, the LORD rejected Saul.

God's ultimate choice was David, the great-grandson of the converted Moabite heathen, Ruth. David was a poor shepherd, a non-obvious choice for King, and a still more non-obvious choice for the Patriarch of the hereditary line from which the Messiah would be prophesied to spring.

David defeated the mighty Philistine warrior Goliath with a stone. But he became King of Israel by defeating Saul with the mightiest weapon of all: faith.

David was truly a great King. The people loved him and they followed him faithfully (most of the time). In battle, he and his soldiers were nearly invincible.

He founded the city of Jerusalem around the hill called Mount Tzion (Mount "Zion" in the King James Bible), and he brought the Ark of the Covenant there.

Over the years, the Kingdom of Israel originally established by David grew to great size, extending almost from the Nile to the Euphrates Rivers at its peak. But this glory was not to last.

David, like even the most exalted of those who came before him, was not perfect. He committed adultery with Bathsheba, and then successfully plotted to have her husband, Uriah, killed. God was not pleased, but apparently God forgave David even this sin.

If the matter had ended there, it would have been more forgettable than it is. But David *married* Bathsheba, and he promised her that if she bore a son, that son would reign as King after him. Her first son died, but subsequently she bore Solomon, who came to epitomize both the best and the worst of Israel.

Under the reign of Solomon, the Kingdom of Israel grew tremendously in size. But the growth was achieved by marriages to princesses of surrounding Kingdoms, not through military conquests. Thus, in the end, Solomon had a huge empire, and 900 wives and concubines.

But in acquiring wealth beyond reckoning and innumerable wives, Solomon forgot about the commandments of God, through His prophet Moses, forbidding the King of Israel to "multiply wives to himself, that his heart turn not away" (*i.e.*, from God); and warning that he should not "greatly multiply to himself silver and gold" (Deuteronomy 17:17).

The evil which these commandments sought to prevent was *not* prevented. Solomon, in his old age, was overcome by relentless pressure from his wives, many of whom were foreign and maintained loyalties to their native religions based on idolatry. Thus, in the end, Solomon allowed the restoration of exactly the same abominable false religions which God had promised to drive out of Israel to make way for His chosen people. In those few final years, the entire spiritual progress of the Jewish nation was undone.

How ironic! Israel rose up from slavery through a long and painful process, lasting centuries, only to be stripped of its underlying principles in a *single generation*. And the cause? The allure of worldly rewards; of power, money, and sex. These worldly rewards turned Solomon's head, and once the head of the King was turned, the heads of the citizens of the nation quickly followed.

No sooner did King Solomon die, then civil war broke out. The nation was permanently split into two Kingdoms (Figure 3-1).

The Northern Kingdom, comprising 9½ of the 12 Tribes (the Tribe of Levi was divided between North and South), turned firmly to idolatry, and turned its back on God. It retained the name "Israel", but was frequently referred to by the name of its capital city, "Samaria".

God sent the great and mighty prophet Elijah, truly a towering figure in Judeo-Christian-Muslim history, to be a source of constant vexation to the evil Kings of Samaria. Through the performance of astounding miracles, Elijah temporarily turned the hearts of the people back to God, but the effect was extremely short-lived. Samaria, in the end, remained hopelessly pagan. The Second Book of Kings, Chapter 17, describes the terrible end of Samaria at the hands of the Assyrian invaders.

Not only were the Samaritans driven into exile (or carried off in chains), but the Assyrians went even farther, settling foreigners in the land of Israel so that the Northern Kingdom could never be re-established by returning exiles. The 9 tribes thusly dispersed are called the "lost Tribes of Israel". The Bible explicitly prophesies that they will someday re-appear, which means that they must somehow be "found". We will consider this matter shortly.

As for the Southern Kingdom, called Judah, consisting of 2½ Tribes (Judah, Benjamin, and some Levites), it survived the Assyrian invasions, because it never turned entirely from God. It's strength came from God, and was proportional to its devotion to God. Most of Judah's Kings maintained Judaism as the state religion, but they also tolerated worship of foreign gods in the land. To the extent that they allowed idol worship, they were offensive to God, whose Law explicitly forbid even the slightest tolerance of idolatry.

Several of the Kings of Judah were overwhelmingly evil. The worst was Manasseh, who removed the Ark of the Covenant from Solomon's Temple, and desecrated the Temple with pagan idols. Moreover, he "shed innocent blood very much, till he had filled Jerusalem from one end to another" (II Kings 21:16). It has been convincingly argued that it was during the reign of Manasseh that the Ark was removed from Jerusalem by the priests, to save it from destruction[11].

---

[11] Graham Hancock, *The Sign and the Seal*, Crown Publishers, New York, 1992, pp. 400-464.

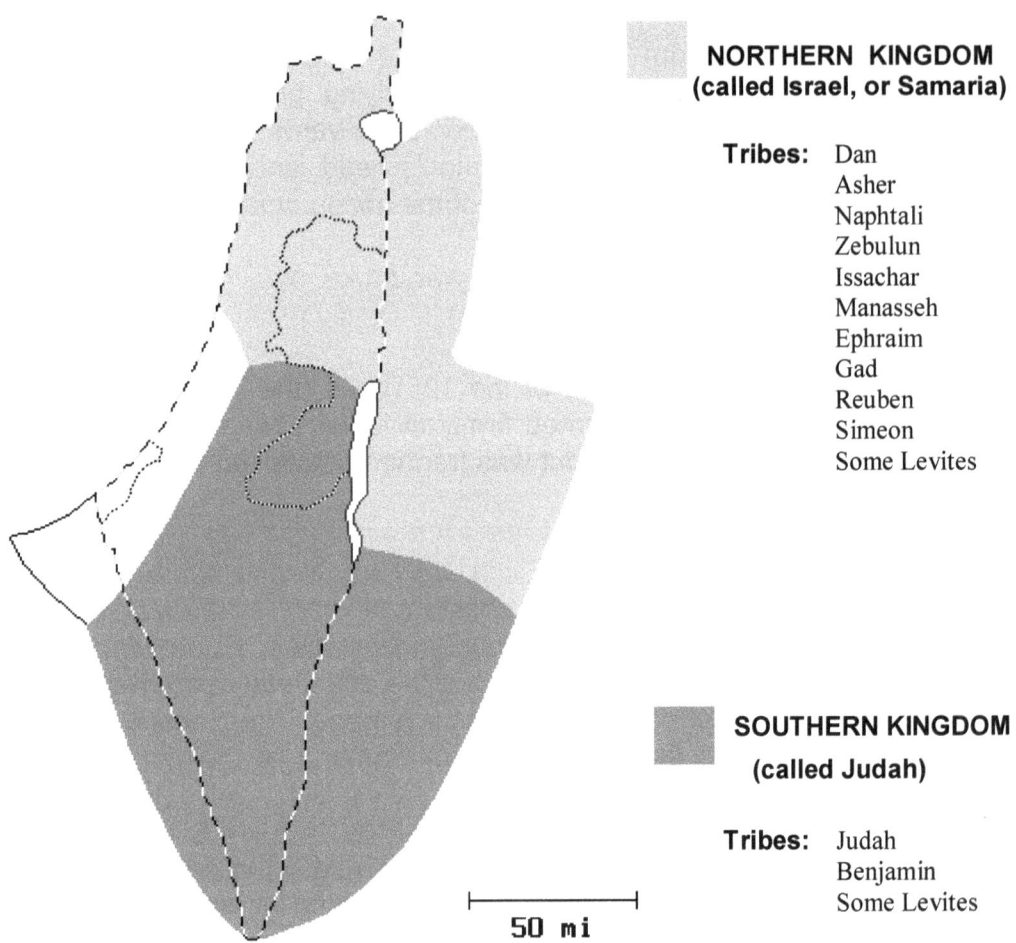

Figure 3-1. This map shows the approximate boundaries of the Ancient Kingdom of Israel after the Civil War which followed the death of King Solomon. The Twelve Tribes had been assigned to their respective areas by Moses. The Levites, or Priests, were not assigned to a single block of land, but rather were dispersed throughout both Kingdoms. Otherwise the Tribes were located wholly in either one Kingdom or the other.

There were nine Tribes in the Northern Kingdom (Manasseh & Ephraim, the descendants of the children of Joseph, are generally counted together as a single Tribe). They were driven permanently into exile by the Assyrians, and are today referred to as the "Lost Tribes" of Israel.

There were two Tribes in the Southern Kingdom, Judah & Benjamin. These, and the Southern Levites, were the forefathers of the Sephardic and Ashkenazi Jews; *i.e.*, virtually all readily-recognizable Jews living in the world today.

The boundaries of modern-day Israel are shown as a heavy dotted line. The lighter dotted lines indicate the West Bank of the Jordan River and the Gaza Strip. The latter is within a territory which, in ancient times, was the home of the Philistines, indicated here as a white area on the left-hand side of the map.

The best of the Kings of Judah, Hezekiah and Josiah, walked in the ways of the LORD with "all their hearts, all their souls, and with all their might" (see II Kings 23:25). There can be no doubt that Jerusalem was saved from the Assyrian invaders under Sennacherib by the faith of Hezekiah and of his chief prophet, Isaiah. It was certainly not military might that saved Judah; the tiny little nation was no match for the mighty armies of Assyria. Only the hand of God saved it.

A word is in order about the "abominations" of idol worship, for those readers who imagine the Jewish Law to be an arbitrary and capricious exercise in religious prejudice. The abominations which the evil King Manassah re-introduced to Judah, and which were removed by the great Kings Hezekiah and Josiah, included such practices as in-temple ritual sodomy and prostitution, institutionalized legal and social corruption, and burning of children as human sacrifice. Unfortunately, even the life-long efforts of these extraordinary Kings did not turn the Lord from the "fierceness of his great wrath" (II Kings 23:26). In the end, He delivered the Southern Kingdom of Judah into the hands of the invading Babylonian King Nebuchadnezzar. The Jewish nation was utterly destroyed, and Solomon's Temple, perhaps the most famous building ever built, was burned to the ground.

All the elite of Judah were carried off in chains to Babylon, inaugurating the period of Jewish history called the "Babylonian Captivity". It was a time of such misery that it is still commemorated by Jews today as the solemn fast-day of Tisha B'Av, observed annually on the date that Nebuchadnezzar is believed to have destroyed Solomon's Temple.

Thus, after a painful developmental process lasting over a millennium, the Jewish nation, around the year 600 BC, came abruptly to an end. This was the first of the Jewish Diasporas. Then an amazing thing happened.

The simultaneous appearance of Oriental religions

Yes, the Babylonian Captivity was a time of tragedy for Israel. But it was not a time of tragedy for everyone. While the Jewish people were enduring these hardships, the rest of the world was simultaneously enjoying what popular historian Bernard Grun, author of the "Timetables of History", calls the "zenith of human wisdom and achievement"[12]. How is such a thing possible?

The same century that saw the eclipse of the Jewish nation also saw the birth of no less than six new religions: Buddhism, Jainism, Taoism, Confucianism, Zoroastrianism, and the current monotheistic form of Hinduism. In short, the whole of modern day Oriental religion arose in a single century! And that's not all. This was also the century of the "Seven Wise Men" of Greece, the pillars of

---

[12] Bernard Grun, *Timetables of History*, Simon Schuster, 1979, p. 10.

the Western intellectual world, who began to repudiate polytheistic mythology and to sew the seeds of modern philosophy, science, literature, poetry and democracy. It's almost as if everything in the world of enduring spiritual and philosophical value, with the sole exceptions of Judaism, Christianity and Islam, came about in a single moment in time.

Was this mere coincidence? And what does it have to do with God?

To answer these questions, we need to place the Oriental religions on our time line. We may then ask questions about the probabilities associated with the simultaneous occurrence of any two of them. Here's the time line again, with our new additions:

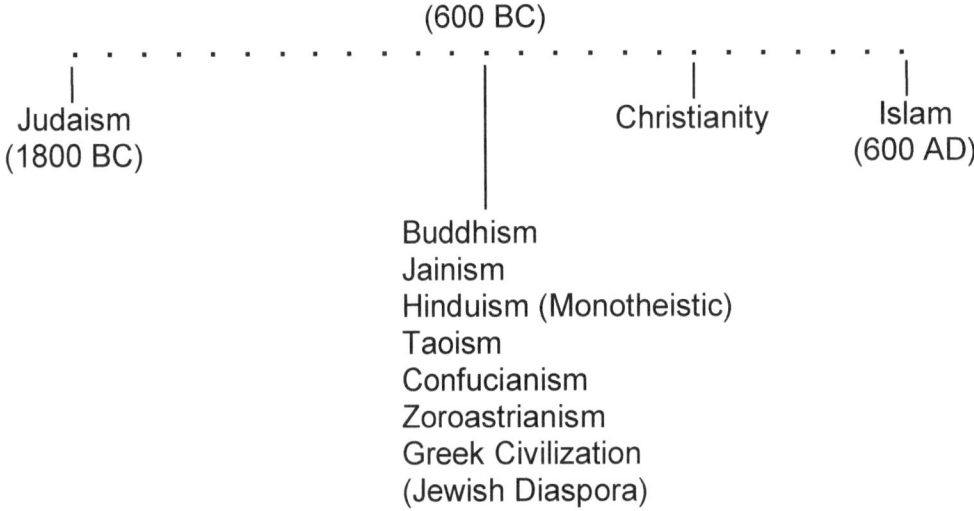

In this time line, we take Judaism as being the oldest religion, and Islam as being the youngest. Thus, our time line extends from 1800 BC to 600 AD. Some may feel that the time line should start earlier, and/or end later. It doesn't matter. Even if you ran the line back to the Garden of Eden (about 4,000 BC) or extended it right up to the present time, the argument you are about to see would have the same outcome. In fact, it would be stronger.

The period from 1800 BC to 600 AD encompasses 25 centuries. In the graphical representation above, each dot therefore represents an entire century. Now please note carefully the following: *All of the Oriental religions arose under a single dot*; i.e. at the same moment in history!

What are the odds of such things happening by chance?

The short answer is that the odds are impossibly *low*. There were 25 centuries between Judaism and Islam. Regardless of which century Buddhism happened to have arisen in, the odds of Taoism having arisen in the same century are obviously 1-chance-in-25. But what are the odds that in the same century, the Hindus would suddenly decide that there was, after all, only **One** God, and that all the other gods of the Hindu pantheon were different manifestations of that **One** God? Obviously the odds are:

$$\frac{1}{25} \times \frac{1}{25} = \frac{1}{625}$$

One-chance-in-625 is simply not very probable, but one can imagine it happening as a coincidence, just as one might see a roulette player in a gambling casino play a single number, and win twice in a row. But you'd have to go to a lot of gambling casinos, and watch a lot of roulette tables, before you'd see that.

We're not even halfway through our list. What are the odds of Buddhism, Taoism, monotheistic Hinduism, Jainism, Confucianism, and Zoroastrianism *all* arising in the same century? This is no mere gambling casino coincidence, but a miniscule probability with a denominator of huge proportions:

$$\frac{1}{25} \times \frac{1}{25} \times \frac{1}{25} \times \frac{1}{25} \times \frac{1}{25} = \frac{1}{9,765,625}$$

Thus, approached as a pure problem in statistics, it can be seen that the probability of all these religions arising in the same century is just under one chance in *10,000,000*. It can therefore be stated with *absolute certainty* that the simultaneous appearance of these religions in the same century was no coincidence.

Note that we have not even considered the "Seven Wise Men" of Greece in this calculation. If we throw that in also, treating the rise of Greek Philosophy as being tantamount to a new religion of sorts, then the number gets so unwieldy that it's difficult to even imagine as a mathematical probability:

$$\frac{1}{25} \times \frac{1}{25} \times \frac{1}{25} \times \frac{1}{25} \times \frac{1}{25} \times \frac{1}{25} = \frac{1}{244,140,625}$$

How can we even form a picture of this improbability? If you are one of those who have difficulty with statistics, please try imagining that God Almighty created a world just like Earth on every planet in a Milky Way type of galaxy with 244 *million* star systems. On how many planets in this galaxy would the historians report that all the Oriental religions coincidentally arose in the same century? The answer is "1". On how many would they *not* all have arisen in the same century? The answer is "243,999,999" !

I think it's worthwhile to harp on this a bit more, because I want you to be absolutely convinced of one thing: that the simultaneous appearances of these Oriental religions was not a matter of mere chance. What the explanation *was* is surely open to discussion, but coincidence is *not* one of the viable explanations.

Let us play the "devil's advocate" for a moment. Suppose, for example, we question whether the dates of the origins of the Oriental religions have been accurately represented here. Admittedly, these dates are not known exactly. But the length of the period during which Oriental religion arose, if not exactly 100 years, was surely not more than 200 years. The problem then consists of dividing the time line between Abraham and Muhammed into 200-year periods instead of 100-year periods. There were *twelve* 200-year periods between Abraham and Muḥammad. The odds of all six major Oriental religions arising in the *same* 200-year period are now:

$$\frac{1}{12} \times \frac{1}{12} \times \frac{1}{12} \times \frac{1}{12} \times \frac{1}{12} = \frac{1}{248,832}$$

This is, relatively speaking, a "much greater" probability than the one we derived above, but it is still inconceivable that these simultaneities were a matter of mere chance. Let's try to assess this improbability on a personal level. If someone said to you: "Jump out the window. It's a lot of fun on the way down", would you? Of course not. You're not ready to die. What if the same person said "Don't worry! Of every 248,000 people who jump, one survives!", would you then jump? I think not.

Note again that we have not considered the rise of Greek Philosophy here. If we throw that in, then our probability estimate reduces to an astronomically small value of about one chance in *3,000,000*.

I shall not dwell further on the mathematics of these great coincidences. I presume you can see that the simultaneous appearances of the Oriental religions could not possibly have been a matter of mere chance. If you are a person who cannot accept arguments based on numbers, then just keep in mind that lightening does not strike twice in the same place unless there is a lightening rod of some sort. Hardly anyone ever wins a lottery, and only a few people in history claim to have won twice. *No one* has ever won three times.

When too many supposedly-different things happen at the same time, there has to be an explanation.

If not chance, then what?

If even two things happen at the same time, common sense suggests the possibility of a relationship between them. In this instance, we have not two things, but *eight*:

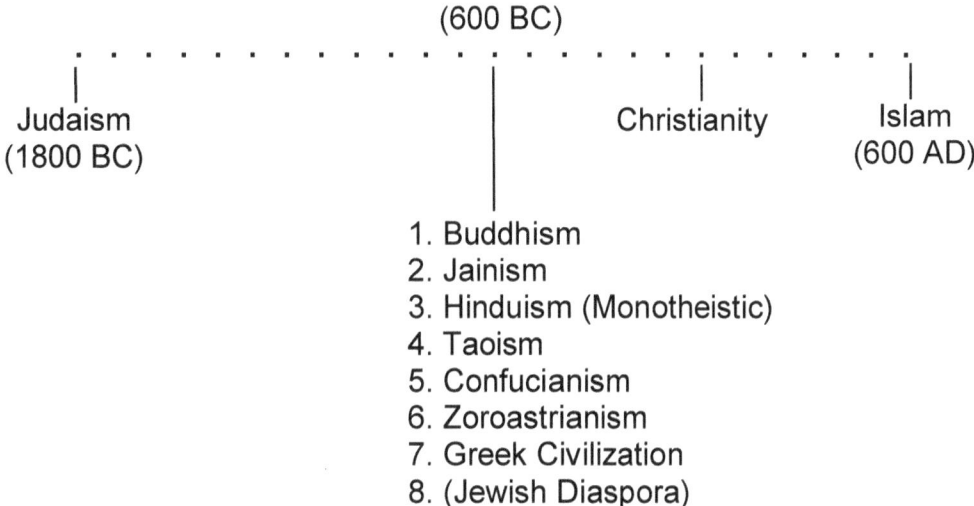

If you will concede that the apparent "coincidence" of these simultaneous occurrences reveals a single underlying cause, then I agree, and much of the purpose of this book has already been served. But I can assure you that certain followers of the above faiths will not be quick to agree.

Let us therefore examine all possibilities. If Oriental religions did *not* appear in response to a single underlying cause, then why did they start at the same time? In our investigation, let's leave no stones unturned. How about *telepathy*?

Perhaps a more acceptable term than "telepathy" would be "collective unconsciousness", an idea advanced by the psychiatrist Karl Jung. This means that everyone in the world got the same idea at the same time—not by chance, but by some sort of primitive, powerful, and poorly-understood form of global unconscious communication.

But that doesn't really help us. *Why* did everyone think the same thing at the same time? That never happened before or since!

Furthermore, if we concede that religion is a positive force for good in society, then in addition to the unlikely event of everyone thinking the same thing at the same time, we find that it is a *good* thing that people thought. And *that* has surely never happened before or since!

Therefore, even if the explanation for these apparent coincidences is rooted in telepathy, further explanation is still required. *Who*, or *what*, put the same idea into the minds of all the people of the world at the same time?

Could the rapid rise of Oriental religion have been the result of communication through trade caravans?

A typical scenario could have gone something like this: Hindu traders could have arrived in China, trembling with excitement because they had just learned that God, in the form of Krishna, had appeared to one of them, and had explained that He was the *only* God, and that He was **One** God, and that all the other Hindu gods were merely different manifestations of Himself.

This, according to the scenario, would have directly or indirectly prompted the Chinese *prophets-to-be* to roll up their sleeves and get to work. People like Lao Tzu, the legendary founder of Taoism, might then have retreated to the mountains to meditate, emerging with a confirmation that there was, indeed, a single ultimate Reality, but reporting that the Reality which appeared to him was not best described as an all-powerful "God", but rather as an all-powerful "*Way*". The word "Tao" means "Way", or "Path", and Taoism, the religion generally attributed to Lao Tzu, consists of the following of this Path.

Could this sort of hypothetical caravan-borne teaching have been the mechanism of coincidence in the simultaneous appearance of Oriental religions?

Sure. But this still leaves the questions unanswered. Although the "Silk Road" from Europe to China was wide open in those days, the people traveling it were *business* people, not proselytizers. If traveling businessmen were so good at changing people's religions, then why did *earlier* ones not cause each nation to adopt the false idols of its neighbors? What was so special about the caravans of the 6th century BC, that everywhere they went, they left behind radical changes in the people's most fundamental and dearly held beliefs; changes which have survived to this day?

Isn't it necessary, if we are to make sense out of this scenario, to assume one thing further—namely that any profound religious/philosophical teachings being carried by the 6th century caravans were *true* teachings? Then the scenario starts to look more plausible: It was not caravan travel *per se* which caused these changes, but the fact that the Truth was somehow "in the air" in 600 BC, and that men and women everywhere were talking about it.

But if this is so, and if Truth itself was the thing which gave rise to Lao Tzu's "Tao", Buddha's "Enlightenment", and Socrates' "Idea of the Good", then doesn't that also mean that all these were the same thing (or at least very closely related)?

If you now believe that the Tao of Lao Tzu, the Enlightenment of Buddha, and the "Idea of the Good" of Socrates all sprang from the same eternal underlying Truth, then the purpose of this book has been served. But I suspect that most readers are not yet convinced, and so we must proceed with our analysis further.

Hypothesis of a "supercharged" proselytizer

We move now to an hypothesis that begins with the assumption that the monumental religious changes of the 6th century BC were a result of caravan communication, but that additionally, certain of the caravans were "supercharged" proselytizers of some sort.

This hypothesis is fully consistent with the underlying belief system of the Mormons, who say that a prophet named Nephi, of the Israeli Tribe of Joseph, led a group of people out of Jerusalem in the 6th century BC. They traveled through Asia for a number of years, enduring many hardships, ultimately sailing across the ocean to America.

Since Jews, in those days, were enthusiastic proselytizers ("Ye compass sea and land to make one proselyte..."; Matthew 23:15), one could imagine a wandering Tribe of Jews gradually making its way across Asia, leaving a wake of monotheistic thought in its path. But did such a thing happen?

There are certainly archaeological findings in the Americas which support the Mormon point of view. The more incontrovertible of these include the pyramids in Mexico and Central America, which demand a comparison with the pyramids of Egypt and Iraq, and the statues of Negroes in pre-Columbian Mexico and Central America, which suggest that Africans (converts from the first Jewish Diaspora?) sailed there long before the great medieval black kingdoms of Timbuktu and Spain even existed.

Nevertheless, outside of the Book of Mormon itself, there is no independent historical evidence for a single, unique "supercharged" proselytizing group of Jews which migrated across Asia to the Americas. Nor does the Book of Mormon propose that Jews started Oriental religion.

Is there a simpler answer?

What about the original 12 Tribes themselves?

When 8 things happen simultaneously, then it is entirely reasonable to presume that they had a common cause. Perhaps, for example, 1 of the 8 things caused the other 7. If so, then 1 of the 8 things ought to stand out as being clearly different from the other 7. It just so happens that in this case, one does:

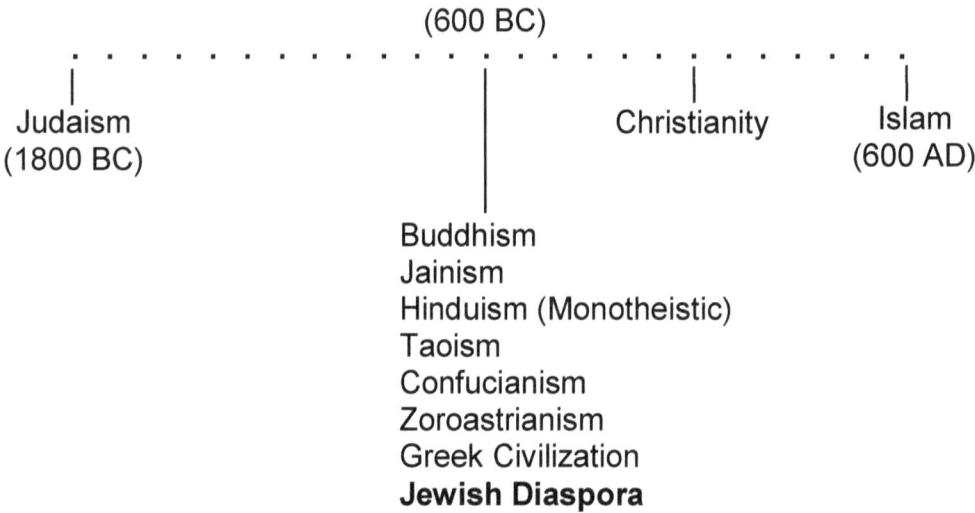

One civilization fell, and *seven* new ones were born. The Kingdom of Israel fell, and the "kingdoms" of Buddhism, Jainism, Hinduism (monotheistic), Taoism, Confucianism, Zoroastrianism, and Greek Philosophy were born. We shall now show how these events were connected.

The Prophets of the Old Testament were unanimous about one thing. The nation of Israel would be destroyed and scattered for apostasy, not to be restored until the End Times, when the House of David would rise up again, and the Jews would be gathered together in Israel.

This scattering began with the first Jewish Diaspora, which started when invaders stormed in from the nation now called Iraq. (No, the world has not changed much in 3,000 years).

There were *two* ancient empires whose capitals were located in the territory of modern day Iraq: the Assyrian Empire, with its capital in Nineveh, and the Babylonian Empire, with its capital in the City of Babylon.

The first phase of the Diaspora began in the latter years of the 8th century BC, when the Assyrian Kings Shalmaneser V (also called Tiglath-Pileser, 726-721

BC) and Sargon II (721-705 BC) invaded, subjugated, and totally decimated Samaria, the Northern half of the divided Kingdom of Israel.

The Prophet Isaiah had warned the Kings of Samaria of the impending doom, but the warnings were not heeded. The Assyrians must have had a real hatred for the Northern Israelites, because, as we noted above, they did not simply conquer them, they exiled them and moved large numbers of foreigners into their lands, so that the Israelites could *never return*. When one considers the work involved in such a venture, compared with the much more familiar military scenario of conquering, killing, plundering and leaving, one begins to grasp the depth of hatred involved. These Assyrians were not interested in mere plunder; they wanted total and irreversible destruction.

How many Israelites were dispersed? According to the Bible (Numbers 2:32), the nation of Israel, at the time of the Exodus from Egypt, contained 603,550 men of fighting age. This number excluded the Tribe of Levi, who were priests, and as such were not enumerated as fighting men. It also excluded the young, the elderly, and the women. So the total population of Israel at the time of the Exodus was surely in the neighborhood of 2 million people.

The Exodus occurred in approximately 1200 BC. So the Assyrian invasion of the Northern Kingdom of Israel occurred 500 years after the Exodus; a length of time adequate for the births and deaths of about 25 new generations. Now, these 500 years were years of growth and prosperity for Israel. Consequently, the population of the Northern Kingdom must have been in the millions. Therefore, the number of people involved in the Assyrian stage of the Diaspora was very large.

Even though we don't know the exact number, we can form an impression of how large it was by considering later population statistics for world Jewry. At the time of the destruction of Jerusalem by the Romans six centuries later, the population of Jews living outside Israel was *already* 5,000,000, of whom 4,000,000 lived within the boundaries of the Roman Empire and 1,000,000 without[13]. In view of all this, it is impossible to doubt that the number of Jews driven into exile in 600 BC was at least several hundreds of thousands, and it could surely have exceeded a million people.

The second phase of this Diaspora occurred a century after the destruction of the Northern Kingdom, when the Southern Kingdom of Judah got *its* "medicine" at the hands of the Babylonians. The Prophet most closely associated with this Babylonian phase of destruction was Jeremiah. The history of his ministry is recorded in the book of the Bible which bears his name.

---

[13] Encyclopedia Britannica, article "Diaspora".

Jeremiah lived in the Southern Kingdom of Judah at a time when memories of the horrors of the destruction of the Northern Kingdom were fresh in everyone's minds. That notwithstanding, the people paid no attention to his warnings.

Jeremiah correctly predicted the impending invasion by the Babylonians. He counseled the Kingdom of Judah to submit, rather than to risk utter destruction. This was an earnest warning, from the heart, meant to avoid the tragic mistake of embarking on a war which Judah could not win. But the worthless "yes men" whom the King employed as his personal court prophets and seers violently disagreed with Jeremiah. Naturally, as has happened over and over again throughout history, the viewpoints of the "yes men" prevailed.

The false prophets of the Court were also well-liked by the people. Jeremiah, whose prophecies *alone* came to pass, was hated. He was arrested twice, his scrolls were cut up and burned, he was thrown down a well to die (but was rescued by an Ethiopian), and finally he was exiled to Egypt, where he is believed by some[14] to have been murdered.

Jeremiah represented a culmination of over a century of prophecies of impending doom, which began during the years of Isaiah and his contemporaries. With the fall of the Northern Kingdom, and the visible and alarming growth of military power in Babylon, the people of the Southern Kingdom of Judah had much to fear.

If one tries to put oneself in the place of the God-fearing Israelis of those centuries, one can readily imagine that a certain number of them would have felt compelled to relocate to places far away from Israel. Concerning the numbers of those who relocated, no record is known. But concerning the existence of such refugees, there can be no doubt. It's simply a fact of life: When people's lives and freedoms are threatened, many will move.

The Bible reports that in the year we now call 587 BC, the Babylonian King Nebuchadnezzar conquered Judah, destroyed the Temple of Solomon, and "carried away all Judah captive into Babylon" (II Kings, Chapter 24). Historians tend toward the opinion that only artisans and craftsmen, *i.e.* people who would have been useful to the Babylonians, were forcibly relocated. But one thing seems certain: many must have fled, to *avoid* captivity and/or death.

The situation must have been analogous to the situation for Jews in Nazi Germany in the pre-World War II years. Those who had the wherewithal to do so, left. The rest either perished, or were taken captive.

Since there are no historical records of mass migration from Judah, we can only guess at the number of people who left. But with the example of the decimated

---

[14] Others believe that he survived and moved to Ireland, taking with him the two daughters of the king. In Britain this point of view is greatly favored.

Northern Kingdom a century earlier, and with the warnings of Jeremiah and the other God-fearing Prophets, and with the sounds of the hoofbeats of Babylonian horses in the wind, it is impossible to doubt that substantial numbers of people must have taken the hint, and moved on to safer territory. And, since there was already a large Diaspora population of Jews from a century earlier, there would have been many safe places to choose from.

It is important to note that those who escaped captivity in Babylon included many who fled the nation in much the same spirit as Noah boarding the Ark. That is, they knew in their hearts that they were fleeing from a punishment being inflicted on the nation by God Himself.

In Noah's case, the Word of God came directly to him. In 600 BC, the word came principally through the mouth of the Prophet Jeremiah. As we have seen, Jeremiah was hated by most of the people. So those who fled from the Southern Kingdom according to Jeremiah's word were a *God-fearing minority.* Since Jeremiah preached that Israel would be scattered because of *sin*, it follows that this message would have been carried by them, to every country to which Jews fled.

Now Israel, in those days, was a great nation—an almost legendary land of renown. This message, of the great nation being destroyed by the Hand of God Himself because of sin, must have been a sobering message to the citizens of the pagan lands to which the Jews re-located.

In conclusion, for over a century, from about 726-587 BC, the two halves of the Jewish nation were threatened with extinction from enemies without. The great Prophets of the Old Testament warned the people of the impending doom. Before, during, and after the prophecies came to pass, large numbers of Israelis were scattered, either forcibly or of their own free will. The total number of people dispersed was at the very least in the hundreds of thousands, and could easily have been over a million. A minority of these people went in chains to Babylon, and some of those eventually returned. The majority, however, never returned. These are the "Lost Tribes of Israel". Where are they now?

What were the final destinations of the Jews of the first Diaspora?

Perhaps the most succinct answer to this question was given by Strabo, the great Greek historian/geographer. His "Geography" is described by the Encyclopedia Britannica as "the only extant work covering the whole range of peoples and countries known to both Greeks and Romans during the reign of Augustus (27 BC-14 AD)". Strabo himself had traveled throughout the length of the Roman Empire, from Tuscany through Europe and Asia Minor down to Egypt, and up the Nile River to the border of Ethiopia. Concerning the Jews, Strabo wrote:

> **"These Jews have penetrated to every city, and it would not be easy to find a single place in the inhabited world which has not received this race, and where it has not become master."**[15]

We do not, for our current purposes, need to look at "every place in the inhabited world", but only at those countries within which Oriental religion arose: Persia, India and China. Where there Jews there? If so, is there any evidence that they were involved in the establishment of the native religions of those countries?

Persia and India

The peoples of Persia (Iran) and India were much more closely linked in ancient times than they are today. This is because they were both invaded and conquered by the same group of central Asian nomads, known as "Aryans". These were Caucasian Indo-European people, believed to have originally emanated from the land between the Oxus and Indus Rivers (corresponding to the modern-day nation Uzbekistan). It was from the term "Aryan" that the modern name "Iran" was derived.

After settling in Iran, one or more waves of these light-skinned Aryan invaders crossed the Hindu Kush Mountains into India between 2000-1000 BC, changing the nature of that country forever. The original inhabitants of India, sometimes referred to as Dravidians, were black. Centuries of warfare pushed the Dravidians toward the south, but in the end, intermarriages gave rise to a new people, the Indians of today.

From the time of the Aryan invasions until about 600 BC, the ancient religions of Iran and India developed in parallel. They were both extremely polytheistic. Their gods had similar names. For example, the two very important gods "Indra" and "Mitra" of India were called "Intar" and "Mithra" in Iran. Their ceremonies involved the use of a hallucinogenic drug, which is believed to have been an extract of a particular species of mushroom. This drug was called "Soma" by the Indians, and "Haoma" by the Persians.

Considering the ancient linkage between the two nations, it is not surprising that when profound changes occurred in Iran, they quickly spread to India, its spiritual cousin.

---

[15] Strabo, *Geography*, quoted in: J.H. Hertz, Ed., *Pentateuch & Haftorahs*. Soncino Press, London, 1987, p. 812.

And, when Diaspora Jews arrived in Iran, profound changes most assuredly took place.

Were there Jews In Persia (Iran) in 600 BC?

This may seem like a silly question to readers of the Babylonian *Talmud,* but to others it may be less obvious. Let us, therefore, answer the question, leaving no stones unturned.

The Bible reports that in the late 8th century BC, the Assyrian invaders of the Northern Kingdom of Israel (Samaria) deported the Jews to "Halah and in Habor by the river of Gozan, and in the cities of the Medes" (II Kings 17:6).

Now, concerning the latter cites, there is no question about who the Medes were. Media was the northwestern part of modern-day Iran. It was an alliance between Media and Babylon that overthrew the Assyrians in 612 BC, giving rise to the Babylonian Empire.

We have already seen that there were plenty of Jews in Babylon; taken there as captives by Nebuchadnezzar in the 6th century BC. Thus, the alliance between the Medes and the Babylonians was an alliance between two nations which eventually developed large Jewish populations. When, in the course of time, the Medes and Babylonians were themselves conquered by the Persians, the new Persian Empire "inherited" many Jews.

The Persians were the inhabitants of the southern part of Iran. They considered themselves to be descendants of the Aryan invaders we made mention of above, and they considered themselves to be ethnically distinct from the Medes.

The Persian conqueror Cyrus II, known as Cyrus the Great, conquered the Medes in 550 BC, inaugurating one of the great empires of world history, the Persian or *Archaemenian* Empire. This empire rapidly grew to encompass much of the "known" world, extending west into Egypt, and south into upper India. It lasted until its overthrow by Alexander the Great.

We need look no farther than the Bible to see the important role Jews played in the Persian Empire. In the *Book of Daniel*, we can see clearly that the Jews, in spite of the fact that they were in so-called "captivity" in Babylon, actually occupied favored positions. Daniel himself was clearly a man of great power and prestige. It seems, in fact, that he occupied much the same position of power in Babylon that Joseph had occupied in Egypt a thousand years earlier. Joseph was Governor of all Egypt, second in power only to Pharaoh himself, and if Daniel was lower in prestige than that, it cannot have been very much lower.

Whenever King Nebuchadnezzar needed advice, he consulted with Daniel. This was a most favored "captivity" indeed! Now, Kings of Babylon came and went, but not Daniel. In Chapter 5 of his book, we find Nebuchadnezzar gone, but Daniel *still there*, serving a new King, Belshazzar. Daniel's prestige in this new court was such that he could predict, right to the King's face, that the King would die that night as a punishment for his transgressions. This is surely not the sort of thing a lowly "captive" would say to a mighty King. Without a doubt, Daniel was a man of considerable power in Babylon.

How powerful? After hearing this dire prediction of death (which came true!), the King, instead of having Daniel drawn-and-quartered, "clothed [him] with scarlet, and put a chain of gold about his neck, and made a proclamation concerning him, that he should be the third ruler in the kingdom" (Daniel 5:29)! Again I say, if this was "captivity", it was a captivity of a most favored nature!

Perhaps more significant than the prediction of death itself for the King, was the prediction that his Kingdom would be "given to the Medes and Persians" (Daniel 5:28). And, indeed, in Chapter 6 of the *Book of Daniel* we see that the conquest of Babylon by the Persians was complete, with Daniel occupying the same favored position with the new Persian Emperor, Cyrus the Great!

Cyrus is a name highly esteemed in Jewish history. It was he who, in the year 523 BC, allowed the "captive" Jews to return to Israel to rebuild their country and their Temple. But they did not all return! It is obvious that many of the Jews had taken a liking to Babylon, and they remained there. The mere existence of the Babylonian Talmud is testimony enough to the fact, well-established in any event, that Babylon was a center of Jewish life for centuries after the Persian conquest.

Rise of Zoroastrianism

Around the time of the destruction of Solomon's Temple in Jerusalem, a sudden change came over the religion of Persia. As we have seen, the ancient religion of this country was a familiar sort of pagan idol worship, whose many gods were similar in name to the gods of the ancient polytheistic religion of India. Then, sometime not too far from 600 BC, the great Persian prophet Zoroaster suddenly began teaching that the multitude of gods were actually only "angels", and that there was only **One** true God, whom he called *Ahura Mazda*, which means "Wise Lord".

Subsequently, the Zoroastrian religion came to dominate the Middle East; a state of affairs which persisted for a thousand years, up to the time of Muḥammad.

Many believers survive to this day. Most of them now live in India, having been long since driven out of Iran by Muslim persecution.

How can we account for the sudden appearance of monotheism in a pagan, idol-worshipping people? The only historical event of sufficient magnitude to account for it was the arrival of the Diaspora Jews. Does this mean that Zoroaster studied with Daniel and the other Rabbis? Not necessarily. It may be that the mere sight of the Jewish prisoners, arriving in chains from the legendary land of the glory of Solomon, put the fear of God into the Persians. In any event, for whatever reason, they put away their idolatry forthwith, and began worshipping **One** God.

If it was God who sent the Jews into exile, then it must have been God who appeared to Zoroaster, to cause him to convert the Persians. Who else but the LORD, King of the Universe, could have taught a nation of idol worshippers that there is only one God?

Were There Jews in India in 600 BC?

Jews were already involved in trade with the Orient at the time of Solomon, and at all times thereafter. At the very least, it is well-documented that Jews were involved in the silk trade[16], and the so-called Silk Road extended all the way to China.

In India today there are several Jewish populations which trace their roots to the First Diaspora of 600 BC. The best-known of these are the Malabar Coast Jews, located principally in the city of Cochin on the southwest tip of the country. Cochin has been a maritime trading center throughout history. It harbors an ancient Jewish population which considers itself, in no uncertain terms, to be descended of the "Lost Tribes" of Israel[17].

A second population of Jews is found in and around Bombay. They call themselves the Bene-Israel (children of Israel), and they too consider themselves to be, without a doubt, descendants of the Lost Tribes.

A third group was reported upon in the *Jerusalem Post* in 1993[18]. These are called the Tchiang tribe, and they live in the northeast Indian states of Mizoram and Manipur. They number 750,000 people, mostly assimilated, but 5,000 of them are still practicing Jews. They consider themselves to be descendants of one of the Twelve Tribes of ancient Israel, the tribe of Manassah (no relation to the evil King Manassah who desecrated the Temple).

---

[16] J. Henry Lord, *Jews in India and the Far East,* Greenwood Press, Westport, CT., 1976.
[17] Ibid.
[18] Jerusalem Post, International Edition, No. 1709, August 7, 1993, p. 24.

Rise of modern Indian religion

India occupies a unique place in the history of religion, being the "melting pot" between East and West. There are no fewer than four major modern-day religions which began in India (Buddhism, Hinduism, Jainism, and Sikhism).

Each one has it roots in the 6th century BC.

Prior to 600 BC, as we have seen, the religion of India was a primitive form of Hinduism, which was polytheistic. The changes which took place in 600 BC were similar to those which occurred in Iran. The nation went from polytheism to the worship of **One** all-encompassing divine principle.

Buddhism

The reactions against polytheism in India took on several forms. Without a doubt, the most widespread—destined to spread far beyond the borders of India itself—was Buddhism.

Although Westerners think of Buddha as a Chinese man sitting in lotus position, the fact is that he was an Indian. At least one author has earnestly proposed that he was Negro[19]. Since India was a land of mixed race, this possibility should be kept in mind.

What is Buddhism? If Western religion was to be reduced to a single phrase, and if that phrase was ...

{attainment of salvation through devotion to God}

... then Buddhism, if reduced to a single phrase, would be

{attainment of Enlightenment through removal of desire}.

What is Enlightenment? To the East it is, without a doubt, the complete equivalent of what Westerners mean when they say "God". I do not mean that Enlightenment and God are one and the same (nor do I necessarily mean that they are *not* the same). I mean, rather, that Enlightenment, as far as it can be

---

[19] J.A. Rogers. *Nature Knows No Color-Line*. Copyright 1952, by the author, pp. 7-9.

defined, is the single, indivisible, ultimate reality behind the illusions of our worldly existence. The attainment of Enlightenment is said to be a state of bliss which exceeds any earthly pleasure, and, in fact, lies entirely *beyond* pleasure or pain, or any other worldly experience of any sort.

If you consider yourself to be a philosopher at all, you'll have to concede that Enlightenment, if it exists, cannot be too far from God. That is, there cannot be *two* indivisible ultimate realities—only **One**. If that **One** is God, then Enlightenment is either God, or *of* God.

The role of Buddha as a revolutionary in Indian society can only be understood by keeping squarely in mind that India, prior to 600 BC, was a nation of idol worshippers. It can be said, therefore, that Buddha's quest for the **One** indivisible, ultimate reality was the same as Abraham's quest for the **One** indivisible, ultimate God. How can we know this? We can know this because Buddhism, like all the other Oriental religions, did not appear until the arrival of Jews in India following the First Diaspora.

If it was God who drove the Jews out of Israel, then it must have been the same God who drove polytheism out of India. Who else but the LORD, King of the Universe, could have caused Buddha to teach a nation of primitive idol worshippers that there is only **One** enduring, all-encompassing reality?

The importance of removal of desire

Buddhists regard the non-Enlightened state as being a state of suffering, whose end can only be brought about only by the removal of *desires* and *attachments* to things in the material world. This relationship between suffering and desire is referred to as the "Noble Truth About Suffering"[20].

To the "Western" mind, which is filled with desire for wealth, power, fame, comfort, security, sex, and innumerable other worldly things, the idea of removing *desire itself* can be very difficult to comprehend. But the method of working toward Enlightenment turns out to be surprisingly familiar. Known as the "Eight-Fold Noble Path", here are some of its aspects:

---

[20]Source: *The Teaching of Buddha*. This is the most concise and all-inclusive Buddhist reference I know of, and I strongly recommend to all. It is published by the *Buddhist Promoting Foundation* (Bukkyo Dendo Kyokai), an organization established by Mr. Yehan Numata, who was the founder of the Mitutoyo Corporation, a manufacturer of precision measuring instruments. Mr. Numata was an Eastern "Gideon", who used his wealth to spread the word of Buddha throughout the world. Consequently, his book may now be found in many hotel rooms in the Orient, just as the Gideon Bible is found in the West. In America, *The Teaching of Buddha* may readily be obtained from: The Society for Buddhist Understanding, 16925, E. Gale Avenue, City of Industry, CA 91745. The book is free, although a contribution is appreciated. The Internet address of Bukkyo Dendo Kyokai is: http://www.bdkamerica.org/.

The resolution to remove desire. Since human beings are filled with endless and insatiable desires, a Buddhist must take a steadfast vow to cease from vainly striving to satisfy them. If at first this seems unreasonable, consider the opposite: Should we abandon ourselves to gluttony, selfishness, and unrestrained sexuality? Or do we actually agree with this teaching already?

The Law of Cause and Effect. This is simply a statement of a principle which may seem totally obvious; namely that the world is a vast concurrence of causes and effects. The heart of this law is the recognition that our minds, as well as all things in the material world, are in a constant state of flux. Nothing remains unchanged forever. We should not allow ourselves to become attached to things which have no permanence, if we wish to gain that which is Eternal.

Right speech. This means the avoidance of lying words, idle words, abusive words, and double-talk.

Right behavior, and right livelihood. This means not to kill, not to steal, not to commit adultery, and not to pursue any occupation which would bring shame.

Right effort means that at all times, one should try to do one's best to proceed diligently in the right direction.

The similarity of these teachings to those of the Bible is evident.

Jainism

The Jain religion was founded by a man known by the title *Mahavira.* He was a contemporary of Buddha. From the Western perspective, his teachings were similar to those of the Buddhist religion, only more stringently ascetic. He taught the attainment of Enlightenment through rigorous discipline and self-denial. Born of nobility, he left the family palace to wander the highways and byways of India naked for over 12 years, denying himself any and every conceivable human comfort and convenience. In the 13th year, he attained Enlightenment, then became a teacher for other seekers.

Unlike Buddhism, Jainism never spread significantly outside India. Yet, although the number of its adherents is small, it has survived to the present day.

There is no evidence that Buddha and Mahavira knew of one another. Yet their religions were founded at the same time in history—the time of the Jewish Diaspora in 600 BC.

If it was God who drove the Jews out of Israel, then it must have been the same God who the drove the Mahavira out of his family palace, to seek the imperishable truth which lies beyond the transient pleasures of this world. Who else but the LORD, King of the Universe, could have caused the Mahavira to teach his followers, in that nation of idol worshippers, that there is only **One** enduring, all-encompassing reality?

Monotheistic Hinduism

The Hindu religion is very old. No exact date can be assigned to its origin.

We noted above that the religions of Iran and India developed in parallel. The ancient form of Hinduism, like the ancient religion of Iran, was a familiar form of polytheistic idolatry, and was dependent upon consumption of hallucinogenic drugs. These drugs were strictly withheld from all but the high priesthood.

Dramatic changes began to take place during the period of the First Jewish Diaspora. It was around 600 BC that Hindu writers began composing the Upanishads, treatises which proclaim that there is only **One** Ultimate Reality, called "Brahman-Atman". Brahman is God, and Atman is the soul. God, in the Upanishads, is likened to the ocean, and our individual souls to rivers which flow into it. Although each of these rivers, to our eyes, has an apparently independent existence of its own, it may ultimately be perceived that they are all *water*; the same water as the ocean from which they sprang.

Thus, although we are *not* God, our souls are related to Him. Moreover, there is only **One** of Him. With the Upanishads, the age of polytheism in India's primary religion came to an end.

India, however, never wholly abandoned its ancient gods. Instead, there appeared a pivotal work, the *Bhagavad-Gita*, through whose pages it was revealed that there is only **One** God, but that He has *many* appearances.

The Bhagavad-Gita is part of an enormous epic called the *Mahabharata*; a book which is central to most forms of modern-day Hindu practice. It recounts the story of a great war between two clans. Although the book contains no dates, historians believe that the events took place around 600 BC.

The principal human character in the Bhagavad-Gita is Arjuna, whose charioteer, Krishna, reveals himself to be God. Krishna teaches Arjuna that he, Krishna, is the **One** and only God in the universe; all the innumerable others being merely various manifestations of Himself. He then transfigures Himself, before Arjuna's eyes, into His true form, which is too awesome for a mortal to behold. Arjuna, overwhelmed, begs him to return to human form. After doing so, Krishna reveals a set of moral precepts which do not differ significantly from those of the Old Testament.

Modern Hinduism lies between Western and Eastern religion, having absorbed and incorporated into itself the basic tenets of both. It is explicitly taught, in the Bhagavad-Gita, that desire for the goods of the world binds people to it, and the pathway to Enlightenment through meditation and discipline is acknowledged. The nature of Enlightenment, however, is the nature of a supreme being—Krishna—who has all the attributes of the God of the West.

If it was God who drove the Jews out of Israel, then it must have been the same God who caused the Hindus to abandon polytheism. Who else could have caused the Indians to suddenly proclaim that all their ancient idols were merely different representations of **One** true God, other than God Himself?

Were there Jews in China?

As in virtually every other part of the world, there are people in China who consider themselves to be descendants of the "Lost Tribes" of Israel.

When the Jesuits established a foothold in China in the 17th century, they found no Christians. But, to their surprise, they found several communities of Jews!

These Jews knew the Old Testament, but not the Talmud. This established them as a very ancient community, well in excess of 2,000 years old, since the Talmud was written in the early Christian era.

By far, the most famous of the Chinese Jewish communities was that of Kaifeng. The historical records (mainly a few stone inscriptions) and the legends of the people themselves showed without much doubt that the community dated back to the period following the First Jewish Diaspora of 600 BC. Not long afterwards, two major changes had occurred in China. The first of these changes was political: Kaifeng (called, at that time, Ta-liang) became the capital of the Wei Dynasty, which controlled most of what we call China today[21].

The dominance of the city of Kaifeng was perhaps due mainly to canals which the Wei built to connect China's main waterways. Whether Jewish trade along the Silk Road helped establish Kaifeng's economic strength, or whether, conversely, Jews were drawn to the city *because* of its strong economy, would be impossible to say 2600 years later.

---

[21] Encyclopedia Britannica, v. 6, articles on "K'ai-feng" and "K'ai-feng Jew".

The second major change which took place shortly after the arrival of the Jews was much more important to the history of China, and of the world. This was the sudden appearance of Confucianism and Taoism.

The Tao

Taoism, the native religion of China, is yet another Oriental religion which teaches that the ultimate reality is an impersonal entity, comparable in all respects to Buddhist Enlightenment.

The major text, or "Bible", of Taoism is the *Tao Tê Ching*, which appeared at about the same time as the Bhagavad Gita appeared in India. The authorship of the Tao Tê Ching is credited to one *Lao-tsu*, about whom essentially nothing is known except his dates. Chinese tradition holds him to be a contemporary of Confucius. Thus, his ministry occurred around 600 BC, in the years following the First Jewish Diaspora.

The **Tao** is the natural order of things in the universe; literally "the Way". The *Tao Tê Ching* is one of the most concerted efforts to describe the indescribable which has ever been undertaken. Consider this passage[22], from Chapter 1 of the book:

> **The way that can be told of is not an unvarying way;**
>
> **The names that can be named are not unvarying names.**
>
> **It was from the Nameless that heaven and earth sprang...**
>
> **Truly, only he that rids himself forever of desire can see**
>
> > **the secret essences;**
>
> **He that has never rid himself of desire can see only the outcomes.**

Like Buddhists, Taoists teach that there is a single all-encompassing reality behind the universe, and that establishing a relationship to it necessitates the removal of worldly desire.

One teaching in the *Tao Tê Ching* which is worth bringing to the attention of Western eyes is found in Chapter 63:

> "**It** (*i.e.*, the Tao) **acts without action, does without doing, finds flavor in what is flavorless,**

---

[22] The translation of the *Tao Tê Ching* is that of Arthur Waley, from his book *The Way and its Power*, Grove Press, 1958.

> **Can make the small great and the few many,**
> <u>*Requites injuries with good deeds*</u>*,*
> **Deals with the hard while it is still easy,**
> **With the great while it is still small".**

Thus, we find that the principle of returning evil with kindness was known in China 600 years before Yeshua (Jesus).

China, like India, was a nation of polytheists before Lao-Tsu. If it was God who drove the Jews out of Israel, then it must have been the same God who drove polytheism out of China. Who else but the LORD, King of the Universe, could have caused all the nations of Asia—from one end of that continent to the other—to simultaneously abandon polytheism, and to turn in worship to a single enduring, all-encompassing Divine Principle?

Confucianism — the "Golden Rule"

The native religion of China is Taoism. Confucianism itself is not really a religion, but a system of ethics. It is a system so highly developed that it is certain that it has never been fully implemented in any nation. That is too bad! For if we all followed Confucius, this world would be a place of justice, happiness, and productivity.

Confucius dwelled, above all, on the relationships between people. He was the first person known to have expounded the "Golden Rule".

The Golden Rule, as we are all taught it in childhood, is to **"do unto others as you would have others do unto you"**. It is one of those few precepts whose truth is intuitively grasped by all people in all places. It's as if we all know *instinctively* that this Rule *works*.

And yet *applying* the Rule to everyday life is far from simple. If you have never tried, you ought to right now. What you will find is that putting yourself in the place of another person, to understand what that other person's hopes and dreams are, is much more difficult than you thought. You have to *work* at it. For people who are selfish and egocentric (*i.e.*, most of us), the task is a mighty one indeed.

And yet throughout history, rare individuals have somehow come to comprehend the incredible fact that the application of this deceptively simple Rule could, almost by itself, bring about a perfect world. Here in the West, it is commonly supposed that the Golden Rule was first enunciated by Yeshua (Jesus). But that is not true. His teachings, as we shall see later, were basically the teachings of the Orthodox Jewish rabbis of his day.

Modern day Jewish commentators, desiring to attribute the Golden Rule to Old Testament Judaism, express the opinion that the Rule is a corollary of the admonition to

"...love thy neighbor as thyself."

This admonition is prominently featured in the New Testament (Matthew 5:43, 19:19, 22:39), but it appeared first in the Torah (Leviticus 19:18).

Hillel, the towering Jewish scholar of the immediate pre-Christian era, and other less-known Jewish scholars in the centuries before him, pronounced negative versions of the Golden Rule. One of the best-known stories of Hillel tells of a heathen scoffer who asked him to condense the whole Law into a single sentence (literally "while standing on one foot"), to which Hillel replied

> **"Whatever is hateful to thee, do it not unto thy fellow:** *this is the whole Torah(!);* **the rest is commentary..."**   (Shabbat, 31a)

Since Hillel is regarded as one of the greatest interpreters of the Torah who ever lived, this puts the Golden Rule squarely at the center of Jewish tradition. But it is never explicitly stated in the Torah! In this particular instance, and in each other instance in which Jewish scholars quoted versions of the Golden Rule, they cited Leviticus 19:18 ("love thy neighbor") as their source.

But the truth of the matter is that the Golden Rule was first stated neither by a Jew nor a Christian, nor, in fact, by anyone west of the Himalayas. It was first explicitly stated by Confucius, and has been preserved in his *Analects*. In this book, the Rule appears no less than three times (Analects 5:11, 12:2, 15:23). Clearly, this doctrine permeates the Confucian philosophy, and forms one of its pillars.

Analects 15:23, to a Westerner, reads like a paraphrase of Hillel. We must remind ourselves that Confucius lived 500 years earlier. In this passage, one of Confucius' disciples asks:

> **"Is there any** *single saying* **that one can act upon all day and every day?", to which Confucius replied: "Perhaps the saying about consideration: 'Never do to others what you would not like them to do to you'".**

Whereas Jewish commentators (and later, Christian commentators) mentioned the Golden Rule, and then went on to expound other matters at greater length, Confucius chose to dwell upon it, giving rise to a conception of a perfect world of productive, joyous and harmonious relationships between people at every level of life. In a Confucian world, people would know their place. Children would respect parents, and the common people their leaders. No one would be worried about "advancement", because advancement based on seniority would come naturally with time, and advancement based on merit would go properly to those most deserving. People would not resent those "above" themselves, because the function of leaders would not be to "lord over" those below, but rather to *serve*. The words of Yeshua come to mind:

> "And whosoever will be chief among you, let him be your servant" (Matthew 20:27).

Confucius recognized the difficulties involved in applying the Golden Rule, and that he himself had not lived up to the ideals he taught. In the Confucian classic, the *Doctrine of the Mean*, he is quoted as having said:

> "There are four things in the moral life of man, not one of which I have been able to carry out in my life. To serve my father as I would expect my son to serve me: that I have not been able to do. To serve my sovereign as I would expect a minister under me to serve me: that I have not been able to do. To act towards my elder brother as I would expect my younger brother to act towards me: that I have not been able to do. To be the first to behave towards friends as I would expect them to behave towards me: that I have not been able to do."

Like other great moral teachers of this world, Confucius was not well-received during his life. But soon after his death, his teachings rose up to become the backbone of Chinese civilization, which they remain to this day (whether acknowledged by the current government or not). Attempts to stamp him out have failed. The great emperor Ch'in (c. 221 BC), who unified China by force, and who built the Great Wall and named the whole country after himself, sought to eliminate Confucianism, which he perceived to be contrary to his militaristic aims. He had hundreds of Confucian scholars buried alive. But as soon as Ch'in died, the spirit of Confucius returned, even stronger than before.

In more recent times, the Communist government of China again condemned Confucianism, declaring falsely that adherence to the principles of Confucius was the cause of all the ills of society, when in fact the truth was the opposite: it was *lack* of adherence to the principles of Confucius which resulted in all the famines and other social ills which plagued China in the early 20th century. Like Emperor

Ch'in before them, the Communists attempted to stamp out Confucianism, but in vain. He has been suppressed, but hardly forgotten.

If it was God who drove the Jews out of Israel, then it must have been the same God who revealed the Golden Rule to the Chinese in 600 BC. Who else but the LORD, King of the Universe, could have caused Confucius to promulgate a doctrine considered to be the fundamental, all-encompassing teaching of both the Jewish and Christian religions?

Greece - the Foundation of the Intellectual World of the West

What happened when Jews arrived in Greece?

Without a doubt, of the ancient idolatrous civilizations whose legacies have been most enduring from our point of view, the most important were those of Greece and Rome. Indeed, the Aristotelian "trivium" (grammar, logic, and rhetoric) and "quadrivium" (arithmetic, geometry, astronomy, and music) were the backbone of our entire educational system throughout the centuries, right up to the soberingly recent past.

Aristotle's pupil, Alexander the Great, proved the utility of the Greek educational system by conquering the whole world. After that, the Greek ideal of education and government survived persistently without any need for further promotion. In fact, it stuck like glue. But where did it come from?

At this point, you're probably anticipating that I'm going to say that "the Jews" did it. You're right. But as I've said in each of the preceding sections of this book, it's not because I believe for a moment that either Socrates, Plato or Aristotle took "Jew lessons". Rather, it's because a consideration of the timing of the monumental changes which took place in Greece, and of their nature (which we shall shortly examine), reveal the truth: that even in Greece, where the full rejection of idolatry was not complete until the arrival of Paul 700 years later, the work of the Hand of God was evident in the 6th century BC, that most critical of times in history.

And the only obvious physical vehicle through which the Holy Spirit could have reached Greece was that same community of Jews whose activities we have been following; fleeing from the Assyrian and Babylonian invasions, and carrying with them terrifying tales of God's awesome power to raise up or destroy whole civilizations according to His whim.

I do not intend to attempt to scientifically prove that large numbers of Jews migrated to Greece in the years of the First Diaspora. The presence of numerous Jewish communities across Europe, from one end to the other, is so well documented that it requires no further attention here. To prove that much of that emigration occurred in the 6th century BC hardly seems necessary. Even if one insisted on postulating that emigration from Israel to Greece took place continuously over the centuries, it would still be inconceivable that a particularly *large* wave of emigrants did not follow closely on the heels of the First Diaspora.

The "Seven Wise Men" of Athens

Historians date the beginning of the great ancient civilization of Greece to the "Seven Wise Men" of Athens, of whom the most important were Solon (630-560 BC) and Thales of Miletus (624-545 BC). The careers of these two men peaked about a century after the Assyrian conquest of Northern Israel, and coincided exactly with the Babylonian Diaspora of the Southern Kingdom of Judah (590 BC). Solon was therefore 40 years old, and Thales 34, when the first Jewish exiles began to appear.

Solon was a poet and statesman, whose political reforms are regarded as having been the forerunner of that world-famous type of government which we know today as "democracy".

In the Greek world into which Solon was born, an aristocracy of birth ruled. Poorer farmers were easily driven into debt, and when unable to pay, were forced to sell themselves into slavery. The middle classes were excluded from government, and they resented it. The prospect of an armed insurrection was looming large at the time that Solon appeared on the scene.

It seems that Solon's rise to power may have begun with, of all things, the reading of a poem. However trivial this may sound, this poem of his must have been a mighty little conglomeration of words indeed, because it seems that it stirred the people of Athens on to an important victory in a difficult war they were fighting.

His career was thus launched. By 594 BC he had risen to become an Archon (annual chief ruler) of Athens, and twenty years later, in the midst of crisis, he managed to obtain nearly complete control of the city-state.

Solon redeemed all forfeited land and freed all the enslaved citizens. Furthermore, he prohibited all future loans secured by the borrowers person. He created new trades and professions, and forbade the export of grain (Athenians were starving, and the rich were selling grain to get richer).

He re-wrote the old Draconian law - not figuratively "Draconian" but literally so - for Draco himself wrote the harsh law in 621 BC. The Draconian law punished all manner of crimes, both serious and trivial, with death. Solon replaced it with a law in which the death penalty was reserved for murder.

These reforms are highly reminiscent of the Law of Moses as expressed by the Torah. Did Solon join a Jewish synagogue and attend yeshiva? I doubt it. But the arrival of Jews and the sudden appearance of these new laws makes me highly suspicious of covert (or simply forgotten) cultural exchange, especially when considered together with the monumental changes going on simultaneously in Persia, India, and China.

The Beginnings of Philosophy

The other one of the "Seven Wise Men" of Greece whom we shall make mention of was Thales of Miletus, widely regarded as the first western "philosopher".

This great scientist-philosopher was the first man to explain cosmology without mythology. Although his cosmology may not seem terribly relevant to us today (he believed that the material substratum of the entire universe was water), his renunciation of mythology as an explanation for the universe was surely a revolutionary event in the intellectual/religious history of Greece.

Did this revolution have anything to do with our God? I think that it did. But it is in the work of Thales' successors, most principally Socrates, that the evidence of the Hand of God becomes much stronger.

Socrates

Socrates wrote nothing down on paper himself, but many of his dialogues were recorded for posterity by his most famous of pupils, Plato. It would be difficult to find an occidental who has attended any school at all who does not know the name Plato. America's greatest philosopher, Ralph Waldo Emerson, had this to say: "Plato is philosophy and philosophy Plato". What can I add?

Plato's most widely-read work has always been his rendering of the immortal Socratic dialogue *The Republic*. In this book, Socrates embarks on a long search for the meaning of the word "justice", but before coming to a conclusion, he and his colleagues diverge widely and variously, touching on numerous related and ancillary subjects, of which the most important are government, and God.

In his day, and right up to the present time, people have tended to take anything Socrates said with great seriousness. When one reads about his life, it's easy to see why. He thought about things a great deal before he spoke. According to eyewitnesses (as recorded in Plato's "Symposium"[23]), he was spied one morning stopping dead in his tracks, apparently lost in thought about some unknown subject. He stood in that one spot for the rest of the day, not budging even as the sun set.

Curious onlookers watched, wondering whether he would continue to stand and think throughout the night also. He did. At dawn, as the sun rose, he finally returned to the animated state and departed, going his way. Do you think he found the solution he was looking for?

Socrates was no "nerd", to use a modern-day slang expression. He achieved renown early in life as an exemplary soldier, fighting in the Athenian army. During that period, he was spied one severe winter's day walking about in a "dreadful frost" without any shoes on, while most others didn't dare emerge from their habitations unless swathed with multiple layers of coverings for body and feet. But the barefooted Socrates astounded his colleagues by "marching over the ice more easily than others did with boots on"[24].

Thus, when Socrates spoke, people listened. And speak he did. It was a day and age when philosophy was highly prized, and a goodly number of Athenian men devoted their lives to following Socrates around and listening to him talk. The Socratic method was "dialectic", or logical argument, which Socrates regarded as the supreme form of human endeavor. When he pursued a single idea, such as the definition of "justice", he pursued it relentlessly as if a war were going on. He refused to give in until both he and his listeners were thoroughly satisfied that the end had been reached. He was inexhaustible in debate, and there is no evidence I know of that he ever lost one.

Socrates' arguments can be so long and drawn-out as to be positively painful to suffer through. It is easy to see why he excelled at debate. In order for one to have had a basis for even *attempting* to refute any of Socrates' deeply and carefully thought-out arguments, one would have had to do what *he* did - spend one's entire life thinking about the subjects under attack.

Since Socrates vehemently denied ever accepting a fee for his teaching services, it is apparent that his achievements resulted from an unlikely coincidence of rare personal ability occurring in the setting of a receptive society. Athens, in the 5th century BC, was in *love* with knowledge, eager to learn "the truth about life", and persuaded that this truth could be known through dialectic. And Socrates, their greatest philosopher, was the unchallenged King of dialectic.

---

[23] All Platonic (i.e., Socratic) quotes and anecdotes are taken from the W.H.D. Rouse translation, entitled "Great Dialogues of Plato".
[24] Great Dialogues of Plato", Symposium, p. 113.

But Socrates frequently used the weapon of logical argument to attack problems which were really *beyond logic* by their very natures. As one reads through Socrates, one is often left with a feeling that some of the premises upon which he based his arguments were axiomatic in nature, and therefore not amenable to, or provable by logical analysis. Furthermore, some of the conclusions do not seem to have been justified by the arguments he presented. His opponents were quick to point these things out, and he himself often admitted it.

As a single illustrative example, Socrates (in *The Republic*, Book X) says that "the same part of the soul cannot possibly hold contrary opinions at the same time about the same things". To be sure, this is a fascinating proposition. But is it true? Who can say? Yet before we have had time to decide for ourselves whether such premises are true or false we find ourselves on various roller-coaster rides of logical argument designed to prove, for example, that art, poetry, and the theater in general corrupt the morals of society (because their imitations of life are inferior to life itself, and because they emphasize the worse parts of human nature), or that the soul is immortal and never dies (because of a logical argument too complex to repeat here).

In spite of the fact that Socrates' premises often seem arbitrary (although it would hardly be fair to call them "capricious"), he nevertheless always seems to come to the same conclusions as the other great philosophers and religious leaders who have been revered by mankind throughout the ages: justice is better than injustice, the soul is immortal, and God lies behind everything.

The religion of Socrates was his own personal religion. It seems to me, from the prospective of the 20th century, that he was, for all intents and purposes, a sort of Hindu. That is, he accepted the pantheon of Greek gods on some level, and talked often about "the gods" (i.e., many gods), but always reverted to talking about "God" (i.e., **one** God) whenever the subject was of great importance.

The answer to the question of whether Socrates was a "henotheist" (i.e., one who speaks of the god-of-the-moment as "God", whoever that god-of-the-moment happens to be), or a monotheist in the Hindu-Zoroastrian sense (where all the many gods and goddesses of mythology are regarded as being either inferior demigods or manifestations of a single true God who lies behind all) may be considered impossible to know today, 2500 years later. But the more one reads Socrates, the more apparent it becomes that there is, in fact, an answer to this question.

Socrates' most famous concept was of the "Idea of the Good", which, loosely stated, means that all the things of this world, whether of mind or of matter, are mere reflections or shadows of real objects which exist in the higher spiritual plane, which he calls the "world of the mind". If Socrates actually believed (as he said he did in *The Republic*) that even a mundane item such as a *bed* is a reflection of an ideal, *perfect bed* which exists in this higher spiritual plane, then how can we doubt that by analogy he *must* have believed that the Greek *gods* were a reflection of a *higher God* which could only be known through the exercise of reason, and not through mere study of mythology?

Thus it seems clear, at least to me, that Socrates paid his respects to the pantheon of Greek gods as a matter of practicality and convenience, but that he knew perfectly well that God was something other than that; something far greater.

There is, in any event, an ultimate proof that Socrates was a monotheist at heart. This proof is that he gave his life for his beliefs. At his famous trial in 399 BC Socrates (then 70 years old) was accused of "impiety and of the corrupting of young men" (as recorded in Plato's "Apology"). The affidavit of his accusers stated that he was "a criminal, who corrupts the young and does not believe in the gods whom the state believes in, but other new spiritual things instead."

The Dialogues "Crito" and "Phaedo", which chronicle the events which took place at the end of Socrates' life, show unequivocally that Socrates had ample opportunity to escape from prison, and from the death sentence imposed upon him. But he chose to stay and die, ignoring all the exhortations of his pupils, friends, and family members. There can be no doubt that he believed in his cause, and that he voluntarily died for it.

Let us turn now to the actual words of Socrates, as recorded by Plato. Anyone who has not read Plato, and who remains convinced that such a reading can only reveal pagan idolatry, albeit finely clothed in secular humanistic philosophy, will surely be surprised to read such statements as:

> **"The just man...will be scourged, racked, chained, have his eyes burnt out; at last, after every kind of misery, he will be hung up on a pole."**
>
> (*The Republic*, Book II),

or,

> **"...the more [people] value money the less they value virtue; in truth, we may imagine riches and virtue as always balanced in scales against each other."**
>
> (*The Republic*, Book VIII).

Did Socrates secretly receive a pre-publication proof of the New Testament? Here are some of the things he says about God, starting with an excerpt from a dialogue in which he attempts to refute the commonly held belief that the Greek gods have a habit of appearing on earth, disguised as human beings:

> **SOCRATES:** "...God and what is God's is everywhere in a perfect state...would he change and alter himself?"
>
> **ADEIMANTOS:** "...He must change for the worse if he does change, for I suppose we shall not say there is a lack in God of beauty or virtue".
>
> **SOCRATES:** "Quite right, and if thus perfect, do you think, Adeimantos, that anyone, god or man, would willingly make himself worse than this in any respect?"
>
> **ADEIMANTOS:** "Impossible."
>
> **SOCRATES:** "Then it is impossible that God should wish to alter himself".
>
> (*The Republic*, Book II)

Again, in Book II, we read:

> "The spiritual and divine is wholly without falsehood...altogether, then, God is simple and true in word and deed, and neither changes himself nor deceives others".

In Book VII of *The Republic*, Socrates gives his famous "cave" analogy ("Plato's Cave"), which compares ordinary human existence to being shackled in a dark cave, in such a way that only shadows of real things can be seen. Dialectic and logical argument are the tools of escape from this dark "cave" - escape to the freedom and dazzling radiance of the "world of mind". "But", says Socrates after spinning this elaborate analogy, "*God knows* if it is really true".

In fact, we are left repeatedly with the feeling that Socrates is cheating us when he insists that his conclusion - that God exists and is the power behind everything - is a *logical* conclusion. Actually, we get the feeling that Socrates *knew* that in advance, and is only using logic as an *excuse* to present a conclusion that he had already come to fully before the arguments ever began.

He himself eventually admits (in Plato's "Apology") that he is, and has always been *guided by an inner voice* since his childhood. He does not tell us exactly what the nature of this inner voice was, but whatever it was, it evidently counseled him to believe in a real God, even when threatened with death by the leaders of Athens. So his arguments about God, although logical-sounding, were never really based on logic, but were only clothed in the language of logic to make them more acceptable to a generation of idol worshippers.

In the end, however, the idol worshipper slew him.

If the appearance of a school of philosophical thought, culminating in a rigorously logical monotheistic refutation of pagan idolatry, coincided with the dispersal of the Jews of ancient Israel, and if that notwithstanding, skeptics insist that Greek philosophy was in no way reflective of the work of the Hand of God, then whose hand was it?

The Socratic Ideal of Perfect Government

It is not inconceivable that Socrates gave the subject of government more thought than anyone else who has ever lived. Besides, if anyone has thought about it more, it is far from certain that any written record of such a person would be easy to locate at this time.

I therefore propose that the Socratic ideal of perfect government not be brushed aside casually, but studied. It is really rather remarkable that as we read through *The Republic*, we encounter in-depth discussions of much the same problems and debates which trouble society today, and it would be a serious error to assume that the "ravings" of a philosopher of 2500 years ago ought to be dismissed on account of the passage of time.

We read, for example, that in *The Republic* Socrates carefully considered the role of women in his perfect city, concluding that there was no reason why they should not be qualified to fill all roles without exception, including supreme ruler or guardian. So "women's liberation" is not uniquely of the 20th century after all. Again, the philosophy of Socrates touches on such subjects as love, sexuality, marriage, work, war - in short, just about everything which concerns society today. Truly, there is "nothing new under the sun".

Socrates' observations about perfect and imperfect government are so filled with relevance to the world today that it is positively frightening to think that 2500 years of history have not resolved the issues involved. Because he foresaw all of our current political problems (which we ourselves have not done), I believe that his solutions ought to be given great consideration.

Socrates' "perfect city" was to be ruled by a special class of "guardians" who would be specially bred (from pre-existing guardians) and trained from youth to be free from material craving, cowardliness, lust for power, and all the other ills which usually afflict leaders in the real world. This training was no joke - it was to take 50 years; most of the guardian's life, in fact.

During my own reading of the rather long discussion of the training of guardians, I found myself becoming increasingly concerned about the question, not answered or even addressed, of exactly *who* it was who was of such towering wisdom that he/she was qualified to *supervise* such an educational program.

It is not until late in Book V of *The Republic* that Socrates reveals the secret of the identity of the supervisors of the training program for guardians. The answer is: the philosopher himself. The form of government being proposed, therefore is an aristocracy. An "aristocracy of the best", Socrates calls it. Until cities are under the rule of "true philosophers", he says, they can never achieve their full potential (or even the greater part of it).

Socrates himself readily admits that the possibility of philosophers taking over the reins of government in a world of violence and deceit, *i.e.* a world such as the one we all live in, is remote indeed. But he refuses to concede that such a thing is impossible. At the close of Book IX he states with firmness that whether or not the perfect city exists on earth, it is laid up in heaven as a pattern for mankind to follow.

I shall show, at the end of this book, how the Socratic ideal of perfect government can be applied to the world today. Once you have accepted, as I have, that it was the Spirit of God which was behind Socrates' philosophy, then the logic of employing his ideas about government in the modern-day world becomes evident. For *no one* has thought more about government than Socrates.

But we have much ground to cover before we will be in a position to discuss perfect government in the world today.

The Four Degenerate Types of Constitution

Having identified a philosopher's aristocracy as the preferred form of government, Socrates proceeds to describe the four "degenerate" types of constitution in a city's government. It is here that we see many reminders of our own present-day governments, frighteningly depicted.

The "four degenerate forms of constitution" are as follows:

1. The aristocratic constitution *degenerates* into the **timocratic** (or honor-loving) constitution when factions appear in the guardian class; one faction cleaving to money and property, and the other to traditional virtue. It is presumed by Socrates that the money-loving faction would prevail, to a greater or lesser extent. This results in a society which is increasingly devoted to money, power, glory, and honor at the expense of truth, justice, virtue, and principle.

In other words, true virtue is no longer a viable way of life in the timocracy. But the degeneration has not gone so far that the *appearances* of justice are not publicly maintained.

2. The timocratic constitution *degenerates* into **oligarchy** (the rule of the few) when love of money prevails entirely, so that honor, or even a pretense thereof, comes to be worthless, and only those with money can prosper. The laws are ignored or perverted so that the rich become richer, and the poor poorer.

3. The oligarchic constitution *degenerates* into **democracy** (the rule of the people) when those who are hopelessly impoverished rebel violently against their assigned roles in society, seizing the power and wealth of their rich overlords. All are then set free to do as they wish. This, says Socrates, is even worse than oligarchy. Whereas the oligarchic ruler at least maintains a sense of thrift, the democratic ruler casts even that aside, yielding to each and every desire and bringing the state to the brink of chaos.

As an interesting aside, Socrates points out that the democratic constitution itself (that is, the written document - not the *reality* of life under such a constitution) is

> "the most beautiful of constitutions...decked out ...as a *robe of many colors*...and what could be more beautiful!"
>
> (*The Republic*, Book VIII)

This analogy, to a "robe of many colors", is not exactly the most common of metaphors. We have previously asked, with tongue-in-cheek but only barely so, whether Socrates perhaps had a pre-publication proof edition of the New Testament at his disposal. Now we may also ask, in considerably more earnest, whether he had perhaps the Old Testament as well.

4. At last, the democratic constitution *degenerates* into **tyranny** when the people themselves rebel against lawlessness. The leaders of the democracy, says Socrates, habitually seize whatever property they can, distributing part of it to "the people", but keeping most of it for themselves. When the people can stand no more, they find themselves a strong man who restores order. He raises a private army to suppress the irresponsible elements in society. After being received initially as a deliverer, he quietly goes about establishing a dictatorship.

The character of the dictator, as described by Socrates, is so familiar in our own world today that reading this portion of *The Republic* is like reading a current newspaper. No sooner has the dictator taken power than he must begin to destroy anyone with enough intelligence or ability to question him, especially his own friends and colleagues who helped put him into office. He is thus the opposite of a physician - he clears away the best and leaves the worst.

He next begins to go about stealing the temple treasures, and the goods of each and every one of those citizens whom he is able to victimize, finally even including his own relatives and friends. As his power expands, his soul unleashes the most bestial and savage of desires; desires which in ordinary men are unleashed only in sleep, or in drunkenness, or in madness. "If he finds any opinions or desires in himself accounted honest and modest, he slays them and casts them out of himself, until he has purged himself of temperance and filled himself with foreign frenzy" (Book IX).

In order to illustrate the misery of the tyrant; a man who, in effect, enslaves an entire people; Socrates creates a clever analogy to a rich man dropped into a desert with all his property and slaves. It is easy to see how, in the isolation of the desert, without the protection of society, the rich man would be in constant fear of being robbed and murdered by his own slaves. By analogy, the tyrant, who has enslaved an entire nation, lives in constant fear of his subjects. He is the most miserable of men.

As one reads through this proposed cycle of degenerations, one sees at every step mirrors reflecting the state of things today, in modern America and in the other nations of the world. But Socrates has proposed a solution to the suffering and turmoil of bad government (which, in his day as well as ours, was *all* government).

The Socratic solution, which is a bit complicated, is derived by consideration of the analogy between people as individuals, and society as a whole. In individuals, Socrates sees three divisions of the soul:

      1. The Reasoning Part,
      2. The Spirited Part, and
      3. The Desiring Part.

The first Part is characterized by a love of knowledge, and it seeks the highest goals and ends at all times.

The second is characterized by a love of honor and glory, and is easily stirred up to action. The things it seeks are, at times, worthwhile, but at other times it finds that its actions have brought about results which were not intended or foreseen.

The third is characterized by a love of gratification of the senses, and a yielding to the base physical instincts. It neither knows nor cares what the outcome of its actions will be.

It is very easy for Socrates to show that peace within the individual can only come about when the Reasoning Part rules over the other two. It is the only Part whose decisions will never result in harm to the other two Parts, because it is the only Part which always considers what is best for the individual as a whole.

When the individual is ruled over by the Reasoning Part, allowing the Spirited and Desiring Parts to function according to their abilities whenever it is in the best interests of the individual for them to do so, then the soul is at peace. This, says Socrates, is the one and only definition of "justice" within an individual.

In a *society* of individuals, the analogous definition of "justice" is found to lie in the distribution of the various functions of society to those best qualified. In other words, for example, farmers will not meddle in the affairs of soldiers, nor soldiers in the affairs of government. Nor, for example, will the rulers or guardians arbitrarily or capriciously meddle in the affairs of those over whom they rule, voluntarily limiting the exercise of their power to those areas directly relevant to the governing of the state only.

This, says Socrates, is the only definition of the word "justice" which will stand up to scrutiny. And if, in the individual, the Reasoning component of the soul is the only component qualified to rule over the others, what is the analogous component in a society of individuals? It is what Socrates calls the "aristocracy of the best", which can only come about when society voluntarily puts itself under the yoke of the philosopher.

In the history of the world so far, there is no instance in which this has happened (at least no enduring instance of which historians have retained a written record). Philosophy (and religion) have always had to struggle to survive, and governments have always fallen into the hands of the rich and powerful, which has always meant rule by either tyrant or mob.

If one analyzes the reasons why the Socratic ideal (of government presided over by philosophers) has never been achieved, one can readily see that *threat of destruction from without* is at the head of the list. That is, a society where reason and law prevail will never be a match for a warmongering neighbor, if that neighbor is willing to devote all efforts and all resources to the art of aggression.

It has thus always been necessary to put *survival* at the head of the list of priorities of any nation, and philosophy, with few exceptions, has become the enemy of those who rule. The saying "render unto Caesar the things which are Caesar's, and unto God the things that are God's" (Matthew 22:21) expresses the need to resign oneself to this "harsh reality" which prevails when nations are continually at war.

But on a planet in which a one-world government, for better or for worse, is *already* quietly evolving, it seems to me that we will have an unprecedented opportunity to apply, for the first time in history, the principles of ideal Socratic government. You see, *there are no longer any external enemies*, and there are thus no longer any valid excuses for tolerating any government other than right government. Unless you really believe, deep down in your heart, that the world must arm itself to prepare for an invasion from space aliens, then ask yourself this: Why, in the 21st century, should we "render" unto a new Caesar, when there is no longer anything to gain from war? And who is to blame if we continue to accept bad government as a "necessary evil"?

But we must act soon, because the "New World Order" is already developing, and there is *no* "aristocracy of the best" forming in parallel. This "New World Order", which is really an old order of corruption and influence, is growing in strength daily, because there is nothing decent to oppose it.

I therefore propose that, for the first time in history, a perfect Socratic government be instituted without delay. To see how this can be done in the world of the 21st century, see the final chapters of this book.

Why did God create Oriental Religion?

The answer to this question no longer seems mysterious, at least not to me. I believe that mathematics is a form of Truth. I understand and accept the overwhelming statistical significance of the arrival of the Diaspora Jews in the countries of the Orient on the one hand, and the simultaneous appearances of all our Oriental religions on the other. I therefore *must* believe that Judaism was somehow the catalyst for all this. I don't know how it happened, and I don't imagine I ever will, but I have to believe in it all the same.

If God drove the Jews out of Israel in 600 BC, then, in the final analysis, God started the Oriental religions. That is why their teachings are the same as the teachings of Western religion. They were started by the same God.

But why?

As we have said before, in the beginning, before Adam and Eve ate from the Tree of Knowledge of Good and Evil, there *was* no "religion". God was present, and we knew Him personally. Because we disobeyed Him, and fell from grace, we have taken upon ourselves the task of finding the way back.

Long after the fall from Grace, God decided to establish a *Covenant* with the Jewish people. But the Jewish people did not live up to the terms of the Covenant.

Failing to heed the numerous warnings of the Prophets, Israel fell into sinful ways again and again. So the Northern half of the Kingdom was given into the hands of the Assyrians, and the Southern half into the hands of the Babylonians.

Hundreds of thousands, and maybe even millions of Jews were scattered abroad across the face of the entire world. This was the First Diaspora of 600 BC.

These Diaspora Jews were the living proof of the Truth of *the futility of turning against God*. Everywhere they went they successfully transmitted that essential message. It is thus perhaps not surprising that everywhere they went, profound changes in religion occurred.

Evidently, God, while promising not to wholly abandon the Jewish nation, nevertheless decided to bring His word to the other nations, *never again to have knowledge of Himself confined to one people*. This was the method that He chose; the mechanism whereby His Spirit burst forth from Jerusalem, bringing new revelations to the nations of the Orient.

As the Bible reports, that Spirit will also *return* to Jerusalem in the End, according to the prophet Micah, whose prophecy we have read previously:

> **...in the last days it shall come to pass, that the mountain of the house of the LORD shall be established in the top of the mountains, ... and people shall flow unto it. And many nations shall come, and say, Come, and let us go up to the mountain of the LORD,...<u>all people will walk every one in the name of his god</u>, and we will walk in the name of the LORD, our God, forever and ever.**

(Micah 4:1-5).

It is profitable to believe that God is the Father of Oriental religion, for that is the path to peace.

To deny it, just because your parents denied it, or because it was not preached from the pulpit of your church, is a sure path to a godless "one-world" dictatorship of wealth and privilege. You see, over in the Orient, they're also denying *you,* and in a world of universal mutual denial, the only principle which can stand is money.

The choice is yours.

Chapter 4

Where Is "David" Now?

The Genetics of "Jewishness"

When people speak with excitement about the Bible as the *living* Word of God, such excitement is invariably found to be based upon the Bible's prophecies about the End Times. In the End, a Deliverer will come, and under his[25] reign the world will become a paradise.

English-speaking people frequently refer to the coming Deliverer as "Messiah". This word, however, is never used in the Bible to describe a Deliverer-to-come. Nevertheless, the word is so ingrained in our culture that it's almost hopeless to avoid continuing to use it.

We will read about the characteristics of the End Times world later. For now, it is enough to note that, in the End, the following two facts must pertain:

1. **The House of David must rise up again, and rule the world.**

2. **The Deliverer (Messiah) must be a descendent of King David.**

We are talking about the salvation of the whole wretched world. The identity of the Deliverer, therefore, is a matter of great importance to believers and non-believers alike, all of whom shall be possessed with a burning desire to know exactly *who* it is who shall rule over them.

A deliverer is expected in virtually every religious tradition. In the modern Jewish religion his title is invariably given as "Messiah". Muslims call him "Maḥdi" (with a

---

[25] It should be noted that the number of Deliverers is not necessarily limited to one. In the Dead Sea Scrolls we may discern evidence for as many as three: a King, a Priest, and a "Teacher of Righteousness". In some places in the Bible, the language describing the Deliverer is explicitly male. In other places, however, the language is less clear, alluding to a rising up of the House of David generally. There is no doubt that the House of David can be, and in fact has been under the rule of women more than once in its history. It therefore cannot be excluded that one or more of the Deliverers might be a woman.

soft, guttural "h"). English-speaking Christians more often refer to him as the returning Christ. In the East, however, people are awaiting the returning Buddha.

Because the belief in a Deliverer is so widespread, billions of human beings have been anxiously keeping watch, day to day, hour to hour, for whole lifetimes, through the centuries. They watch the skies, they watch the land, and they watch the sea, waiting patiently for the arrival of the Deliverer. From whence shall he come?

In the West it is agreed upon by all that he must be a descendant of the House of David. This means that he must be a great-great-great...(etc.) grandson of the original King David. Now, most people are unable to trace their own genealogies back much beyond their grandparents. How will it be possible to know that someone *is* or *isn't* a descendent of King David, a man who died 3,000 years ago—a period of time corresponding to a hundred generations?

The genetics of being "David"

When a man has sexual intercourse with a woman, he passes to her a "sperm" cell which contains half of his genetic material (DNA). This sperm enters into, and combines with the woman's "egg" cell, which contains half of *her* genetic material. The product is a "fertilized egg", which contains a full complement of DNA, half from the father, half from the mother.

The DNA of human beings is wrapped up into 46 things called *chromosomes.* Twenty-three of your chromosomes originally came from your father, and 23 from your mother. For simplicity, in the following graphic representation, we will show only 2 of these chromosomes, since the principles which emerge are the same for any chromosome count:

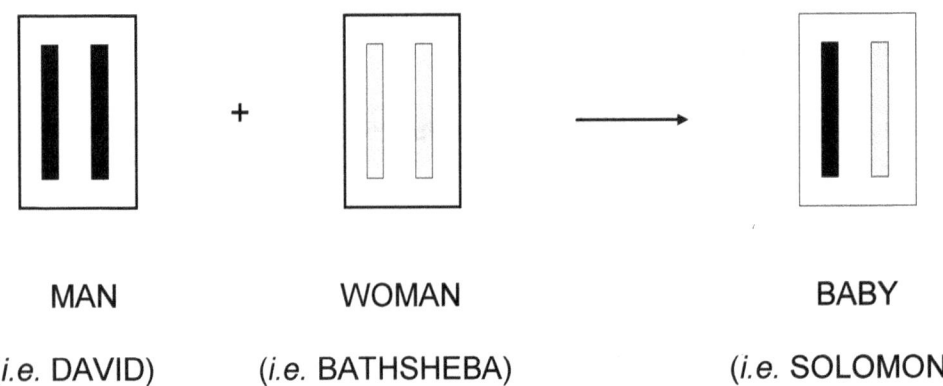

MAN   WOMAN   BABY

(*i.e.* DAVID)   (*i.e.* BATHSHEBA)   (*i.e.* SOLOMON)

Where is "David" Now?

In this drawing, the genetic material of an imaginary David is represented as 2 heavy black lines. The chromosomes of Bathsheba are represented as lighter gray lines. Note that baby Solomon has one of each: a black line from David, and a gray line from Bathsheba.

Is this simple enough? The important thing is that only *half* of baby Solomon's DNA comes from daddy. The other half comes from mom. But there's not a Bible scholar in the world who wouldn't call Solomon a "full-blooded" descendant of the House of David. The point is that you don't need *all* of your father's genes to be a legal descendant of him; only *some* of them.

This means that you may not look like your father, and you probably *won't* look like your grandfather. You certainly won't look anything like your great-grandfather. Yet you're still the lawful "full-blooded" descendant of all of them when it comes to matters of inheritance.

Let us, for brevity, refer to any lawful descendant of King David as being a "David". Where is "David" now?

You'll be surprised at the answer.

The number of "Davids" increases rapidly

Let's now give our imaginary David *more* than one child. Let's give him two:

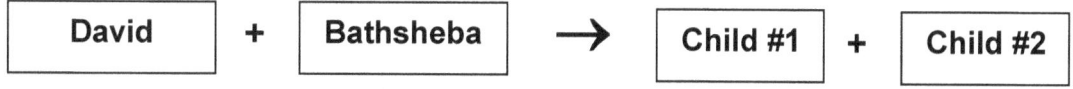

Let's call David and Bathsheba the "First" generation and the two children the "Second" generation. What's happened to the number of "Davids"? It's *doubled.*

Both of these children are "full-blooded" descendants of David, entitled to all the rights of inheritance. It doesn't matter what they look like. Whether or not they resemble their father physically, they're legally "Davids".

Let's now let our imaginary David and Bathsheba die, leaving no other offspring behind. What has happened to the number of "Davids" in the world? It's *doubled*—even though the number of people in the family has not increased. There were two parents; now there are two children. Yet in the First generation, there was only *one* "David", *i.e.,* David himself. In the Second generation, there are now *two*.

What will happen in the 3rd generation? If these two children grow up and marry, and each has only two children, then the number of "Davids" will again *double:*

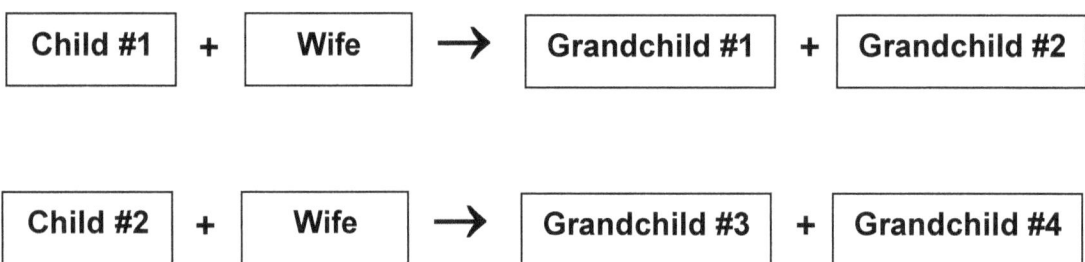

Look what's happened. The two children married, and had *four* grandchildren between them. So there are now *four* "Davids". Please note that the population of Israel has *not* increased. When the four parents die, there will be four children—the number of people has not changed. The only thing which has changed is the number of "Davids", which has again *doubled.*

Even if we assume that the historical David had only 2 children, and that the population of Israel did not increase at all in the centuries following his reign, we can see that the number of "Davids" will nevertheless have doubled in each generation. These grandchildren and great-grandchildren may not have looked anything like grandpa David, but they were still 100% "full-blooded" legal descendants.

Now let's look at the real facts—the Biblical facts, that is. David had at least 10 wives and concubines, and probably many more. The Bible names 19 sons and 1 daughter. If he had 19 sons, it is virtually certain that he had many daughters who weren't named. There is also a strong implication that he had numerous unnamed concubines in addition to those wives and concubines who are specifically identified (I Chronicles 3:1-9).

It is thus safe to assume, as a minimum estimate, that David left behind *dozens* of offspring. If any of them were at all like his most famous son, Solomon, who had nearly 1000 wives and concubines, then the number of Davidic grandchildren running around Jerusalem after Solomon's death must have been hundreds, if not thousands.

According to the Encyclopedia Britannica[26], the population of the ancient world, estimated to have been 300,000,000, didn't change much from 1000 BC to the

---

[26] Encyclopedia Britannica, 15th Edition, 1988. Macropaedia, volume 25, "Population", p. 1045.

time of Yeshua (Jesus). Nevertheless, we may still assume that after the Civil War which split Israel into two nations, the number of "Davids" approximately doubled with each generation (in accordance with our diagram above, which shows that a doubling takes place *even in the absence of population growth*). Starting with a few hundred, it is not difficult to see how a *large number* of "Davids" must have been alive in the world by the year 600 BC, the approximate date of the First Jewish Diaspora.

How large a number? Well, people in the ancient world married a lot younger than they do today. Between Solomon (1000 BC) and the Diaspora (600 BC), a period of 400 years, there was time for anywhere from 12-16 generations. Let us assume that a generation took about 33 years, *i.e.* a third of a century (surely an underestimate back in those days—who waited until they were 33 to get married in ancient times?), and let us take the generation after Solomon as the first generation, with a starting number of "Davids" as being 100 (again, surely an underestimate). How many "Davids" were there by the time of the Diaspora? The number will approximately double every generation:

Approximate Year	Generation	# of "Davids"
1000 BC	1st	100
967	2nd	200
933	3rd	400
900	4th	800
867	5th	1,600
833	6th	3,200
800	7th	6,400
767	8th	12,800
733	9th	25,000
700	10th	50,000
667	11th	100,000
633	12th	200,000
600 **(Diaspora)**	13th	400,000

Since Solomon surely had more than 100 children, and since people generally got married way before the age of 33, these are to be regarded as rock-bottom minimum estimates. Furthermore, these 400 years were years of growth and prosperity for Israel. We might therefore consider this number, 400,000, as being the smallest possible number of "Davids" living in Israel at the time of the great Diaspora of 600 BC. That's a lot of "Davids"!

Remember that it doesn't matter what they looked like, or what sorts of people they were. Even if some of them were low-down dirty scoundrels, each one of them was a "full-blooded" legal descendent of the Line of David.

Where did they all live? In the beginning, they probably lived in or close to Jerusalem. But in this world, no one stays in the same place for very long. By the time 400 years had gone by, the "Davids" were certainly scattered to the four corners of the Israelite nation, both the Northern and Southern Kingdoms.

What this means is that there were "Davids" literally everywhere in Israel, and when the Assyrian and Babylonian invaders dismembered and scattered the nation, they drove **hundreds of thousands** of "Davids" into exile.

What happened to the number of "Davids" in the Diaspora?

We have already seen that there were Jewish immigrants who relocated to Europe, Persia, India, China,... in fact, *everywhere* (including Africa, as we shall shortly see). Let's look at a single country, China. Suppose that one hundred "Davids" moved there in 600 BC. What will happen to that number over time? The answer is in the table above. It shows that after 400 years, or 13 generations, there will be *400,000 "Davids"!*

Let's get realistic. We're interested in *today,* not ancient times. We want to know how many "Davids" there are in China, and in other countries, *today,* right now. So we need to start with realistic numbers.

The number of Jews who moved to China in 600 BC was probably a lot *more* than 100. And the time elapsed since then is a lot more than 13 generations. Allowing 33 years per generation, the amount of time which has now elapsed since the Diaspora is up to at least *80 generations.* If one hundred "Davids" becomes 400,000 in 13 generations, how many "Davids" will there be after 80 generations?

The number is staggering. It can only be represented as a "6" followed by 25 zeros (*i.e.* 6×10^{25})—a number so large it has no name. It's like the number of grains of sand on the beach.

Note that these "Davids" no longer have any physical resemblance to Israelites. Most of them have long since intermarried, and in every subsequent generation they have looked more and more like natives of the country, and less and less like Israelites. Nevertheless, the genes of King David have thusly penetrated deep into the gene pools of Asia, Africa and all the other continents of the world.

It makes no difference that there may exist relatively inbred communities of Jews which have resisted intermarriage. It is a demonstrable fact that most Jewish refugees are indeed assimilated into the local population into which they move. That is why the total world population increases relentlessly, but the total world *Jewish* population never changes much.

And all the assimilated "Davids" remain "Davids", whether or not they practice Judaism, and whether or not they know who they are. God knows who they are.

I would suggest to you that most of the people in the world today, whether black or white or yellow, are of the Line of David. Many readers will find this hard to believe, but the mathematics make it painfully clear, and well-nigh incontrovertible.

Therefore, if an Oriental man runs a 2-page ad in the newspapers proclaiming himself to be Messiah, you may believe him, or you may disbelieve him, but if you disbelieve him because you think an Oriental can't be of the Line of David, you may be seriously mistaken.

The Messiah can therefore come from any of the four corners of the earth. Anyone who believes in the Messiah, but who doubts that the Messiah could come from literally any nation, at literally any time, is fooling himself.

The Messiah is the King of Israel, who will rule over the raised up House of David. We now see, however, that the House of Israel is no longer a "race". Who, then, are the "Children of Israel"? Perhaps we can understand now why Yeshua (Jesus) said:

> **...whosoever shall do the will of my Father which is in heaven, the same is my brother, and sister, and mother.**
>
> **(Matthew 12:50)**

Chapter 5

Yeshua Moshiaḥ

Jesus Christ

The man whom the English call *Jesus Christ* stands at the heart of this book, as he does at the heart of history — everyone's history.

This is evidenced in numerous ways. It was 2000 years from Abraham to Jesus, and it has been 2000 years since. So he is literally at the center of the timeline of world religion.

While it is self-evident that he is the heart of the Christian religion, his importance does not stop there. In the Jewish religion his denial, which, as we shall see, was in fulfillment of scripture, constitutes a negative tradition which has come to rival even observance of the Law itself in importance. Do you doubt this? Even in some of the most reformed of synagogues, where virtually anything *else* can be freely discussed, including witchcraft or sorcery, the name of Jesus cannot be openly pronounced. When he is brought up at all, he is referred to by appellations such as "the founder of Christianity", or simply as "that *other* guy". The name "Jesus" is virtually never uttered out loud in a synagogue.

Consequently, even though it has been in a negative sense, it can truly be said that from one point of view, Jesus has been the focus of Judaism for 2000 years.

What about Islam? Surely Muḥammad is the Prophet thought of as being the heart of that religion, and yet that Prophet taught his followers that he was sent to them by Jesus (Qur'an 61:6).

Doesn't that make Jesus a lesser figure in Islam? Not so fast. If the Prophet was established by the authority of he that sent him, then by the same authority, the following saying must be taken into account here: "Verily, verily, I say unto you, the servant is not greater than his lord; neither he that is sent greater than he that sent him" (John 13:16).

I approach the subject of Messiah with great trepidation, because his nature remains a mystery to humans. I have failed repeatedly through the years to reduce his story to an acceptable text, and yet I am called upon to try. Where does one begin?

Yeshua Moshiaḥ

I suppose we can begin by calling him by his real name: Yeshua ben Yosef, *i.e.* Yeshua, son of Joseph the carpenter of Nazareth, known to the Greeks as "Iasous", which the translators of the King James Court inexplicably felt compelled to turn into "Jesus", a name I have reservations about.

I believe in all the prophets, including the Arab prophet, Muḥammad, and I agree with the prophet Muḥammad that "all the prophets came bearing the same message, and all are to be equally revered". Wherefore then do I declare one of them only, Yeshua ben Yosef, as "standing at the heart of history"?

Because in his role as prophet, he did indeed come with the same message as the others. But he was also something else which no one else has ever been, or can ever be. He was the Messiah, who was sent into the world to die for our sins. This simple-sounding statement is as deep as the ocean, and cannot be understood by the wisest of people. Nevertheless, we are bidden to try. Those who reject it without even having thought the matter through are not fully educated, no matter how much schooling they have had.

No writer, designer, architect, planner, plotter or schemer could have even dreamed of the story which actually came to pass 2000 years ago, much less executed it. What makes it all the more remarkable is that it was entirely foreseen, and hated by some, and yet it came to pass, and is still coming to pass today, as a juggernaut, or as a steam-roller of immense size which is moving forward and cannot be stopped. Knowledge of its route does not empower anyone to prevent its journey; it proceeds regardless of the acts of men.

No one asked for it. It was said, it was done, and it cannot be undone.

What was done? What cannot be undone?

Israel was the repository of the Word of God. The prophet Moses clearly foresaw that the people would fall into evil ways after he died. Had he been able to see them later, their behavior would therefore not have surprised him in the slightest. They became worse even than the idolators whom the LORD displaced when He brought them into the Promised Land. So the LORD removed them, and scattered them around the world, as they are to this day.

But the LORD promised that He would raise up the House of David again in the End. Why, we cannot say. That is what He said He would do. But how would He do it?

The Children of Israel had to be punished and humiliated, in a very large way, but in a way which did not discredit them so much that they could not still be admired and respected for being the repository of His Word. How can a nation so humbled and humiliated be "admired and respected"? The answer is two-fold. First of all, there must be, buried somewhere within that nation, a kernel of Truth so precious that it shines through the dirt. Secondly, the rest of the world must be at least as wicked, or even more wicked, than Israel itself.

Both those conditions do in fact exist.

The punishment which was inflicted upon Israel was that they would slay an innocent man, whose *cause* would be taken up by the gentile world. This *cause* was so vital and essential to the completion of God's plan for the salvation of humankind that the plan had to be suspended. And so it is suspended. It cannot be completed until that cause returns to Israel, and is wholeheartedly taken up there.

At the same time, the kernel of Truth which Israel holds cannot be received in its entirety by any other nation, because it entails obedience to a law so contrary to human greed and ambition that even the great majority of Jews cannot stand to adhere to it. I refer not even to the vast collection of allegedly-implied law known as the Talmud, but merely to the Law as stated in Torah. Even the most observant of Jews do not follow this law entirely. Most Jews do not even try. And most Christians and Muslims believe that the Law is "cancelled" in Christ.

So Israel safeguards the Law, though it cannot follow it. The gentile nations safeguard the Messiah, who came to complete the Law, though they cannot comprehend the Law he came to complete. In chess, this would be deemed a "stalemate".

Is the Law really all that difficult to comprehend? The Rabbis of today declare it to be so obscured by innumerable levels of complexity that it cannot be understood; not even by the wise. Thus the Talmud stands in its place.

This is not, however, true. The "levels of complexity" alleged to conceal the Law are not "levels", but "level". A single level. And that level is the refusal of all people, in all times and places, to ponder the meaning of "love thy neighbor", a commandment known as supreme in every time and place. It is, however, a commandment merely proclaimed, never obeyed.

Aside from that, there is no "complexity" to the Law. Some parts of it may seem irrational, but in a mad, mad, mad, mad world—one which pursues outright falsehood on a daily basis—the pursuit of this Law instead could be accomplished with the greatest of ease. And it must be, or there will be no peace, ever. Forget about the "United Nations". You can't legislate morality.

How can all this be brought on by slaying an innocent man? What? *One man?* How many men, women and children have been whipped, tortured, mutilated, drowned, raped, impaled, burnt, and utterly destroyed in body, and in reputation, and in spirit, that we should care about the death of one man?

Let's find out.

The prophecies

Iasous Christos, *i.e.*, the Jew, Yeshua ben Yosef, was a prophet of the Jewish religion. The same was the man who said

> **"Till heaven and earth pass, one jot or one tittle shall in no wise pass from the law, till all be fulfilled".**
>
> **(Matthew 5:18)**

This "law" is the Law of Moses, of course. Yet Jews today deny that the Messiah has come, even though some among them have known, from the beginning, that the Messiah did indeed come, and that Yeshua was he. Why is this? Yeshua himself gave the answer:

> **"And whosoever speaketh a word against the Son of man, it shall be forgiven him: but whosoever speaketh against the Holy Spirit, it shall not be forgiven him, neither in this world, neither in the world to come."**
>
> **(Matthew 12:32)**

The Christians proclaimed that Yeshua was God. Although it is well-established that many Jews believed that Jesus was Messiah, there was a sharp division of opinion concerning this doctrine of divinity. Many regarded it as outright idolatry, which was the supremely forbidden sin. Surely, the Rabbis decided, it was safer to deny the Son of Man in error, which Yeshua himself said would be forgiven, than to risk speaking against the Holy Spirit, which would result in eternal damnation.

Where did the Christians get the idea that Yeshua was God? There is not much evidence that this doctrine was known at the time of his ministry. Most of what was known at that time came from Isaiah, Chapter 53, which we must now examine.

Chapter 53 of the Book of Isaiah is not a continuation of Chapter 52, nor is it a prelude to Chapter 54. It is a free-standing prophecy which seems to come out of nowhere. Although the King James translation of this passage can be disputed, the fact of the matter is that Hebrew is an exceedingly difficult language to translate, and there really isn't any other English translation which can be said to come closer to the "true" Hebrew meaning:

Isaiah 53

1. Who hath believed our report? and to whom is the arm of the LORD revealed?

2. For he shall grow up before Him as a tender plant, and as a root out of a dry ground: he hath no form nor comeliness; and when we shall see him, there is no beauty that we should desire him.

3. He is despised and rejected of men; a man of sorrows, and acquainted with grief: and we hid as it were our faces from him; he was despised, and we esteemed him not.

4. Surely he hath borne our griefs, and carried our sorrows: yet we did esteem him stricken, smitten of God, and afflicted.

5. But he was wounded for our transgressions, he was bruised for our iniquities: the chastisement of our peace was upon him; and with his stripes[27] we are healed.

6. All we like sheep have gone astray; we have turned every one to his own way; and the LORD hath laid on him the iniquity of us all.

7. He was oppressed, and he was afflicted, yet he opened not his mouth: he is brought as a lamb to the slaughter, and as a sheep before her shearers is dumb, so he openeth not his mouth.

8. He was taken from prison and from judgment: and who shall declare his generation? for he was cut off out of the land of the living: for the transgression of my people was he stricken.

9. And he made his grave with the wicked, and with the rich in his death; because he had done no violence, neither was any deceit in his mouth.

10. Yet it pleased the LORD to bruise him; he hath put him to grief: when thou shalt make his soul an offering for sin, he shall see his seed, he shall prolong his days, and the pleasure of the LORD shall prosper in his hand.

11. He shall see of the travail of his soul, and shall be satisfied: by his knowledge shall my righteous servant justify many; for he shall bear their iniquities.

12. Therefore will I divide him a portion with the great, and he shall divide the spoil with the strong; because he hath poured out his soul unto death: and he was numbered with the transgressors; and he bare the sin of many, and made intercession for the transgressors.

---

[27] The Hebrew word ḥa-vu-rah-tho", translated here as "his stripes", can also be interpreted to mean "his friendship" or "his fellowship". Indeed, this is the Masoretic Jewish translation, which is also more acceptable to Muslims, who deny the doctrine of vicarious atonement. The phrase then reads "in his fellowship we are healed". Because of the ambiguities of the Hebrew language, which originally had no vowels (all the vowels having been added in the Christian Era a thousand years later), this interpretation can be defended from the grammatical point of view, although it is awkward in its treatment of the Hebrew root-word for "friend".

Clearly, these passages describe a messenger of God who will fulfill the following criteria:

VERSE	INTERPRETATION
1	This prophesy, of his coming, will not be believed.
2	He will not be recognized when he comes.
3	He will not be accepted, but despised.
4-5	He will be perceived to have been smitten by God, even though the sins he will suffer for are *ours*.
5	"and with his stripes we are healed"... Therefore, the suffering he undertook on our behalf will somehow bring healing to many who are sick.
6	"*All* we like sheep have gone astray"; therefore his message is for *all*, not just for some.
7	He will not raise a finger of protest when he is led off by his executioners.
8	He will be imprisoned, but will be taken abruptly out and condemned to death without a fair trial.
9	He will be executed, and buried in a place reserved for the wicked, or for the rich.
9	He will not, at any time, have committed any violent acts, or uttered any falsehoods.
10	This will all be done according to God's plan, with Whom the responsibility ultimately rests.
10	The acceptance of his death as a sacrifice (an "offering" for sin) will bring fruition to God's plan.
11	He will know, before his death, that his ministry has succeeded, and he shall be satisfied.

12	He will be rewarded for his sacrifice. In some unspecified way, he will be joined with a group of exalted great ones. Whether these are people or angels cannot be determined from the verse.

It will be immediately evident to anyone who is familiar with the life of Yeshua ben Yosef, *i.e*, Jesus, son of Joseph, the carpenter of Nazareth, that Chapter 53 of the Book of Isaiah is a concise biography of that life.

For the first thousand years of the Christian Era, there were considerable numbers of Jewish followers of Jesus. But these virtually disappeared from the face of the earth after the Crusades.

Excepting a handful of specially-trained anti-missionaries, modern day Jews never read Isaiah Chapter 53, either in synagogue or out. Jewish scholars argue that the chapter refers *not* to the Messiah, but to the entire *nation* of Israel. In other words (they now say) it is *Israel* which will be despised and rejected. Therefore, they say, this passage is not "messianic" at all. Furthermore, since the nation of Israel was *always* despised and rejected, the commentary is totally superfluous now, as it was when it was written. That is why it is never read in synagogues. It simply doesn't say anything worth repeating.

It is self-evident, on reflection, that the modern Jewish view represents a significant departure from a previous Jewish interpretation. For if we assume that the ancient Rabbis considered Isaiah Chapter 53 to be about the entire nation of Israel, we run into some logical absurdities. The main such absurdity is that we must therefore assume that no one in ancient Israel was expecting a *suffering servant* to die for our sins. If that is the case, then anyone who allowed himself to be killed to fulfill prophecy, was dying for a cause which no one knew about.

Let us assume the worst about Yeshua—that he was a total fraud, who willingly died on the cross just for the thrill of having a moment of fame. Wait a minute. What fame? *Would a man give his life for a cause that no one knew about?*

Obviously, the point of view that Isaiah 53 is about the "entire nation of Israel" is a *new* view, and has replaced an older point of view which was, at some point in history, rejected as being "too Christological".

Modern Jewish commentaries on Isaiah 53 endeavor to suggest that Israel, being the only nation to follow the "true religion", is and always has been less sinful than all other nations (*i.e.*, nations which follow Christianity, Islam, Buddhism, etc.). Therefore, say the Jewish commentators, when Israel suffers at the hands of the other nations, it cannot be for Israel's *own* sins, but must be for the sins of her tormentors, who are morally even *worse* than Israel herself.

This is nonsense. What prophet ever held Israel to be *without sin?* Consider the following four quotes from the "Major Prophets":

> **Isaiah 1:1** "The vision of Isaiah ... which he saw concerning Judah and Jerusalem ... (1:4): 'Ah, sinful nation, a people laden with iniquity, a seed of evildoers, children that are corrupters; they have forsaken the LORD, they have provoked the Holy One of Israel unto anger, they are gone away backward'".

> **Jeremiah 1:14** "Then the LORD said unto me ... (1:16) I will utter my judgments against them (*i.e.*, Israel) touching all their wickedness, who have forsaken me, and have burned incense unto other gods, and worshipped the works of their own hands."

> **Ezekiel 3:17** "Son of man, I have made thee a watchman unto the house of Israel ... give them warning from me... (19) Yet if thou warn the wicked, and he turns not from his wickedness, nor from his wicked way, he shall die in his iniquity..."

> **Daniel 9:5** "We have sinned, and have committed iniquity, and have done wickedly, and have rebelled, even by departing from thy precepts and from thine judgments".

The "Minor Prophets", from Hosea to Malachi, agree. Keeping in mind the words of Isaiah 53:9, concerning the Suffering Servant of the LORD (..."because he had done ***no violence***, neither was any ***deceit*** in his mouth..."), let us ask ourselves: is this *really* about the entire nation of Israel? No violence? No deceit? Here's what the "Minor Prophets" said:

> **Hosea 4:1-2:** "Hear the word of the LORD, ye children of Israel; for the LORD hath a controversy with the inhabitants of the land, because there is *no truth*, nor mercy, nor knowledge of God in the land. By swearing, and lying, and *killing*, and stealing, and committing adultery they break out, and blood toucheth blood."

> **Malachi 1:1** "The burden of the word of the LORD to Israel ... (1:6-7) 'A son honoreth his father, and a servant his master; if, then I be a father, where is mine honor? And if I be a master, where is my fear? saith the LORD of hosts unto you, O priests, that despise my name. And ye say, Wherein have we despised thy name? Ye offer polluted bread upon mine altar; and ye say, Wherein have we polluted thee? In that ye say, The table of the LORD is contemptible'."

Based on these passages, it hardly seems likely that the author of Isaiah 53 was referring to the entire nation of Israel.

(Other nations should take great care not to arrogantly assert their "moral superiority" in the wake of the LORD's condemnation of ancient Israel; nor should they take any comfort in it—in **His** mind, which we cannot know, the other nations of the earth may be even *worse*).

Having taken the trouble to quote all the above Prophets, I must now reveal to you that there actually *is* a way to see Chapter 53 as being about the nation of Israel, and not about a single man. This way involves the concept of a *remnant:* a pure, unspoiled, untainted subset of world Jewry—an exalted minority whose people have never fallen into the sinful ways of the masses.

The sections of the Bible dealing with the End Times are replete with references to this *remnant*. Most of these references are quite explicit, stating, in straightforward language, that the End will be a time of severe trouble, but that a *remnant* of Israel will be raised up. One of the most important such prophecies, although somewhat dense in its complexity, is found in Isaiah, Chapter 6. This is the famous vision of Isaiah, in which he was brought up to the presence of the LORD, and charged with a rather singular task (which we shall describe shortly).

Before being charged with this special task, Isaiah saw and heard Seraphim (flaming angels), who chanted in unison **"Holy, holy, holy is the LORD of hosts: the whole earth is full of his glory"**. This is one of the most familiar lines in the entire Hebrew liturgy; one which is recited by the Orthodox every day of their lives. The rest of this brief chapter, however, is not often discussed at any great length. The words of the Prophet Isaiah:

> **I heard the voice of the LORD, saying, Whom shall I send, and who will go for us? Then said I, Here am I; send me.**
>
> **And He said, "Go, and tell this people, Hear ye indeed, but understand not; and see ye indeed, but perceive not."**
>
> **"Make the heart of this people fat, and make their ears heavy, and shut their eyes; lest they see with their eyes, and hear with their ears, and understand with their heart, and convert, and be healed."**
>
> **Then said I, "LORD, how long?" And He answered, "Until the cities be wasted without inhabitant, and the houses without man, and the land be utterly desolate, and the LORD have removed men far away, and there be a great forsaking in the midst of the land."**
>
> **"But yet in it shall be a tenth, and it shall return, and shall be eaten: as a teil tree, and as an oak, whose substance is in them, when they cast their leaves: so the holy seed shall be the substance thereof."**
>
> **(Isaiah 6:8-13)**

What's this?! The holy Prophet is to *shut* their eyes and ears; to *prevent* these people from attaining understanding? That's surely the face-value meaning of the text. Why would God want to do that?

And what about that last paragraph? It's a bit dense, but if you study it closely, you'll see that what it's saying is that God will preserve only a small *remnant* of the people, perhaps literally 10% ("a tenth"). As an oak tree casts its leaves every fall, leaving only the life-force within the trunk, so will Israel be continually debrided; continually *cut off*, leaving only a remnant behind.

The English translation found in the *Hertz* version of the Hebrew *Pentateuch and Haftorahs* renders the same verse as follows:

> **And if there be yet a tenth in it, it shall again be eaten up; as a terebinth, and as an oak, whose [trunk]* remaineth, when they cast their leaves, so the holy seed shall be the [trunk] thereof.**
>
> *Hertz actually says "stock".
>
> **(Isaiah 6:13)**

Surely, it seems, at first glance, that God intends to punish the larger part of Jewry, sparing only an exalted remnant for an extraordinary destiny. God doesn't even *want* the others to be healed. And what is it that the eyes and ears of the Jews are to be closed to?

I'm not even going to attempt to answer the last question, because I do not have authoritative knowledge about the "one true meaning" of Isaiah 6. I merely wish to show you the plainest interpretation, and to document the existence in the Bible of mention of an exalted *remnant* of Israel. Now we may return to our consideration of Isaiah 53.

Without a doubt, if Isaiah 53 is about the nation of Israel, it must be about this exalted remnant, since all others are heavily burdened by sin. Does not Isaiah say, of the Suffering Servant, that **"for the transgression of my people was he stricken ... because he had done no violence, neither was any deceit in his mouth"** (Isaiah 53:9-10)? It is inconceivable that this refers to the large mass of commoners, since they were roundly condemned as sinners by *all* the Prophets.

This point of view, that Isaiah 53 is about the exalted *remnant* of Israel, was championed by the Karaites, an ultra-orthodox sect of Judaism which arose about the same time as the Talmud, and went to war against it. It will probably not surprise you to find out that the Karaites regarded *themselves* as the exalted remnant.

I find much merit in the Karaite point of view about Isaiah 53. But since I consider Yeshua to be the single most significant visible manifestation of the exalted remnant, I find no contradiction between the Karaite and Christian points of view.

On the other hand, to say that Chapter 53 is about the entire nation of Israel, without any qualifications, is utterly without logical or scriptural basis.

Was prophecy really fulfilled, or did it just look that way?

In the modern age, where 100% of Rabbis say that Chapter 53 of the Book of Isaiah is *not* a messianic prophecy, but rather a triviality of some sort, the fact of suppression of older opinion is evident. Whether this was a minority or majority opinion in 32 AD is impossible to determine now, but the fact that a pre-existing opinion has been suppressed seems virtually certain.

But even if it is conceded that some ancient Rabbis accepted Isaiah 53 as being an explicit messianic prophecy, Jewish critics of Christianity are quick to argue that Yeshua and his disciples merely *contrived* to make it look like his life was a fulfillment of Biblical prophecy. Indeed, for the non-believer, it would not be difficult to find evidence to support this point of view (see, for example, Matthew 21:1-7, where Jesus and his disciples go out of their way to obtain a donkey upon which he shall ride triumphantly into Jerusalem, explicitly for the purpose of fulfilling scripture).

Unfortunately, such arguments have no validity whatsoever. They suggest that unless a person who has fulfilled a Biblical prophecy was *ignorant* that he was doing so, that he was somehow "cheating". But the various prophecies concerning the coming of a Messiah were known to most well-educated Jews, and to insist that a Messiah had to be illiterate is obviously absurd. Besides, the same critics who reject Jesus because he was *not* illiterate also reject the Prophet of Islam, Muḥammad, because he *was* illiterate! Oughtn't we be consistent?

Additionally, the existing historical writings from the period between Isaiah and Yeshua suggest that a large number of false messiahs came and went—not to mention the numerous other latter-day false messiahs who have disturbed the peace of the "modern" era. If, in the midst of fraud on such a large scale, *one and one only has come and still not gone after 2000 years*, then such a thing ought not to be casually dismissed. Yeshua is that "one and one only". There simply has been no other.

Equally compelling is the evidence of the fact that as a result of Yeshua's ministry, a billion Christians and another billion Muslims were brought from idolatry to God. "You can fool some of the people all of the time, and all of the people some of the time, but you cannot fool all of the people all of the time", said Abraham Lincoln. The Word of God was brought to the world, and now, 2000 years later, it is still alive and *growing*, not shrinking! If this is an error, then I suppose the whole world could be held to be one gigantic error.

In the whole history of our civilization, I know of nothing which documents that any large number of Jews has yet accepted Yeshua Moshiah without ultimately winding up being pulled into the mazes of either Christian or Islamic dogma. I, for one, intend to do so. If you wish to join me, be forewarned that you may, in doing so, render yourself unacceptable to either Jews, Christians, *or* Muslims. You may find yourself standing alone.

Historical background

The story of Yeshua begins with the messianic prophecies. We have already quoted one, Chapter 53 of the Book of Isaiah, which explicitly refers to the essential features of his life and ministry. Certain others will be dealt with later.

To see Christianity as an historical phenomenon, we must continue to consider the history of Israel itself. We have gotten as far as the 6th century BC, the time of the Babylonian Captivity. This came to an end in 523 BC, when the Persian emperor Cyrus the Great permitted the Jews to return home.

After the nation, and the Temple in Jerusalem, had been rebuilt, there were about 3 centuries of relative peace in Israel. Although there is precious little written history of this most important period, it is evident in retrospect that exciting new ideas were developing; ideas which were to come to be the backbone of Christianity and Islam, and to be rejected (or at least ultimately ignored) by Jews. These were ideas about resurrection after death, judgment by God, and eternal life for those judged worthy.

The first books we know of which incorporated the new ideas were the Books of the Maccabees. It is evident from passages like 2 Maccabees 12:42-45 that the new concepts, of resurrection and judgment, were already fully formed at that time. In this passage, the author describes a money offering made on behalf of men who had fallen in battle, and who had been found afterwards to have been wearing amulets sacred to the "idols of Jamnia, objects forbidden to Jews by the Law". With the disposition of these fallen men in the next world in mind,

> **...The noble Judas [Maccabee] exhorted the people to keep themselves free from wrongdoing, for they had seen with their own eyes what had happened because of the sin of those who had fallen.**
>
> **He levied a contribution from each man, and sent to Jerusalem the total of two thousand silver drachmas to provide a sin-offering; <u>*a fit and proper act in which he took due account of the resurrection*</u>.**
>
> **Had he not been expecting the fallen to rise again, it would have been superfluous and senseless to pray for the dead; but since he had in view the splendid reward reserved for those who die a godly death, his purpose was holy and devout. That was why he offered the atoning sacrifice, to free the dead from their sin.**
>
> II Maccabees 12:42-45

The Maccabeean author's obvious acceptance of what would today be called "Christian" ideas undoubtedly accounts for the fact that Jews have celebrated Hanukkah with fervent enthusiasm for over two millennia, but have steadfastly refused to extend official recognition to the Books of Maccabees, even in spite of the fact that they are the most important historical sources for this immensely significant period.

Returning to history, we may note that the beginning of the end of relative peace in Israel occurred when Alexander the Great conquered the Middle East (334-332 BC). Although he was a conqueror, the available information suggests that he was not at all hated, and that, on the contrary, he had a sincere respect for Judaism. For another century, the Jewish nation continued to prosper in peace as a territory of the fragmented Greek Empire. But in 176 BC the bubble of happiness burst, with the rise of that most evil of Kings, Antiochus Epiphanes.

Antiochus decided to force the whole world to be Greek, and he set out with a vengeance to stamp out every religion and culture which differed from his own. Although many Jews went along with "Hellenization" willingly, others resisted, some even unto death.

As the Second Book of Maccabees vividly documents, the tortures which Antiochus submitted the Jewish people to were so horrible that they remain shocking to this day. If you can find a copy of the Bible which contains Maccabees, read 2 Maccabees, Chapters 6 and 7. The atrocities described in these chapters will turn your stomach, even if you thought yourself to be totally inured by years of sick, sadistic cinema from Hollywood. Consider, for example, the case of a woman whom tradition has named "Hannah", who watched Antiochus' henchmen murder each of her seven sons, while she was forced to look on. Their crime? They refused to eat pork.

Each, in turn, was subjected to the following tortures: They were first scourged with whips, then their tongues were cut out. Next they were scalped, a procedure quite evidently not invented by American Indians. Then they were "mutilated", which either means that they were castrated, or that their limbs were amputated (depending on how you translate the Greek word for "mutilated"). Finally, they were thrown, still alive, into huge frying pans and slowly burned to death.

None of the seven sons ate pork! They all died, and their mother followed.

The depravity of Antiochus has never been exceeded, although it's possible that it's been matched. His was the ultimate depth of evil—a singleminded and wholehearted devotion to torture, and to murder, and to every other crime against God and man.

Antiochus was the most powerful military tyrant of his day, and he "got away" with all his crimes against *individuals*. But when he put a statue of Zeus in the Temple in Jerusalem, he made a serious error.

The Maccabean revolt

The response to the defilement of the Temple was not long in coming. In the town of Modin, 23 miles northwest of Jerusalem, the local priest, Mattathias, rebelled. A Greek soldier showed up in town, under orders to force the people to sacrifice to the Greek gods. Mattathias refused. When one of the townspeople rose up to comply with the order in his stead, Mattathias became incensed. He drew his sword and slew the traitor. Then he killed the Greek soldier, and tore down the pagan alter.

In reviewing the story of Mattathias and his sons (who came to be called "the Maccabees"), one is immediately impressed with the similarity of the position of Mattathias, the patriarch of this extraordinary family, to that of Elijah of the Northern Kingdom of Israel after the civil war. Just as Elijah was the last Jew in the Northern Kingdom to speak and act for God, so was Mattathias perhaps the last Jew with the courage to stand up to Greece. He was the savior of Israel. One may speculate as one wishes to speculate: There is no evidence whatsoever that *if Mattathias, in 168 B.C., had not struck down that Greek soldier, thus triggering civil war against the pagan Greek Empire, there would be a single Jew, Christian, or Muslim in the world today.*

The Maccabees, with a small army of untrained, ill-equipped men, defeated a much larger force of professional mercenaries who were sent to quell this rebellion. In response the Greeks sent an army of 47,000 soldiers, but the Maccabees, with only 3000 men, each one filled with fiery determination to serve

God, beat a contingency of 6000 of them. The rest fled! The following year the Greeks sent 65,000 soldiers, but Maccabee, with 10,000 men, again put them to shame.

The Greeks were thoroughly humbled and humiliated. So they put together an army of 120,000 men and 32 war elephants. The Jews fought valiantly, but found themselves besieged in Jerusalem. Then word came of an attempt by Antiochus' second-in-command, Philip, to usurp the throne in their capital city, Antioch. So the Greeks made a hasty peace treaty with the Jews and promptly returned home! As faith in God had turned back the Assyrians from the gates of Jerusalem centuries earlier, so once again did faith turn back the Greeks.

But it was evident that the Jews could not win by force of arms. No matter how many glorious military victories they obtained, it had become clear that the Greeks would always send a bigger army. What were they to do?

They made a treaty with Rome.

Israel as a Roman Province

No sooner did Israel sign a treaty with Rome, then the Greeks were promptly expelled. The Maccabbees had won—or had they?

What Greece could not do with unrestrained physical brutality and the shameless shedding of innocent blood, Rome finally succeeded in doing with the Devil's favorite tool—money. Rome never attempted to physically exterminate religion. She simply laughed at it. Then she bought it. Once it was hers, she corrupted it.

When the Jews, in the first century A.D., came to the full realization that they had been bought and corrupted, they rebelled. But at that point in time they had become hopelessly divided, and in any event, they could not possibly have stood up to Rome. In 70 A.D., the Temple and the nation were decimated.

Those who wished to remain Jewish had to flee for their lives. Unlike the exile decreed by Babylon, this one was destined to last for 2000 years[28]. The ancient nation of Israel was *over*, and the Jewish people were scattered abroad, across the face of the earth.

---

[28] In 132-135 AD, the legendary pseudo-messiah Simeon Bar Kochba, in what is perhaps best thought of as an epilogue to ancient Jewish history, led a final military uprising against Roman rule. The outcome was predictable. The Jewish resistance was utterly crushed, and all Jewish studies and outward observances were thereafter officially banned by law. Subsequent Jewish intellectual efforts were directed not toward military goals, but toward the development of the Talmud.

The divisions in Israel which eventually led to its final destruction began immediately after the Maccabeean victories. In the first place, the High Priesthood fell into the hands of the Maccabees, which caused tremendous resentment from certain quarters. A split arose, which eventually became formalized in the appearance of two political parties. One of these political parties was known as the Sadducees. In principle, its members were firmly adherent to the teachings of the written Torah, and they generally refused to accept "oral law" or tradition as having any validity. In practice, however, it is ironic that the Sadducees were the upper class; wealthy, arrogant, and, as such, inclined to compromise with Rome.

In other words, they refused to compromise the ideals of Judaism with Jews, but they did so with Romans. They thus came to be despised by the masses.

The other political party was the Pharisees. While revering the Torah, the Pharisees also accepted the necessity of adhering to certain "oral laws" and other non-Torah-based Jewish traditions in order to accommodate to the ever-*changing* realities of life in the world. Ironically, this party, in spite of its acceptance of the need for change, was the party of hatred of Rome. Apparently, Rome was not the sort of "change" the Pharisees were looking for!

The Pharisees were therefore also the party of "the people", because most of the common folks shared with them a profound hatred of Rome.

In addition to this political split, there was another split which was purely spiritual. This was the split with regard to the question of resurrection. The wealthy and worldly Sadducees rejected all notions of resurrection of the body after death, since the Bible did not say anything about it. But another idea, not fully embodied in any particular Jewish scripture, had arisen, and had found much support among certain of the Pharisees. This idea, stated explicitly in the Books of the Maccabees, was that man, after death, is resurrected by God, and judged according to his deeds in life.

Along with the idea of resurrection and judgment was the perception, which was a *correct* perception, that the war against the Greeks, which had now become transformed into a war against Rome, could no longer be won by military force. Every time the Jews defeated a Greek army, the Greeks simply sent a larger force. Now the enemy had been multiplied overwhelmingly in that the Jews had sold themselves willingly into the hands of Rome, and Rome *was* the world. Would the little nation of Israel now go to war against the *whole world*?

For the first time in its history, Israel began to realize that a new sort of Savior was needed; one who fought not with iron weapons, but with the most powerful weapon of all: pure faith. This Savior was sent. Like many messengers who came before him, he was rejected. But unlike the others, each of whom was eventually "rehabilitated", Yeshua's mission and purpose were never understood by the bulk of the Jewish establishment, and he remains rejected to this day.

Life of Yeshua ben Yosef

We now turn to an examination of the life of Jesus Christ. We will address all the important questions, because we must. This means questions about his birth, his ministry, his Messiahship, and his death and resurrection. These are difficult questions; questions I would much prefer to avoid. But one thing about Yeshua which does not change is that he cannot be gotten around, and he cannot be avoided. Just as it would have been easy for him to have fled from the Garden of Gethsemane the evening before his death, it would be easy for us to simply not address these questions, and to get on with our lives. But this is not to be.

His birth

Here is what is known about his birth. His mother, Mary, conceived him before her marriage to his father, Joseph. She denied having "known" any man, and Joseph believed her. This story became known to Yeshua, and he believed what his parents told him. His disciples believed him, and the whole Christian and Muslim world believes his disciples.

I too believe Mary. Why? Because I know that the Christian religion shows unmistakable evidence of the Hand of God, which I say in spite of my many disagreements with what it has evolved into at the hand of man. It is simply out of the question to suppose that a Holy institution began with a lie.

Furthermore, the virgin birth was a fulfillment of the prophecy of Isaiah 7:14, "Therefore the LORD himself shall give you a sign; Behold, a *virgin* shall conceive, and bear a son, and shall call his name Immanuel". Now, Jewish scholars have maintained, for 2000 years, that the Hebrew word "almah", translated as "virgin" by Christians, simply means a young woman of marriage age, whether she be a virgin or not. They say that the unique and exclusive word for "virgin" is a *different* word: "bethulah". Therefore, saying that an "almah" would conceive is totally superfluous. Like all of Isaiah Chapter 53, Isaiah 7:14, according to these scholars, says nothing worth repeating.

As an exercise in pure semantics, the Jewish scholarly view can be maintained, but it ignores the fact that in ancient Israel—a nation with little tolerance for pre-marital sex—a woman who was an "almah" was fully expected to be a "virgin" as well. That suggests that "almah" and "bethulah" were synonymous. Were they?

In order to find out, we must turn to the Torah, to see how the words were actually used.

We needn't look far. In Genesis we read that Abraham, having no respect for the women of Canaan, dispatched his servant to his ancestral homeland to find a wife for his son Isaac. The servant promptly found *Rebekah*, who was described as a "bethulah" when she first appeared (Genesis 24:16). This was explicitly defined as a *virgin:* "neither had any man known her". The servant explained the purpose of his mission to Rebekah, who promptly invited him to her home. There, only a few short verses later, the servant recapitulated his entire story. This time, however, Rebekah was described as an *"almah"* (Genesis 24:43). Same woman ... same story ... but two different Hebrew words for "virgin". In the face of this, it is difficult for me to accept that the words "almah" and "bethulah" did not have similar meanings.

It is therefore *unreasonable* to propose that the Isaiah prophecy was not what Christians have claimed it to be. I, for one, believe that it was. Because I believe that Isaiah was an *inspired* Prophet, it follows that Yeshua must have been born of a virgin birth.

But this is not to say that I consider myself to have knowledge concerning the mechanism by which Yeshua was conceived. The New Testament says of Mary that "she was found with child of the Holy Spirit" (Matthew 1:18). This could mean that God was indeed the literal father, causing her to conceive divinely. But it could also mean that God was not the literal father, but merely an agent—a divine obstetrician as it were—causing her to conceive biologically by a mechanism about which we can only speculate.

However, I shall refrain from speculating. The prophecy of Isaiah said that a virgin would conceive. A virgin conceived. It's not necessarily for us to know how.

Miracles associated with Yeshua's birth

At least three extraordinary things happened during the first days of Yeshua's life. He was visited by "wise men" from the east. These men, undoubtedly Zoroastrian astrologers, were of sufficient stature that Herod, the King of Judea, demanded an audience with them. They were seeking the Messiah, and they were lead (by a star, according to the New Testament) right to the manger in which the baby Yeshua lay.

Some may find it hard to believe that the wise men were "lead by a star". I'll offer you another way to look at it. Daniel, one of the most towering of all the great Prophets of Jewish history, resided in Babylon around 600 BC, during the great

Jewish Captivity. Toward the end of Daniel's life, Babylon had become the capital of the new Persian Empire. Were there any other towering preachers of monotheism living in Persia at around 600 BC? How about Zoroaster? It's quite a coincidence that Daniel and Zoroaster both lived and worked in the same place at the same time, is it not?

We know quite a bit about Daniel—he was an exceedingly powerful and influential man in Babylon. We know essentially nothing about Zoroaster. Could they have been the same person? I suppose not. Nevertheless, I'll say this: The fact that they both lived and taught in the same empire, at about the same time, makes it virtually *certain* that in Persia, the homeland of Zoroastrianism, the teachings of Daniel were known—most likely, *well*-known.

And what did Daniel teach? Among many other things, he taught that the Messiah would come approximately 500 years after the rebuilding of the Temple in Jerusalem (see below). Clearly, the Zoroastrians must have been very familiar with this prophecy—it was, after all, pronounced from the heart of their own homeland! Therefore, when the "three wise men" came seeking the Christ, they may very well have been following a star, but they *also* knew, in advance, the *timing* of the event (*i.e.*, the early years of what we now call the "Christian" era), and its *location* (*i.e.*, Bethlehem)(see Micah 5:2).

It wasn't only Zoroastrian astrologers who were drawn to Yeshua. Shepherds in the nearby fields were drawn by some mysterious force (angels of the LORD, according to the New Testament) to that same manger, in which lay the newborn Savior.

Then, on the eighth day of Yeshua's life, he was brought to the Temple in Jerusalem to be circumcised. While there, the family was accosted by Simeon, an elderly man who had been told in a vision that he would see the Messiah before he died. When he laid eyes on Yeshua, he immediately identified him as the Chosen One.

It is not at all difficult to imagine the amazement of the family at these things.

Life and ministry of Yeshua

Yeshua was born a Jew[29], he lived as a Jew and he died a Jew. It is therefore impossible for any man to be a wholehearted follower of Yeshua unless he is, first and foremost, a Jew.

---

[29] The term "Jew", as used here, refers only to those aspects of Jewish observance which emanated directly from the Torah. The modern religion of Judaism is undoubtedly different in many ways, as it is based as much or more on Talmud than on Torah.

No number of Gospels, epistles or commentaries of any sort whatsoever can alter this fact. It will never change; nor will the world change until it is believed and accepted.

That Yeshua said that the Kingdom would be taken away from the Priests (Matthew 21:42-46) does *not* change this fact. He was referring to a corrupted priesthood, not to the religion of Abraham. He loved the Jewish people, and devoted his life to their salvation. Many in turn loved him and followed him wherever he went, to hear his words and to be healed.

Any doubt that his message was meant for the Jewish people is dispelled by his comment to a Canaanite woman who beseeched him, that he would heal her sick daughter. He replied:

> **"I am not sent but unto the lost sheep of the house of Israel."**
>
> Matthew 15:24

Notwithstanding this comment, Yeshua, setting the tone for future Christian evangelists, extended himself willingly and wholeheartedly to her and to all other gentiles, as long as they believed in God, the Heavenly Father. That he did so, however, did *not* change the nature and purpose of his ministry. Recall his saying from the Sermon on the Mount:

> **"Till heaven and earth pass, one jot or one tittle shall in no wise pass from the law, till all be fulfilled".**
>
> Matthew 5:18

This saying should have dispelled any doubts in people's minds about the purpose of Yeshua's ministry. He sought to be a living example of the Jewish law, and urged all others to seek to do likewise. That is why I said earlier that the Karaite interpretation of Isaiah 53, namely that it refers to an exalted remnant of Israel, is *not* incompatible with the Christian interpretation. Yeshua was the living, visible manifestation of that exalted remnant.

Although Yeshua was, most assuredly, a great teacher, he was not sent because of that. He was sent to bear witness of He who sent him; his Father in Heaven; who is our Father also. The notion, widely held among Christians, that Yeshua preached a radical new faith, distinct from Judaism, is, to put it plainly and succinctly, *wrong*.

For example, the "Golden Rule", as we have already seen, was first preached not by Yeshua, or by Jews at all, but by Confucius 500 years earlier (see Chapter 3 of this book).

The notion that "love thy neighbor" should be regarded as the second greatest Commandment was, as we have already seen (Chapter 3), almost a direct paraphrase of Hillel, and represented the current teaching among prominent Pharisees of that day.

Even the admonition against divorce (Matthew 5:31-32), an apparent contradiction of the Law of Moses, was a common pharisaic teaching of the day, and cannot be considered to be a unique teaching of Yeshua[30].

For all these reasons, it is wrong to consider Yeshua a radical or revolutionary. A great teacher he surely was, but only of the Jewish law as it was known to the faithful of Israel at that time.

It is for all these reasons, and more, that we must recognize that Yeshua was a Jew. He was born a Jew, he lived as a Jew, and he died as a Jew.

Again, the saying...

> **"Till heaven and earth pass, one jot or one tittle shall in no wise pass from the law, till all be fulfilled"**

... sets the agenda for all those who wish to bear witness of the Messiah. This witness is to live by the Jewish law—the Law of Moses—to the limits of one's ability to do so. I recognize that this is no small matter, and no easy thing to do. But we will discuss this Law later, for if we do so now, we shall never finish the story of Yeshua Moshiaḥ.

Death of Yeshua

Yeshua went to Jerusalem to die. He was appalled at the thought of it, as evidenced by his prayers in the Garden of Gethsemane:

---

[30] *Jewish Literacy*, by Rabbi Joseph Telushkin. William Morrow and Company, New York, 1991. Page 126.

> **"My soul is exceeding sorrowful, even unto death...O my Father, if it be possible, let this cup pass from me: nevertheless not as I will, but as thou wilt.**
>
> Matthew 26:38-39

The 53rd Chapter of the Book of Isaiah stated that God's Messenger had to die. In accordance with this, Yeshua, when he arrived in Jerusalem, spoke the plain and untempered truth. He said and did things which were guaranteed to arouse the hatred and fear of the High Priests, knowing full well that they would seize him and cause him to be sentenced to death.

When he was taken, bound and dragged before the chief Priests and elders, an unruly proceeding by any standard, he surely said nothing which should have warranted a death sentence. According to the synoptic Gospel writers, he was asked, point blank, whether or not he was the Messiah. This is what each of the three writers gave as Yeshua's answer to this question:

<u>**Matthew:**</u> "Thou has said: nevertheless I say unto you, Hereafter shall ye see the Son of Man sitting on the right hand of power, and coming in the clouds of heaven."

<u>**Luke:**</u> "If I tell you, ye will not believe; and if I also ask you, ye will not answer me, nor let me go. Hereafter shall the Son of Man sit on the right hand of the power of God."

<u>**Mark:**</u> "I am: and ye shall see the Son of Man sitting on the right hand of power, and coming in the clouds of heaven."

Thus, of these three principle Gospel writers, only one (Mark) reports Yeshua to have explicitly claimed to be the Messiah. Matthew (one of the original Twelve Disciples, who knew Jesus personally) and Luke have him making vague, cryptic remarks. In the Gospel of John, neither the Messiah question, nor Yeshua's answer, are even reported.

What does it matter anyway? Declaring oneself Messiah is *not* a capital offense in the Law of Moses.

The Law prescribes death for 1st degree murder, and for teaching the worship of gods other than the God of Abraham. Yeshua did not do that. It is also said, in the Law, that a *false prophet* shall die (whether by the Hand of God or of man is not specified). But all of Yeshua's prophecies came true.

Even if one wished to regard a claim of Messiahship as a serious offense, one would still be obligated to obtain credible evidence from a minimum of 2 or 3 witnesses in order to lawfully obtain the basis for a sentence of death. What actually transpired at this "trial"? The only existing document which reports on the proceedings thereof is the New Testament, whose authors report that the witnesses who were called did not agree in their allegations.

Furthermore, this council of elders should have felt obligated to at least *consider* the possibility that the claim was *true*, lest they send an innocent man to the grave. Now consider this: If, as I am certain *was* the case, there existed at least a substantial minority of Rabbis who regarded Isaiah Chapter 53 as being a messianic prophecy, then how could this council of elders have proven that a man was *not* Messiah by killing him? Doesn't Chapter 53 state *explicitly* that the Messiah would be *murdered*, without a fair trial? If the Messiah must be murdered, then how on earth can you prove that a man is not Messiah by murdering him?!

It seems clear that the standards of Jewish law were violated in this "trial". One must bear in mind that the Jews were not lawless people; on the contrary, they gave the world the Mishnah and the Talmud, which formed the bedrock of western law. So why was Yeshua murdered?

With respect to the Sanhedrin[31] itself, the average Christian of today undoubtedly thinks of it as a body of corrupt Shylocks, empowered to perform all manner of barbarous acts according to the arbitrary and capricious nature of its judges. Nothing could be farther from the truth.

In fact, the Sanhedrin was an ultra-academic, finely-tuned legal machine[32]. The judges were highly disciplined men, operating under a strict system of rules and regulations. The mock proceeding against Yeshua represented a complete breakdown of that system. Although the reasons for that breakdown can be debated endlessly, there is, in the end, only one explanation: It was the will of God, and the fulfillment of the prophecy of Isaiah, who stated that *the messenger would be imprisoned, but would be taken abruptly out and condemned to death without a fair trial*.

---

[31] Jewish defenders of the mock "trial" of Yeshua have maintained, through the centuries, that he was never strictly tried in the legal sense, as he was not formally taken before the Sanhedrin. This is undoubtedly true. However, the sentence of death, or the equivalent thereof (and handing a man over to Rome for execution was surely the equivalent thereof), is a serious one, and if the members of the Sanhedrin were actually *not* present during this "trial", they still, in my mind, must be held accountable. It seems to me to be highly probable that some or all of them *must* have been present, and if they weren't, they damn well ought to have been.

[32] *Jewish Literacy*, by Rabbi Joseph Telushkin, William Morrow & Company, New York, 1991, pp. 123-4.

The Crucifixion

Yeshua was nailed to a cross and hung up to die. Three days later, he was seen alive by his disciples. All eleven surviving disciples eventually saw him, and many other people as well, and there can be no doubt about the fact that he was alive.

This has raised the question of whether he was actually killed on the cross. There are both Islamic and atheistic arguments against the usual Christian interpretation of the facts reported in the New Testament. The Muslim argument, which is very subtle, is considered in Chapter 8 of this book. Here we consider only the atheist argument, which is rather blunt.

It is extraordinary that at each and every point in Yeshua's life, questions are raised which cannot be resolved logically, but which ultimately become matters of *faith*. I consider this, in and of itself, to be powerful evidence that Yeshua was sent by God, since God has stated explicitly that He never shows His face (Exodus 33:20). This means, in part, that He never gives us "scientific" or "hard" or "incontrovertible" evidence of His existence, for if He did so, then we would have no further need for faith. Since we were put here to learn to have faith, it follows that if there ever came a time when faith was *no longer needed*, our existence would then no longer have any meaning.

The questions about Yeshua's death arise because of its rapidity. Crucifixion is a hideously slow, painful death, resulting above all from suffocation. Well-developed muscular men could survive several days on the cross. In the average case, it was usually all over within 24 hours. In Yeshua's case it was over in 6 hours.

Just before his death, a sponge was extended to him on the end of a long reed. All four Gospel writers actually agree on this. According to John, "they filled a sponge with vinegar, and put it upon hyssop, and put it to his mouth" (John 19:29).

Next, the Romans decided to break the legs of Yeshua and the two thieves with whom he was being crucified. The reason was that it was the eve of the Jewish Sabbath, and it was unlawful to continue a crucifixion into the Sabbath day. The breaking of the legs had two purposes: In the first place, it caused great blood loss, and secondly, it made it impossible to support the weight of the body on the legs, hastening the process of suffocation.

The Romans broke the legs of the two thieves, but when they got to Yeshua, he was already dead. They pierced his side with a spear, and "forthwith came there out blood and water" (John 19:34). A *rich* man (see Isaiah 53:9), Joseph of Arimathaea, who had been a secret disciple of Yeshua, approached the Roman

Governor, Pontius Pilate, and pleaded for the body. Pilate was incredulous when informed that Yeshua was already dead. He therefore did not take Joseph's word for it, but checked first with the centurion (Mark 15:44-45). But the centurion confirmed the death, and then only, Pilate permitted the body to be taken.

Joseph placed the body of Yeshua in the tomb he had purchased for himself. It was not seen again until the resurrection. These are the known facts regarding the death and resurrection of Yeshua.

For 2000 years the enemies of Christianity—recognizing that Yeshua was seen by entirely too many people to just ignore the eyewitness reports of his resurrection—have taken refuge in the theory that he did not "really die" on the cross, but was taken down alive. The explanation usually given for his survival is that the sponge containing vinegar also contained some sort of drug which induced a death-like state. From the purely technical point of view, this theory might seem plausible since such drugs apparently do exist, although they can hardly be said to be well-known to medical science, even today. Whether they were known at all in ancient Israel is quite impossible to say. It certainly does not seem likely.

According to the Talmud (Sanhedrin 43a), the women of Jerusalem often raised money to provide condemned prisoners with a "goblet of wine containing a grain of frankincense", which was supposed to induce a merciful state of grogginess or unconsciousness (but not necessarily a state so "death-like" as to fool the Roman centurion). Whether this item in the Talmud should be accepted at face value, or whether, instead, it should be regarded with suspicion (since the Talmud was not fully compiled until about 600 years after the event in question), is a matter which every man must decide for himself. Either way, it is ridiculous to suppose that an entire "goblet of wine with a grain of frankincense" was lifted up to Yeshua on a sponge, which, besides, he refused to drink from.

The very idea that Yeshua's emergence from the tomb of Joseph of Arimathaea was the result of a plot defies all reason. It is evident that Yeshua himself knew nothing of any such plot. None of the 12 disciples can conceivably have been involved. Who then could have done such a thing? Where did they get the alleged drug? How did they obtain the cooperation of the centurion? For such things to have happened *spontaneously* would be, in themselves, a miracle.

It is necessary for every man to believe in the resurrection of the dead. For if the resurrection of the dead is not possible, then there is no God. As for Yeshua, the question of whether that sponge had a drug in it is totally irrelevant. The prophecy of Isaiah stated that the Suffering Servant would be "brought as a lamb to the slaughter", and that he would "make his grave...with the rich in his death". And that's exactly what happened. Three days later, as he himself prophesied, he rose up from the grave and preached to his disciples.

If this was not the Hand of God, then whose hand can it have been? To quote the High Priests themselves, "what further need have we of witnesses?"

Is Yeshua Messiah?

Before we address any questions about *who* "the Messiah" is, we'd better first figure out *what* the word "Messiah" means. In current Judeo-Christian theology, the word is generally used to connote a Grand Person who will be Savior to the whole world. But is that what it really means?

In considering the definition of the word "Messiah", it is desirable to turn to the ancient Hebrew text of the Bible. The Jews have maintained this text in its original form with extreme devotion. In modern day Torahs, for example, the Five Books of Moses are *written out* exactly as they appeared 2,000 years ago. Torahs are, by Jewish Law, written out by *hand*. If a letter in the ancient texts was written a little larger than its neighboring letters, then it is copied large in modern Torahs. This is true even if no one knows, anymore, what the significance of the larger letter was.

Similarly, if a letter was a little *smaller* than its neighbors, it appears smaller in modern copies of the Torahs as well.

Even stray dots and dashes, whose meanings may be entirely unknown, are copied, as if they were laden with significance.

Even if a word is suspected of having been misspelled, it is copied anyway, just in case the word may have been spelled that way for a reason.

Thus, although translations of the Hebrew Bible into English and other languages may take substantial liberties at places which are held to be "Christological", and although we may therefore be as suspicious of the *translation* as we feel it appropriate to be, we may nevertheless rely on the original Hebrew text, which has been preserved through the centuries with a fanatical degree of loving care.

The first occurrence of the word "Messiah" in the Hebrew Bible is in the Book of Leviticus, Chapter 6, verse 15 (verse 22 in the King James version). Here, the word of God comes to Moses, instructing him in certain particulars of ritual sacrifice. Now, the first High Priest of Israel was Aaron, Moses' brother. In this particular verse, reference is made to the "anointed priest" who, upon being selected from Aaron's blood descendants, shall minister to the sacrifice in his stead, after Aaron's death.

The Hebrew words for "the anointed priest" are "Cohen ha-Moshiaḥ". "Cohen" (a common Jewish name nowadays) means "priest". "Moshiaḥ" means "anointed". The prefix "ha" is the Hebrew word for "the". So "Cohen ha-Moshiaḥ" means "the anointed priest".

The word "Moshiaḥ" therefore means "anointed". In ancient times, this generally meant having oil poured on your head. This may seem like a silly thing to do nowadays, but you must bear in mind that every drop of oil recovered from the olive, back then, had to be laboriously beaten out by human labor. Moreover, if the cupful of oil was laced with various spices and fragrances from the Orient, each of which had to be transported across thousands of miles of perilous terrain by camel caravan, then you had an anointing unction affordable only by royalty.

In fact, anointing with oil was an act of sheer extravagance, usually reserved for the coronation of kings, or of high priests.

Therefore, we may see that the word "Moshiaḥ", rendered in English "Messiah", means "anointed one", which, in turn, means one crowned as a king, or otherwise selected for service of an extremely lofty nature.

The Greek word for "anointed" is "christou" (*i.e.,* "Christ").

Various renditions and conjugations of the word "Moshiaḥ" appear throughout the Hebrew Old Testament. Sometimes they refer to the anointing of a person or thing so that it becomes suitable to be placed in a Sanctuary of God. In six places in the Books of Samuel, Saul is referred to as the "anointed" of God, which merely means that he was selected, by God, to be King of Israel. No scholar has ever dreamed of suggesting that Saul was a "Savior", sent to "save the world". The very idea is preposterous.

King David was also referred to twice in the same way (*i.e.,* as the "anointed" of God). Now the Bible says that David was the progenitor of the hereditary line from which that Grand Person, anointed to be Savior of the whole world, would arise. Even this notwithstanding, no one yet has suggested that David himself was that Person.

In the entire Hebrew Bible there is exactly and precisely *one* single place where the word *Moshiaḥ* is used in a non-trivial way. That one exception is found in the Book of Daniel, wherein is contained a most singular prophecy, which we must now consider. Some background history is necessary first, however.

Daniel, whom we have made honorable mention of earlier (see above, and Chapter 3 of this book), was one of the distinguished citizens of Jerusalem who were taken into captivity in Babylon following the invasion of the Southern Kingdom of Judah. While in captivity in Babylon, Daniel came to realize the full extent of the depths to which the Jewish nation had fallen. Furthermore, he came to see the relationship of that fall to *sin*, and to appreciate the fact that the entire thing had been prophesied in the Bible.

The nation had been forewarned. The warnings had not been heeded.

Daniel was aware that the great Prophet Jeremiah had predicted seventy years of captivity in Babylon, even *before* the invasion of Judah had begun. Recognizing the greatness of Jeremiah, Daniel, from his standpoint as a captive, embarked on a program of fasting and prayer, pleading with the LORD that he might be shown the full meaning of Jeremiah's "seventy years" (Daniel 9:2 ff.).

Now in retrospect the meaning seems clear enough to us. The Babylonian Captivity lasted from approximately 590 BC to approximately 520 BC, a period of about 70 years. But recall that Daniel was writing from *within* that seventy year period. He had no way of knowing with certainty when his captivity would end, or indeed if it would *ever* come to an end.

Wishing fervently for the restoration of Jerusalem and Judah, Daniel wanted to hear, from the mouth of God Himself, whether Jeremiah's prophecy meant exactly what it seemed to say, or whether perhaps it had another meaning, or even additional meanings.

After much prayer and fasting, Daniel was visited by the angel Gabriel, who revealed to him a prophecy of surpassing importance to the subsequent history of the world. Gabriel told Daniel that the Temple in Jerusalem would be rebuilt, and that seventy *weeks* of years[33] , i.e. 70 x 7, or 490 years, would then pass, after which something extraordinary would happen **"to finish the transgression, and to make an end of sins, and to make reconciliation for iniquity, and to bring in everlasting righteousness, and to seal up the vision and prophecy, and to anoint the most Holy"** (Daniel 9:24).

The subsequent verse (Daniel 9:25) reveals that the mediator of these extraordinary events would be a *man,* whom Daniel refers to as **"the Messiah, the Prince"**. This is the one and only place in the entire Hebrew Bible where the word *Moshiaḥ* (Messiah) appears in reference to a personal Savior of the world. This, therefore, *must* be taken as the legitimate definition of the word "Messiah", when the word is used in reference to a personal Savior. What other definition can there be?

Because of the peculiar language of Daniel 9:25, the exact *timing* of the coming of the Messiah is somewhat ambiguous. Now, entire books have been written on

---

[33] The Biblical language device where years are referred to as "days", and seven-year periods as "weeks", is well-established and widely accepted by both Jewish and Christian scholars. Thus, although the interpretation of "seventy weeks" as meaning 490 years may seem far-fetched at first glance, it is virtually certain that that is precisely what it means. See Ezekiel 4:6 for an explicit use of the literary device of days for years.

this subject, and therefore I shall not even attempt to review the multitude of oft-conflicting interpretations. Suffice it to say that some authors have gone as far as drawing up calculations "proving" that all the key events of Yeshua's life can be predicted, *to the day,* by the prophecies of Daniel, and others have used the very same verses to predict the precise timing of the Second Coming of Christ. These speculations can be complex in the extreme.

The governing aspect of this prophecy, however, is the shell of "seventy weeks", or 490 years. Whatever the timing of the various events is held to be, they all *must* lie within this shell. For this reason, the entire nation of Israel was gripped with "messianic fever" at the time of Yeshua's arrival in Jerusalem, which, if not precisely 490 years after the rebuilding of the Temple, was certainly not very far from it.

Gabriel also revealed to Daniel that in the midst of the Messiah's ministry, he would be "cut off, but not for himself: and the people of the *prince that shall come* shall destroy the city and the sanctuary" (Daniel 9:26).

To restate these prophecies concisely, employing round numbers, they said that the Temple in Jerusalem would be rebuilt, and that approximately 500 years later the Messiah would come, establish righteousness, and then be killed; and that subsequently the city of Jerusalem and the Temple would again be destroyed.

We have the benefit of the hindsight of history, which, as they say, is "20-20" in its accuracy. The rebuilding of Solomon's Temple in Jerusalem, which spanned a number of years, may be placed approximately at 500 BC. Therefore, according to Daniel, the Messiah would come approximately at the year which we now call zero BC. This would be followed shortly by the invasion of, and destruction of Jerusalem, and of the Second Temple.

If you've never thought about it before, you should now understand why there was a tense atmosphere of expectation in Jerusalem just prior to the coming of Yeshua. Based on the time-frame given in the Book of Daniel, the appearance of the long-awaited Messiah was widely held to be imminent. But who came? The only Messiah who came was Yeshua. There was no other.

Shortly thereafter, in accordance with prophecy, Yeshua was murdered, and Jerusalem and the Temple were destroyed by the "prince to come", *i.e.* Rome.

Those of us who are non-Christians are therefore left in a most awkward position. Either Yeshua, *i.e.* Jesus, was the Messiah of Daniel, or else Daniel was wrong.

If Daniel was wrong, then the Bible is discredited, which means that the Old Testament and, by implication, the New Testament and the Qu'ran, are all wrong. This means that all religion would be wrong. This would make the world's money-worshipping atheists and agnostics very, very happy.

But the Bible is *not* wrong, and since the only Messiah who came 500 years after the end of the Babylonian Captivity was Yeshua, it follows as a purely logical conclusion that Yeshua was the Messiah whose coming was prophesied in the Book of Daniel.

But wait a minute. Yeshua, and everyone else in Jerusalem at that time, *knew* about the prophecy of Daniel. Couldn't he and his disciples have merely *contrived* to make themselves look like they were fulfilling prophecy?

We have raised this question earlier in this chapter, and I shall not repeat the argument, but instead refer the interested reader to that earlier discussion.

And the answer is that Yeshua was certainly the Messiah of Daniel.

But this does not complete our inquiry. We must now ask an additional question. Are there *other* Messiahs, or was Yeshua the only one?

The Messiah of the End Times

The only place in the Old Testament where the word "Messiah" is used in the sense in which it is understood today, i.e. the Savior of the whole world, is in the Book of Daniel. And yet the Judeo-Christian-Muslim conception of "Messiah" is broader than that.

From the broadest point of view, the Messiah, as prophesied by the four "major" Prophets (Isaiah, Jeremiah, Ezekial and Daniel), and the twelve "minor" Prophets, is he who will come at the end of this godless era. His appearance will usher in an age of peace and prosperity such as the world has never known. He must be of the line of David, and his destiny is to restore the house of David to Kingship in the world, with Jerusalem at the center of the world's religious worship.

It seems desirable to focus on those messianic prophecies whose meanings are *not* hotly disputed by Jews, Christians, and/or Muslims. One good example is the 11th Chapter of the Book of Isaiah, because its meaning is generally agreed upon by all. If you have never read this passage, read it now, because it will surely come true, and it contains all the basic prophecies for the Messianic Age:

> **1. And there shall come forth a rod out of the stem of Jesse, and a Branch shall grow out of his roots:**

2. And the spirit of the Lord shall rest upon him, the spirit of wisdom and understanding, the spirit of counsel and might, the spirit of knowledge and of the fear of the Lord;

3. And shall make him of quick understanding in the fear of the Lord: and he shall not judge after the sight of his eyes, neither reprove after the hearing of his ears:

4. But with righteousness shall he judge the poor, and reprove with equity for the meek of the earth: and he shall smite the earth with the rod of his mouth, and with the breath of his lips shall he slay the wicked.

5. And righteousness shall be the girdle of his loins, and faithfulness the girdle of his reins.

6. The wolf also shall dwell with the lamb, and the leopard shall lie down with the kid; and the calf and the young lion and the fatling together; and a little child shall lead them.

7. And the cow and the bear shall feed; their young ones shall lie down together: and the lion shall eat straw like the ox.

8. And the sucking child shall play on the hole of the asp, and the weaned child shall put his hand on the cockatrice' den.

9. They shall not hurt nor destroy in all my holy mountain: for the earth shall be full of the knowledge of the Lord, as the waters cover the sea.

10. And in that day there shall be a root of Jesse, which shall stand for an ensign of the people; to it shall the Gentiles seek: and his rest shall be glorious.

11. And it shall come to pass in that day, [that] the Lord shall set his hand again the second time to recover the remnant of his people, which shall be left, from Assyria, and from Egypt, and from Pathros, and from Cush, and from Elam, and from Shinar, and from Hamath, and from the islands of the sea.

12. And he shall set up an ensign for the nations, and shall assemble the outcasts of Israel, and gather together the dispersed of Judah from the four corners of the earth.

Jesse was the father of David. Therefore "stem (or root) of Jesse" means a descendant of King David. Thus it has been said, for 2500 years, that the Messiah will be of the house of David. Please note that the word "Messiah" does *not* appear in these, or any other End-Times verses. Notwithstanding, this *is* the Messiah whom modern-day Orthodox Jews are anxiously awaiting. He might therefore be called the "Messiah of the End Times". The reader should understand explicitly that this is the Messiah who has *not yet come,* corresponding to the long-awaited Second Coming of Christ in the Christian religion. The Rabbis call him "Moshiaḥ ben David", literally "Messiah son of David", meaning Messiah of the *House* of David—a man, demonstrably descended from the line of King David, who will bring about the fulfillment of the prophecies of Isaiah Chapter 11.

This Messiah will be a just ruler, whose reign will bring about such a profound state of peace that even the wild animals will become tame. Furthermore, in that day the "earth shall be full of the knowledge of the LORD", a very different state than prevails in the "secular humanist" environment of today. And, finally, the lost tribes of Israel, both north ("Israel") and south ("Judah") will be brought back from the ends of the earth to which they have been scattered.

Since these prophecies have *not* been fulfilled, it can be said with certainty that *this* Messiah *has not come*. Christians are not troubled by this, as the words of Christ seem to them to state unequivocally that he will return. Jews, however, have elected to reject Yeshua (Jesus) as Messiah until all prophecies have been fulfilled.

In his life, Yeshua promised that the Son of Man would return in triumph in the End Times. Since he was Messiah, all his words are established, therefore the Son of Man will indeed return in triumph. However, whether he is recognizable at that time as "Jesus of Nazareth" is another question altogether. Most people did not recognize him the first time!

When he returns, will he identify himself as the second coming of Christ (to the delight of Christians), or as the *first* coming of Moshiaḥ ben David (to the delight of Jews)? Or will he return as the Muslim Mahdi? It's not for me to say.

Another important Messianic Era prophecy is Micah 4:1-5, which describes the state of religious practice in the end times:

> "...in the last days it shall come to pass, that the mountain of the house of the LORD shall be established in the top of the mountains, ... and people shall flow unto it. And many nations shall come, and say, Come, and let us go up to the mountain of the LORD,...all people will walk every one in the name of his god, and we will walk in the name of the LORD, our God, forever and ever." (Micah 4:1-5).

The Bible is never wrong. These verses teach us that even in the End, people will all practice different religions, each walking "in the name of *his* god". This notwithstanding, all people shall recognize the God of the Bible as being supreme, or perhaps as being the supreme manifestation of their own god. Aside from this basic underlying agreement, however, it seems that there will never be a "one-world religion".

What do Jews *really* believe?

About a thousand years ago, after a millennium of bickering, the Orthodox Jewish Rabbis finally reached a durable consensus on these matters. The public position of essentially all Judaism, since that time, has been that there will be *two* Messiahs, *neither of whom has yet appeared on earth.* And Jesus is NOT either one of them!

In the Talmud, these two Messiahs have names. The foremost of them is the one we made mention of above, "Moshiaḥ ben David", *i.e.,* the Messiah of the House of David, *i.e.,* the Messiah of the End Times—the Savior of Isaiah Chapter 11. We note again that the Hebrew Bible never explicitly refers to this Savior by the title "Messiah", or, for that matter, by any other title. He is never named!

The second of the Talmudic Messiahs bears the Hebrew title "Moshiaḥ ben Yossef". This means "the Messiah, the son of Joseph". This title, in and of itself, would appear to teach of a Savior who will arise from the House of Joseph, or from the hereditary line of Joseph. Orthodox Jewish students are taught that this Messiah is quite *inferior* in glory, having the non-enviable role of *dying a violent death* in the process of preparing the world for the *greater* Messiah, Moshiaḥ ben David.

Where did he come from? The Bible makes no mention of a Messiah from the House of Joseph. Wherefore a "Moshiaḥ ben Yosef"?

The answer is that he is not drawn directly from Biblical prophecy, but rather from convoluted interpretations of scriptural verses, some of which seem far indeed from anything one might consider to be a messianic prophecy. Consider, for example, Genesis 30:23, where Rachel, after years of being barren, finally conceives a son for her husband, Jacob. That son was Joseph. Here's how Genesis 30:23 reports this event:

> **And [Rachael] conceived, and bare a son; and said, God hath taken away my reproach.**

According to the current rabbinic point of view, the messianic implications of the above passage are derived from Isaiah 4:1.

Isaiah 4:1 is part of a passage which is generally regarded as being a prophecy of the state of affairs which will prevail during the period of *terrible troubles* which will herald the start of the End Times, or Messianic Era. This is the period of trouble corresponding to the Christian "Tribulation". Among other things which are predicted to happen is the following:

> **And in that day seven women shall take hold of one man, saying, We will eat our own bread, and wear our own apparel; only let us be called by thy name, <u>to take away our reproach</u>.**
>
> Isaiah 4:1

In other words, the Tribulation of the End Times will be so hard that any "eligible bachelor", who can provide any degree of protection and/or sustenance whatsoever, will be hotly pursued by an army of women! Each of these women will gladly forego the traditional gifts, honors and privileges which normally accompany marriage. And all this will be done **"to take away [their] reproach"**. Thus, according to this rather far-fetched analogy, Racheal's mere utterance of the words "God hath taken away my *reproach*" are supposed to prove that she was thinking of the Tribulation when she said that! And since she was thinking of the Tribulation, we are to believe that she must have been thinking that a descendant of her new son, Joseph, was going to be a Messiah of that Tribulation period!

A more plausible argument for the existence of a "Moshiaḥ ben Yosef" comes from the Prophet Obadiah. Commenting on the ultimate victory of the God-fearing over the God-hating in the End Times, the Prophet said:

> **...Upon mount Zion shall be deliverance, and there shall be holiness; and the house of Jacob shall possess their possessions.**
>
> **And the house of Jacob shall be a fire, <u>AND THE HOUSE OF JOSEPH SHALL BE A FLAME</u>, and the house of Esau for stubble, and they shall kindle in them, and devour them; and there shall not be any remaining of the house of Esau; for the LORD hath spoken it".**
>
> Obadiah 1:17-18

This surely implies an important role for the House of Joseph in the End Times, does it not? Maybe not. At the time these words were written, the term "House of Esau" had evolved into a common Biblical metaphor for *all* heathen nations, and "House of Joseph" was often a reference to *all* Israel. Even if one accepts this passage as a prophecy of a special role for the descendants of Joseph, it cannot, by itself, be taken as proof that the Prophet Obadiah was expecting an individual, *personal* "Messiah" from the house of Joseph.

Besides, no one knows where the House of Joseph is anymore. It's one of the "Lost Tribes".

Aside from a few passages like the above, there is nothing in the Bible which explicitly, or even *implicitly* predicts the emergence of a Messiah from the house of Joseph. So what's all this business about a "Moshiah ben Joseph"?

It is interesting to note that this same "Moshiah ben Joseph" tradition holds that the Biblical passage Zechariah 12:10, a Christian favorite (**"and they shall mourn for him, as one mourneth for his only son"**), is a lamentation for none other than this same Moshiah ben Joseph, after he is cut down in the course of carrying out his exalted role in God's great Tribulation. Could this be a clue as to this Moshiah's true identity?

I shall now present the solution to this mystery. It's so obvious that it would be almost comical, if not for all the people who have been murdered through the ages because of it. Think about the title: "Moshiah ben Joseph", and keep in mind what the Rabbis themselves say the title implies (although their wording might differ a bit):

> **Moshiah ben Joseph**: "The Messiah, the son of Joseph, *who will die a violent death in preparation for the final Messiah* (*i.e.*, of David) *of the End Times"*.

Do you know of any historical figures who fit this description?

We have seen that Yeshua of Nazareth was *the Messiah* prophesied by Daniel. He was *the son of Joseph,* the carpenter from Nazareth. *He died a violent death*, on the cross, in preparation for the final reconciliation of the End Times. So why do the Rabbis say he has not yet come?

No history book answers this question directly. There are, however, known facts which suggest an answer. It is known, for example, that there were followers of Yeshua in the Talmudic academies for centuries, even though they may have been a powerless minority. It is known also that the Karaites—the Rabbis opposed to the writing of the Talmud—accepted Yeshua as an important Jewish teacher (even though they did not accord him the status of Prophet). Why were these forms of Jewish belief utterly stamped out?

The Christian Church, as it developed in Medieval times, adopted beliefs which were anathema to Judaism. These included the abandonment of circumcision and of the Kosher laws, which alone would have made European Christianity unacceptable to Jews. On top of that, they declared God to be a "Trinity", one part of which was the man, Yeshua. Some of them even made statues of Jesus, Mary and Joseph (suspiciously Italian in their facial characteristics) and prostrated themselves before them. No Jew was going to go along with that. Finally, they declared that Jesus himself was returning, and that the First and Second Comings of the Messiah both involved exactly the same person—Jesus of Nazareth.

These doctrines and beliefs were frozen forever at the Councils of Nicaea, Chalcedon and Ephesus. After these Councils, there would be no further tolerance for challenges to established Christian doctrine. All of it was carved in stone, and anyone disputing any small part of it was excommunicated or destroyed.

The Muslim response to this rigidity was an equal and opposite reaction, setting the stage for the bloody Crusades, a nightmarish series of wars which, from many points of view, are not over even today. The Jewish response was a total denial of Jesus. The Rabbis were not concerned about their immortal souls for taking this step, since, as we have already seen, Yeshua himself said

> "And whosoever speaketh a word against the Son of Man, it shall be forgiven him..."
>
> (Matthew 12:32)

So they spoke against the Son of Man, and they do so to this day. But in the beginning, many knew perfectly well who he was.

Was Yeshua God?

Like every other question about Yeshua, this one has no simple answer. There are many powerful arguments against it. He had to be baptized by his cousin, John the Baptist. Why would God have need to baptize Himself?

After his baptism Yeshua went into the desert for 40 days, to be "tempted by Satan". It is taught that Satan was a fallen angel, hence a creation of God. How could God be "tempted" by one of His own creations?

God is perfect. Was Yeshua perfect? Not in his own eyes. He made numerous comments which bear witness of this. In Matthew (19:16-17), someone addressed Yeshua as "Good Master", to which he replied...

> "Why callest thou me good? There is none good but one, that is, God".

Again, in Matthew 11:11, Yeshua says...

> "...Among them that are born of women there hath not risen a greater than John the Baptist; notwithstanding **he that is least in the kingdom of heaven is greater than he**."

Wait a minute. Yeshua was born of a woman, was he not? Concerning his paternity, there may be controversy. But concerning his mother, there is no controversy. He was the son of Mary, and was, without a doubt, "among them that are born of women". Was he, therefore—by his own testimony—*less than the "least in the kingdom of heaven"*?

Notwithstanding all the above, the matter cannot be said to be resolved. For there remain, for us to consider, a number of most thought-provoking messianic prophecies, typified by that of Zechariah, Chapter 2, verses 10-11:

> **10. Sing and rejoice, O daughter of Zion: for, lo, I come, and I will dwell in the midst of thee, saith the LORD.**

> **11. And many nations shall be joined to the LORD in that day, and shall be my people: and I will dwell in the midst of thee, and thou shalt know that the LORD of hosts hath sent me unto thee.**

Evangelical Christians are in complete agreement that the Messiah (*i.e.*, Jesus) is the subject of these verses. Among Jews, there is a division of opinion. Some, especially among the less faithful, trivialize these verses, stating that they merely refer to the rebuilding of Solomon's Temple, which was underway during the days of Zechariah. "I will dwell in the midst of thee", according to this interpretation, means that through the *symbol* of the rebuilt Temple, God will, figuratively speaking, "dwell" amongst the people of Israel.

But many Orthodox Jewish commentators concede this passage to be an explicit reference to the Messiah of the End Times, *i.e.*, the Messiah of the House of David. There is therefore a substantial body of opinion among both Jews and Christians that the "I" of verse 10; that is, the person who will "dwell in the midst of [Israel]", refers to *the Messiah*.

Who, therefore, *is* this "I"?

In verse 11, God says again "I will dwell in the midst of thee", but then, the grammar abruptly changes, and the text says "and thou shalt know that *the LORD of hosts hath sent me unto thee*"(!).

If "I" in the previous verse is God, announcing His own coming, and if, when He comes, He does so in the form of an earthly messenger who is also "I", then it follows that the messenger *is* God!

All the English translations of the Bible which I have seen, both Jewish and Christian versions, are in virtually complete agreement with respect to the English word-for-word translation of these two verses. There are no language controversies here. Therefore, if this passage is indeed messianic, it can be said that when the Messiah comes, the distinction between him and He who sent him becomes blurred. If so, then the belief in the Messiah as God-on-earth, incomprehensible though it be to the human mind, cannot be categorically denied.

There are other passages in the Books of the Prophets where the distinction between God and His Messenger is blurred. Let's consider one more, from the 48th chapter of the Book of Isaiah. Here God, in the midst of a stern reminder to Israel of the fact that He alone is the creator of all, says

> **Come ye near unto me, hear ye this; I have not spoken in secret from the beginning; from the time that it was, there am I: and now the LORD God, and his Spirit, hath sent me.**
>
> Isaiah 48:16

Once again we have God speaking, then suddenly the sense changes and the same voice becomes the voice of God's messenger, saying that God *sent* him. It would appear that the messenger, as well as God's Spirit, are one and the same as He who sent them.

The Rabbis have considerable difficulty with this passage, and the others like it. They call this an "intermingling of words", and try hard to avoid the most obvious interpretation, which is that he whom was sent by God *was* God.

These passages have been cited by Christians through the centuries, as evidence that Yeshua was God-on-earth.

The Muslims see it differently, however. Muḥammad taught that the Messiah was a prophet, *not* God. Furthermore he stated emphatically that all the prophets were equal.

The fanaticism with which Muslims have denied the divinity of Yeshua is such that they carved the following inscription in stone, in the Dome of the Rock in Jerusalem (the actual inscription, of course, is in Arabic):

> "O you People of the Book, overstep not bounds in your religion, and of God speak only the truth. The Messiah, Jesus, son of Mary, is only an apostle of God, and His word which He conveyed into Mary, and a Spirit proceeding from Him. Believe therefore in God and His apostles, and say not Three. It will be better for you. God is only one God. Far be it from His glory that He should have a son."

I believe that Muḥammad was a prophet of God, and that the Qur'an is an inspired document. How can I reconcile this with the suggestion, embodied in the Biblical scripture just quoted, that the Messiah is not entirely distinct from He who sent him?

I have found that the Hindu religion provides a good framework for understanding in this regard.

Understanding the "Nature of Christ" through the Bhagavad Gita

We have discussed previously (Chapter 3) that Hinduism reconciles the irreconcilable, namely the age-old "controversy" between East and West, as to whether the ultimate reality is *Enlightenment,* or *God.* India lies between East and West, and has successfully absorbed the ideas of both, accepting them without conflict. Hindus acknowledge Enlightenment and recognize the path of removal of worldly desire, but they picture the end of that path as being restoration to the presence of the living God.

The Hindu religion also provides reconciliation between the apparently irreconcilable Christs of the New Testament and the Qur'an, in that God, in the Hindu scriptures, is presented as having a dual nature, at least insofar as the way in which He appears.

The premier scripture of modern Hinduism is the Bhagavad Gita. In this book, God first appears as *Krishna* the charioteer. The chariot he drives is the chariot of *Arjuna*, who is the human hero of this story. There is no particular moment of revelation of the true identity of Krishna to Arjuna. In other words, at the time that Krishna begins preaching to Arjuna, it is clear that Arjuna *already knows* that he is in the presence of God, and that God, for His own good reasons, has elected to appear to him as a man.

Therefore Arjuna, at that point in the book, might in good faith had informed his colleagues that he had "seen and talked to God", and he would have been telling the truth insofar as he understood it.

But the matter does not end there. Midway through his sermon, Krishna decides to reveal Himself to Arjuna in his true form, as God Almighty. He transfigures Himself into a form so awesome that it requires the full superlative powers of human language to even give an impression of His overwhelming majesty. This form is so terrifying that Arjuna quickly begs God to resume his human appearance. It is highly significant—and readers should take note—that the very vision that all religious men and women have craved through the ages, namely the vision of God Almighty Himself, is so *terrifying* that when finally apprehended, we promptly beg God to hide us from his Glory. This sobering fact is confirmed in the Book of Exodus, where God responds to Moses' request to be permitted to see Him with the words "thou canst not see my face: for there shall no man see Me, and live" (Ex 33:20).

Arjuna's vision was both awesome and terrifying:

> [God]...revealed...His supreme form, with countless mouths and eyes, displaying multitudes of marvels, wearing numbers of divine ornaments, and raising divine weapons beyond count. And this form wore celestial garlands and robes, it was anointed with the perfumes of the gods - it was God Himself, infinite and universal containing all miracles.
>
> If in the sky the light of a thousand suns were to rise at once, it would be the likeness of the light of that great-spirited One. In that body of the God of gods [Arjuna] saw the entire universe centered, in its infinite differentiations. [Arjuna] was stunned, and he shivered. He folded his hands, bowed his head and said:
>
> "I see all gods in your body, O God,
> And all creatures in all their varieties...
>
> Your own infinitude stretching away,
> Many arms, eyes, bellies, and mouths do I see,
> No end do I see, no beginning, no middle,
> In you, universal in power and form...
>
> Immeasurably burning like sun or the fire.
>
> You are the imperishable, highest of truths to be known,
> The highest foundation of all this world.
> Unchanging, the eternal keeper of right,
> The Person Eternal I hold you to be.
>
> At the sight of (you)...the worlds are in panic and so am I!"

(Bhagavad Gita, 11:9-23)

Arjuna was overcome with fear, and he begged God to return to His previous man-like form of Krishna the charioteer.

Now, a very interesting and important question arises. Having seen God's full Glory, what would Arjuna think if one of his colleagues, seeing Krishna the charioteer drive by, said "I have seen God"? Would Arjuna agree, or disagree? He had been aware from the beginning that Krishna the charioteer was God. But after witnessing Krishna's transformation into God Almighty, he surely would have felt differently. Clearly, *there was more to God than was evident in seeing Krishna the charioteer.*

Would Arjuna then call another man a liar, if the other man saw Krishna the charioteer and said "I have seen God"? Since Krishna *was* God, the other man would be telling the truth. But if Arjuna said "you haven't *really* seen God", he would be telling the truth also.

What does this have to do with Christ?

What did the Apostles of Yeshua actually see?

When one reads the Gospels—especially the synoptic Gospels, but even the Gospel of John—one is hardly impressed with the feeling that the disciples of Yeshua understood themselves to be in the presence of God Himself. Even in the Transfiguration, it is not made explicitly clear *whom* it was in whose presence they felt themselves to be.

When Yeshua asked his disciples "Whom do men say that I the Son of man am?" (Matthew 16:13), he received a potpourri of answers! Only one of them, Peter, said "Thou art the Messiah, the Son of the living God". But even so, what does "Son of the living God" mean? The closest Yeshua came to providing an answer was in John 10:31, where "the Jews" tried to stone him because, in their words

"...thou, being a man, makest thyself God"

John 10:33

Yeshua's answer was:

Is it not written in your law, "I said, Ye are gods"?

John 10:34

All commentators understand this to be an explicit reference to Psalm 82:6-7, which says:

> **<u>Ye are gods</u>; and all of you are children of the most High.**
> **But ye shall die like men, and fall like one of the princes.**

This response of Yeshua does not justify anyone in claiming that Yeshua made himself equal with God. If it does not rule it out either, so be it, but the matter remains unsettled. We really do not know *what* Yeshua wanted us to think that he was, other than to believe that he was the promised Messiah of God, foretold by Daniel and Isaiah.

In the vision of Stephen, the Christian Church's first martyr (Acts 7:55), we see the first instance of Yeshua being beheld in a strictly supernatural setting. Paul's famous vision follows shortly (Acts 9:3-6). Aside from Paul's two dreams, this was the last encounter with Yeshua reported by anyone in the New Testament prior to the Revelation, the dream of the Apostle John.

In all three instances, *i.e.*, Stephen, Paul, and the Revelation of John, the supernatural vision of Messiah was as a distinct being, at the Right Hand of God. It is therefore unknown whether any one of these three men perceived Yeshua to be God Himself.

We may therefore feel safe in proposing that the viewpoint which says that Yeshua was God-on-earth was a *logical* deduction, based on passages such as the two quoted above (Zechariah 2:10-11, Isaiah 48:16). There is no passage in the Gospels or Epistles in which any Christian prophet or saint says "I have seen the Messiah, and He *is* God".

The resolution of the "war" between Islam and Christianity about the so-called "nature of Christ" can be comprehended through the understanding of the Bhagavad Gita as a parable (or as literal history, if one is able to see it that way).

To most observers, Krishna was Arjuna's charioteer—*i.e.,* an ordinary man. Why should they think otherwise? Unless they talked to him, and got to "know" him, they would be basing their assessment upon ordinary observations of the five senses. Likewise, many have considered Yeshua to be a man.

Among those who knew Krishna would be some who understood him to be a Holy Man; one possessing great wisdom. Likewise, many have considered Yeshua to be a Holy Man; a man of great wisdom.

Others might have understood Krishna to be a heavenly messenger. Some might even have known him to be "God" in some sense of the word. Likewise, many have considered Yeshua to have been a heavenly messenger, even the Son of God.

Only Arjuna was blessed by being shown Krishna in His true, awesome form, which may be compared to our ultimate Western God, God the Father (the Jewish "Eloheim", the Supreme Being embodying a "plurality of majesty"). Therefore, we may ask the question "to whom, in the Western world, has God the Father revealed Himself in his Full Glory, showing Himself to be one and the same as his Messiah?"

The likely answer to this question is "no one". At least, no one of the prophets of Western religion. God appeared to Abraham and Jacob as a man (Genesis, Chapters 18 and 32 respectively). He appeared to Moses "face-to-face, as a *man* speaketh unto his friend" (Exodus 33:11). He appeared to Yeshua's disciples as a risen divine being, at the Right Hand of God. And He appeared to Muḥammad as Gabriel, the archangel originally introduced in the Biblical Book of Daniel.

In other words, there *is* no exact parallel to Arjuna in the Western world. Whether any man has ever seen the full glory of God is impossible for us to say.

Some believe that every appearance of God in the Bible is Christ, in which case Christ is God. It's not for us to say. God has the attribute of *plurality* in His majesty, and He has the ability and authority to appear as any number of persons, or in any number of ways.

Therefore, it is my logical conclusion that the revelations to the Christian and Muslim churches, irreconcilable though they may seem, must stand until God Himself resolves the matter. This doesn't really need to be said, since neither church has the slightest intention of retreating from its position anyway.

Can anyone ever really "know" the "nature" of Christ?

I often wonder whether God, in His infinite wisdom, has preserved the Hindu religion for all these years, in spite of its obvious strong ties to ancient idolatry, because it provides a complete religion to India, and also an important parable to Westerners who insist that Christ have only a single nature, when in fact Christ may have many natures, each one apparent to some people, but not others.

It is worth noting, at this juncture, that there exists a parallel Eastern argument over whether *Buddha* was merely a man who attained Enlightenment and taught others (as enshrined in Theravada Buddhism), or rather an earthly manifestation of Enlightenment itself—*i.e.*, the appearance in human form of a Supreme Being analogous to our God (as embodied in Mahayana Buddhism). This is the same as the argument we entertained above about God and His Messiah. This is the "nature of Buddha" argument; one entirely parallel to, and every bit as insoluble as the parallel dispute about the "nature of Christ".

Can God have a son? Yes, God can surely have a son, if He so chooses. Whether or not Yeshua should be literally regarded as such is not for us to say.

We do not, and cannot, "know" God. Do you deny this? If you "know" God, why have you kept your knowledge secret from all the churches of the world?

On the other hand, those of us who desire to be humble before God have realized that we do not "know" God. Therefore, it follows that *to the extent that the Messiah is God-on-earth, that is the extent to which we cannot "know" the Messiah either.* That is why it is hopeless to attempt to understand the "nature" of Christ, or the "nature" of Messiah. And we most assuredly do not increase our understanding by killing those who disagree with us.

Let us instead contemplate our *own* natures, and try to figure out how we came to be separated from the presence of God, and how we might reverse the error of Original Sin.

Chapter 6

Islam

Part I

History of the Covenant Between God and Man

We have seen that the Jewish people were a disappointment to God, and that He scattered many of them throughout the earth in the 6th century B.C., even as far as China. But, in accordance with His promise, he surely did not abandon them. Rather, He made them bearers of His Spirit, to carry the Word of Himself to the far-flung corners of the orient.

We also saw the Jewish people, in the days of the Maccabbees, doubt that pure faith in God could save their nation from being engulfed by Rome, turning instead to worldly militaristic ambition. When a messenger, Yeshua Moshiaḥ (Jesus Christ), was sent to them later, bidding that they return to faith in God, the messenger was slain. The Word, however, spread like wildfire in the hands of his followers; not so much among the Jews, but among the gentiles.

We have seen further that the Jewish rejection of Yeshua was prophesied a half-millennium before it happened, and that his rejection was necessary for the fulfillment of scripture.

If the story had ended there, then the Jewish people would stand condemned, and there would be no obvious reason for God to ever raise them up again. Nor would there be any obvious way for prophecies of the resurrection of the House of David to be fulfilled. Therefore, the story could not end there.

No, there had to be a further chapter. There was, and there is. The Lord God created a whirlwind of dissent about the "nature of Christ"—a slew of opinions as numerous as the languages God imposed upon man at the Tower of Babel. This made it impossible for the new religion which grew up around Yeshua to ever be put into a "final form".

The first serious attempts to quell this dissent were the Christian councils of Niceaea, Chalcedon and Ephesus, which we shall discuss presently. At these councils, the Roman Church came to triumph over the East, forcing upon them a dogmatic doctrine of Christ as God-on-earth. For those who continued to dissent, the penalty was excommunication.

For large numbers of Eastern Christians, a burning *resentment* was the enduring result of the councils. To prevail over Rome, however, they needed more than heightened emotions. They needed Divine Guidance. This Guidance was sent to them as a revelation—a revelation through the mouth of an illiterate Arab merchant named Muḥammad.

His religion, Islam, completes what we shall presently see to be a *circle*, a continuous geometric shape which has no beginning and no end. We will return to this concept later.

The story of Islam, in its capacity as a separate faith distinct from both Judaism and Christianity, cannot be understood without an understanding of its roots. The seeds from which these roots sprang were planted in the days of the revered patriarch of Judaism-Christianity-Islam, father Abraham.

Abraham

At the end of Chapter 11 of the Book of Genesis, we were introduced to Abram, whose name God later changed to "Abraham", which means "father of many nations" (Genesis 17:5).

A father of many nations indeed! As the great patriarch of Jews, Christians, and Muslims, his portion among nations amounts to no less than half the souls alive on earth today. And the mathematical arguments we have seen earlier in this book convey the powerful implication that much of the other half of the world's population may fall under his domain as well.

Abraham was originally from Ur, a city in southern Iraq. This is the region called Mesopotamia ("between the rivers")—the *fertile crescent* between the Tigris and Euphrates rivers. Let us review Genesis, Chapter 12, which records the divine order to move:

> **Now the Lord had said unto Abram, Get thee out of thy country, and from thy kindred, and from thy father's house, unto a land that I will show thee:**
>
> **And I will make of thee a great nation, and I will bless thee, and make thy name great; and thou shalt be a blessing:**
>
> **And I will bless them that bless thee, and curse him that curseth thee: an in thee shall all families of the earth be blessed."**

The first part of the above quote (Genesis 12:1) deserves special mention. It became necessary for Abraham to leave his home and his people in order to obtain the Lord's blessing. The same was true for all who followed him, as was later true for all who followed Yeshua (many of whom perished at the hands of the Romans), and as was still later true for the followers of Muḥammad (all of whom eventually had to flee for their lives, from Mecca to Medina). It is therefore the duty of every believer in God to be prepared, if and when the call comes, to again uproot himself; if not physically, then at least spiritually.

In Abraham's case, the physical and spiritual move were one and the same: he relocated to the land we know today as "Israel".

A "revolutionary war" in the Middle East

Now the Middle East, in those days, consisted of two great empires: Babylon (*i.e.,* Iraq) and Egypt. In between these lay a seemingly indomitable frontierland, corresponding to today's Israel. Has anything really changed?

In the days of Abraham, Israel was a collection of petty kingdoms which paid tribute to Babylon. A "king" back then was probably no more than what we would today call a "mayor" of a city today. Chapter 14 of the Book of Genesis describes a rebellion of a coalition of such Israeli mayor-kings from the region south of Jerusalem. The members of this coalition refused to pay their annual tribute to Babylon, undoubtedly knowing full well that a military reprisal was certain.

Jewish scholarly opinion states that Amraphel, the power behind the Babylonian force sent to quell the uprising, was none other than Hammurabi, the great Babylonian king and law-giver. If so, then we are dealing, in Genesis Chapter 14, with a major political upheaval. To me, as an American, it is reminiscent of the rebellion of the Thirteen Colonies against England during our own War of Independence in the 18th century.

The Babylonian army inflicted a serious defeat upon the rebellious Israeli kings, but Abraham used his own private army to turn the tide of the battle. The Babylonians were routed.

The Israeli kings were subsequently indebted to Abraham, but he refused to accept any spoil from the battle. What he did get, however, was peace for himself and his people.

Prior to this war, Abraham was in a state of continuing unrest, such as might have been seen in the American Wild West upon the arrival of a new stranger in a frontier territory. Subsequent to the war, however, Abraham was clearly established as a man to be feared and respected. After purchasing a piece of land in a place called "Machpelah", in which to bury his deceased wife Sarah (Genesis Chapter 23), Abraham was legally established in the land. The troubled history of Israel, the Nation, had begun.

The children of Abraham

In the Book of Genesis, the origins of the best known of the families of Abraham are described. There are many of them. In Genesis 13:16, God tells Abraham "I will make thy seed as the dust of the earth, so that if a man can number the dust of the earth, then shall thy seed also be numbered". This, of course, required that he be married and have children.

We gave a short account of the story of Abraham's two wives, Hagar and Sarah, in Chapter 2 of this book. Let us look at the rest. The Bible reports that Abraham was married to his half-sister, Sarah, but that she was barren. So she gave Abraham her Egyptian maid, Hagar, to be his second wife, in accordance with the customs of the day. You see, it appears that the children of a woman's maid were counted as her own. The issue was inheritance: Without a male child, a wife inherited little of her husband's property; less, even, than his sister did.

Unfortunately it was true then, as it remains true today, that people cursed themselves with a heavy burden of jealousy. When Hagar the maid became pregnant, she grew proud and refused to submit to the rule of her mistress, Sarah. The latter flew into a jealous rage, and demanded permission from Abraham to throw Hagar out of the house. Hagar's pregnancy had not yet come to term, and as yet there were no offspring for Abraham to be attached to. Perhaps for this reason, or perhaps for other reasons, he gave his consent. Hagar was ejected forthwith (Genesis, Chapter 17).

But the angel of the Lord visited Hagar and counseled her to return, and to submit to her mistress. She did so, and shortly thereafter gave birth to a son, Ishmael. In the birth of Ishmael, Sarah's wish for a full inheritance was granted.

But then God caused *Sarah* to conceive, and her own son, Isaac, was born (Genesis, Chapter 21). Now she could have her full inheritance through her own "flesh and blood". Without delay, she again demanded that Hagar, and Ishmael with her, be cast out from the house. This time, it was to be permanent. She had no further use for either of them.

Now, Abraham loved Ishmael, and this request grieved him greatly. But the voice of God told him to consent to Sarah's wishes, and he did so. He "took bread and a bottle of water, and gave it unto Hagar, putting it on her shoulder, and the child, and sent her away" (Genesis 21:14).

On that very day, the religion known today as "Islam" was born.

Since God Himself suffered the expulsion of Ishmael to take place, it may be clearly seen that it is His will that Islam exist.

Hagar nearly perishes in the desert

Hagar's bottle of water was soon spent, and she got lost in the wilderness. She sat down to die, placing Ishmael a "bowshot" away. "Let me not look upon the death of the child", she said (Genesis 21: 16). But they did not die. God brought forth water from the earth, and saved the two of them. This spring of water is identified by Muslims today as the well of Zamzam, located far from Israel, within the precincts of what is now the al-Haram Mosque in Mecca. At the center of this Mosque is the holiest site in Islam, the Ka'bah, a temple said to have been built by Abraham himself, with his son Ishmael.

God advised Hagar not to despair. As was recounted in Genesis 16:10, Hagar had been visited by the angel of the Lord, who said to her "I will multiply thy seed exceedingly, that it shall not be numbered for multitude". And, as for Ishmael, Genesis 17:20 stated "I have blessed him, and will make him fruitful, and will multiply him exceedingly; twelve princes shall he beget, and I will make him a great nation".

God did not forget these prophecies, a fact which is attested to by the one billion Muslims of the planet earth, many of whom trace their ancestry to Abraham through Hagar and Ishmael.

As for Sarah, promises were made regarding her as well. In Genesis 17:16, God said to Abraham "I will bless her, and give thee a son also of her: yea, I will bless her, and she shall be a mother of nations: kings of people shall be of her". This prophecy was fulfilled in the birth of Isaac, whose son, Jacob, was the father of the twelve tribes of Israel.

So the prophecy of Genesis 13:16, that Abraham's progeny would be as numerous as the dust of the earth was fulfilled through many tribes: the twelve tribes of Ishmael and the twelve tribes of Israel, at the very least.

But modern day Muslims have managed very nicely to put God's word out of their minds. Thus, they recall the prophecies made regarding Hagar and Ishmael ceaselessly, but manage somehow to forget the prophecies made regarding Isaac.

Similarly, modern day Jews and Christians have, equally remarkably, forgotten about Ishmael. On those few occasions where the memories of Hagar and Ishmael are evoked, this is done so with an air of contempt. Perhaps this is because Hagar was a maid.

Or perhaps its because of the "wild ass" hoax we described in Chapter 2 of this book.

We also saw in Chapter 2 that there is powerful evidence that God made a Covenant with all the descendants of Abraham. The token of the Covenant was circumcision. Both Ishmael and Isaac were circumcised. So who is it who "owns" the land of Israel? Is it Jews, is it Muslims, or is it someone else? Besides, what is a "Jew"? And what is a "Muslim"?

Considering all the ambiguities involved, and considering the fact that the waters of truth have been muddied by serious transgressions of the Law of Moses by all parties involved, isn't it true to state that, at this point, the definition of a "Jew" or "Muslim" or "Christian" is none other than the definition given by Yeshua when he was told that his "brethren" wished to see him?

...whosoever shall do the will of my Father which is in heaven, the same is my brother, and sister, and mother. (Matthew 12:50)

Chapter 7

Islam

Part II

The Christian Councils

If Islam was "born" the day Sarah threw Hagar out of the house, then it was "confirmed" by the Christian Councils of Nicaea, Chalcedon, and Ephesus.

In no way can the rise of Islam be held to be independent of the developments of early Christianity, which we shall therefore now examine.

<u>Paul</u>

It must be conceded that the greatest evangelist in the history of the world was Paul. The armies of Muhammed got just as far, but Muḥammad himself never left Arabia. Buddhism spread just as far to the east, but Buddha himself never left India.

Paul, on the other hand, single-handedly carried Christianity the full length of the Roman Empire, from Israel all the way to Spain. The magnitude of this feat staggers the imagination. And he had no army, he himself bearing only a single weapon: his vision of Yeshua (Jesus), whom he had never personally met.

Having expressed such profound admiration, it must now be added that for Jews and Muslims, Paul has proven to be one of history's great trouble-makers, for the new religion he founded allowed for peaceful coexistence with no doctrine other than itself.

The story of Paul is well-known to all Christians. His Hebrew name was "Saul", and he first appears in the New Testament as "Saul of Tarsus", a city which still exists in modern-day Turkey.

Paul's was a rich Jewish family. He was a Roman citizen, which conferred considerable privilege on a man at that time—a privilege which was to save him when he was later arrested for his Christian activities (Acts, Chapter 22). He went to Judea to study and eventually to live.

While in Judea, he, exercising fully his aristocratic prerogative, became very much involved in the effort to stamp out the "new religion" which was being spread by the disciples of Yeshua. It cannot be over-emphasized that at that early date, the "new religion"—today called "Christianity"—was indistinguishable from Orthodox Judaism, save in one respect only: that it expressed reverence for Yeshua as the promised Messiah.

Paul was present at, and zealously involved with the murder of Stephen, the first known martyr of the fledgling Judeo-Christian Church. Thus, Paul was a man who believed in the appropriateness of killing those whose religious views differed from his own.

We should not be surprised, then, to note that now, 2000 years later, nothing has really changed. Jews, Christians and Muslims still seek each other's blood.

Paul's conversion was one of the most momentous happenings in western history. With characteristic vehemence, he had obtained a fistful of arrest warrants, and was on the road to Damascus to arrest any Christians he might find there. While on the road, he heard the voice of Yeshua himself, from heaven, saying "Saul, Saul, why persecutest thou me?". And Saul said "Who art thou, Lord?". The voice answered "I am Yeshua whom thou persecutest: it is hard for thee to kick against the goads" (Acts, Chapter 9).

Paul arose from this vision, to find that he had been stricken blind. He was led by the hand to Damascus, where, instead of persecuting the early Church, he joined it!. His eyesight was then miraculously restored, and his career was launched.

At Damascus, Paul astonished the early Christian Church members by proclaiming the glory of Yeshua instead of arresting his followers. There is no doubt that they regarded him with great suspicion at first. Later on, they accepted the sincerity of his conversion, and sent him out to spread the Word.

The favored evangelical assignment must surely have been Jerusalem, but Paul, as a newcomer, was sent north to visit the gentiles. I'm sure that the gentiles listened attentively at first, but when he explained to them that they had to give up all their favorite foods and cut the flesh from around the tips of their penises, they balked.

It was one of those great bottlenecks of history. Something had to be done, or the early Church would have died a neonatal death. So Paul became a politician. By his own admission (I Corinthians 9:19-24), he tried to be all things to all people. Like a candidate for office, seeking votes from different ethnic groups, he endeavored to speak their languages, eat their foods, and, as far as possible, be one of them. As long as they would listen to him talk about Yeshua, he would accommodate himself and his religion to their needs, and to their limitations.

A glimpse into the world of the early Church which sprung from proselytizers such as Paul is offered in the book of Revelation, Chapter 2. The author, usually presumed to be the Apostle John, had a dream or vision in which he heard the voice of Yeshua addressing himself to the early Churches in Asia Minor. For example, regarding the Church at Pergamos, the voice of Yeshua in the dream/vision said...

> **"I know thy works...thou holdest fast my name, and hast not denied my faith, even in those days wherein Antipas was my faithful martyr, who was slain among you...**
>
> **...But I have a few things against thee, because thou hast there them that hold the doctrine of Balaam, who taught Balac to cast a stumblingblock before the children of Israel, to eat things sacrificed unto idols, and to commit fornication (Revelation 2:12-16)".**

A "few" things? This Church, and the others mentioned in Chapter 2 of Revelation, were obviously motley affairs indeed; places where acceptable religious practices mingled freely with pagan obscenities. In no way could such things have been tolerated by the Jewish-Christian Church in Jerusalem.

That latter Church, the Church in Jerusalem, was the Church of Yeshua Messiah as Jew. It was persecuted; first by "traditional" Jews, then Romans, then by the Christians themselves. But the final blow, as we shall presently see, was Islam.

Abrogation of the Law of Moses

Paul and his co-workers to the north of Israel were at obvious odds with the early Judeo-Christian Church in Jerusalem. Paul's way of dealing with gentiles was to declare them free to eat any food, and free to renounce the Covenant of circumcision. Some hint of the trouble which arose because of these teachings may be obtained by reading the latter half of the Book of the Acts of the Apostles, especially Chapters 15 and 21.

With respect to the Jewish dietary laws, Paul obviously failed to prevail over the gentile taste for pork and other foods forbidden to Jews. Either according to his own ideas, or perhaps proceeding on the basis of the famous dream of Peter

(Acts 10:10-17), he declared, to the gentiles, that belief in Yeshua Messiah caused their food to become "clean".

If the transgressions of Jewish law had ended there, subsequent world history might have been very different. But Paul dispensed with circumcision.

Even in today's most ultra-reformed Jewish congregations, where the great majority of Jewish laws have been abrogated, and where even the existence of God Himself is openly questioned, there neither is, nor ever has been any serious discussion about abandoning the Covenant of circumcision.

Thus, in reneging on the most fundamental token of God's Covenant with man, Paul crossed a line which no devoted follower of the Law of Moses would ever cross with him.

True, the prophets of old had taught that circumcision of the flesh was of no value if the "heart" was not circumcised also (Deuteronomy 10:16, Jeremiah 4:4 and 9:26, Ezekiel 44:7-9). The converse, however, that circumcision of the flesh was *obviated* by "circumcision of the heart", was *not* the word of God, but of Paul.

On the contrary, God declared circumcision to be an "*everlasting* Covenant" (Genesis 17:13). Since Time has not ended, the commandment to circumcise male offspring is presumably still current. Sound's horrible? Is it worse than the suffering the uncircumcised world inflicts upon itself? How about two World Wars? How about the Turkish slaughter of 1,000,000 Armenian Christians, or Pol Pot's negligent/intentional homicide of 3 million Cambodians?

The abrogating of the Covenant of circumcision, in the interest of spreading the word of Yeshua, proved to be the death blow of the early Judeo-Christian Church. Unremitting hostility from the chief Rabbis of Jerusalem ultimately prevailed, and the Israeli branch of the early Church was outlawed.

The surviving branch of the early Church was the branch which was physically outside the reach of the Rabbis; the branch created by Paul and his co-workers in Europe and Asia Minor.

These Pauline Christians did not follow Jewish law. In particular, they renounced the Covenant of circumcision. There was no chance of reconciliation between this church and Judaism.

Modern world history had begun.

The "nature" of Christ

The followers of Yeshua never regarded him as "only" a prophet, but as much more. At the very least, he was regarded as the Jewish Moshiach, the promised Messiah.

Immediately, there was trouble. As we have already seen (in Chapter 5 of this book), the writings of the prophets about the so-called "End Times" required the fulfillment of a number of important prophecies which had *not* yet been fulfilled. The "lion" was surely *not* lying with the "lamb", and all nations were surely *not* flowing to the "Mountain of the Lord" in Jerusalem. Something was wrong. What was it?

There is no exact answer to the above question, yet. Truthfully, the doctrinal problems of those days are still very much with us today—none of them has really been solved. Insofar as he died for our sins, and our sins are still upon us, it can be said in a figurative sense that Yeshua is *still* on the cross... waiting for us to decide.

Thus, the members of the early Church were in a state of suspense. They were adrift in the knowledge that the End Times prophecies were not yet completely fulfilled, and they needed something to hold onto in the meantime. Therefore, the notion that the Messiah would have *two* comings was proposed, and accepted. The First Coming was the one the world had already witnessed in Yeshua. The Second Coming would be the return of the Son of Man in His full glory, at the End of Time.

But this did not solve all the problems. According to Biblical Prophecy, exemplified in Zechariah 2:8-11...

> **"Thus saith the LORD of Hosts...I will dwell in the midst of thee...and thou shalt know that the LORD of Hosts hath sent me unto thee..."**

...the Son of Man in his full glory was so holy that the distinction between the Messenger and He who sent him would be blurred. To many bishops of the early Christian Church, this meant that Yeshua had to be God Himself; literally the Word made flesh. Thus was born the controversy about the "nature of Christ", an evil controversy which has resulted in a state of endless war, and misery beyond reckoning.

Whenever I think of this controversy, I think of it in terms of an imaginary dialogue between a Jew and a Christian. The following is fictional, but I think it illustrates the sorts of arguments which led to a total polarization of opinion about the "nature" of Christ:

JEW:	Yeshua was merely a philosopher.
CHRISTIAN:	Not so, he was a prophet.
JEW:	If Yeshua was a prophet, he was a *false* prophet.
CHRISTIAN:	Yeshua was a *true* prophet. He was *more* than a prophet—he was the Messiah.
JEW:	Yeshua was nothing more than a good-natured schizophrenic!
CHRISTIAN:	He was nothing less than the Son of God!
JEW:	He was a troublesome, meddling lunatic!
CHRISTIAN:	He was God Himself, God-on-earth, the Third in the Holy Trinity!

These two imaginary debaters, arguing about the *mystery* of who Yeshua was, are unable to agree. So they force each other to extreme positions, each one, in the end, asserting that there's "no mystery at all"—he and he alone understands the "nature of Christ" fully.

This dialogue is imaginary, but it illustrates the process whereby the *mystery* of Yeshua came to be systematically denied by those in power. A profound event in history—Yeshua's life and ministry—was reduced to trivial terms, to cater to people's needs for simple explanations to complex problems.

A total polarization of opinion rapidly developed in the early Christian era. Either you regarded Yeshua as a deadly enemy, or you regarded him as God Almighty Himself—here on earth as a man. Those were your choices.

For a century or two, there were people who desperately tried to maintain a middle ground, but they were subjected to abuse and persecution from both sides. In the process of time, almost all of them either reverted totally back to "pure" antichrist Judaism, or surrendered to the growing Christian majority, accepting Yeshua as God, and perhaps even bowing to statues of him. Anyone who continued to proclaim himself a middle-of-the-road Judeo-Christian was branded an "heretic".

As a result of books like Irenaeus' *Against the Heresies*, and Councils such as Nicaea, Chalcedon and Ephesus, the pure water of early Christianity came gradually to be replaced with the muddy waters of man-made doctrine.

The First Council

By the fourth century, Christianity had become the official religion of the Roman Empire. The believers in Christ as the literal Son of God (or as God Himself, on earth as a man) were in the majority. But dissenters were prevalent, and the fighting was hot and heavy.

Historically, one of the most durable of the early dissenters was Arius, a presbyter of Alexandria. Arius taught that Christ was created, not eternal, and that he was not of the same substance as God. His bishop disagreed, holding that Christ was eternal and of the same substance as God. The controversy which resulted from this ridiculous and non-resolvable dispute was so severe that Emperor Constantine called the Council of Nicaea in 325 AD, at which 300 bishops, men, voted that Christ, *i.e.* Yeshua, *was* God. Religious "democracy" was born; Arius was exiled and condemned as an "heretic".

Influential friends, including the Emperor's daughter Constantia, succeeded in effecting a compromise solution which made possible Arius' return from exile and his re-admission to the Church. But, before this could take place, he dropped dead while walking in the streets of Constantinople.

But Arianism did not die; not then and not ever. Full-fledged Arian Christian groups flourished for centuries; a constant thorn in the side of the Catholic Church. Among the most prosperous of these were the Visigoths, who played a major role in the history of Europe, especially the regions now known as France and Spain, where Arianism prevailed until the Muslim conquest of 711. And today, the Arian concept of Christ survives in Unitarianism and Islam.

More Councils

The Council of Nicaea did not solve the problem of serious divisions in the Roman Church. A century later there remained, in the minds of the Eastern bishops, a burning question. What was the relationship between the human and divine natures of Christ? Were they "co-joined" or did they dwell in him separately? In Europe, it had already been determined (apparently with little dissent) that they were co-joined.

But another world-class dissenter, Nestorius, the presbyter of Antioch, vehemently disagreed. He declared that Yeshua was a man, and that the "divine" component of his nature dwelled within the man. When Nestorius was promoted to the position of bishop of Constantinople, he delivered a sermon against calling Mary the "Mother of God", declaring that she had borne a man, not a God.

Cyril, bishop of Alexandria, took a stand against Nestorius, and the fighting became so fierce that another Council had to be called. At Ephesus in 431 the bishops met again, and in a session laden with political intrigue, Nestorius was accused of reviving the "heresy" of a certain Paul of Samosata, the bishop of Antioch in 260 A.D., who had taught that Yeshua was a man who became divine, rather than God become man.

Nestorius was condemned and banished.

But the banishment of Nestorius did not suppress the dissension of those still within the Church who agreed with the Nestorian point of view. Consequently, it became necessary to convene yet *another* council, the Council of Chalcedon, in 451. At this final Council, the European bishops triumphed over the East, and the fundamental Catholic concept of Christ as undisputed God-on-earth became permanently established. This meant that Yeshua was declared (by democratic consensus) to be God, and simultaneously man, both natures being fully integrated into a simultaneous and unified entity.

In spite of the sound political majority engineered by the West, there remained numerous influential Eastern bishops who refused to cooperate, and the Churches known as Monophysite, Coptic, and Jacobite, which persist to this day, separated themselves from the body of European Christianity. Furthermore, The Nestorians continued to dissent, and Nestorian Churches, some of which survive to this day, spread all the way to India and China.

Racial and ethnic aspects of the Christian Councils

There is a side to the Christian Councils which receives insufficient notice: the aspect of racial and ethnic prejudice.

Those who were most likely to be blood descendants of people who had walked with Yeshua were the relatively dark-complexioned people of Arabia and Egypt. These were the lands in and adjacent to Israel, where the events of Christianity actually took place.

It was among the people of the Middle East and Egypt that the idea that Yeshua was a man, not a god, refused to die out. Since these were the people physically closest to Yeshua, they undoubtedly felt that their concept of him should have carried more weight than it did.

It is an historical fact that the notion of Yeshua as God was championed by the relatively light-skinned bishops of Europe, especially France. These were people who had never walked with Yeshua, and were not descended from people who had.

It is a mistake to regard these differences between East and West as being trivial. In an American court of law, it is difficult or impossible to convict a man of a serious crime upon the presentation of written evidence alone. The spoken testimony of living, breathing eye-witnesses is required. There is no substitute for having been there.

But in the "nature of Christ" controversy, the party which was most representative of those who *had been there*, was overwhelmed by a body of largely European bishops whose knowledge of Yeshua was, for the most part, second-hand.

As one reflects on these events, one begins to see that there was a racial and ethnic side to this story. The Caucasian bishops of Europe had inherited the wealth and political power of the Roman Empire, and they used it to suppress the views of the Arab and Negro Bishops of Africa and Asia. The prevailing view about the "nature of Christ" was thus determined by the politically advantaged, a situation which could not possibly have ended peacefully.

Subsequent fate of Christianity in Africa and Asia

It is certain that the founders of the first African and Asian Churches endured just as much persecution as their European brothers. But in the wake of the Christian Councils, the ultimate "reward" for many of them was excommunication by the Roman Church. This must have been a painful blow.

With the notable exception of Ethiopia, Christianity did not spread very far in Africa. And in Asia, where Christianity first took root, it went on to largely die out. The Nestorian Churches of China disappeared without a trace. In India, a few remain today, but they are no more than a "drop in the bucket" in a nation of a billion inhabitants. Likewise in the countries of the Middle East, only small Christian minorities survive, and most of these are remnants (largely assimilated from the doctrinal point of view) of churches formerly branded as "heretical" by Rome.

Although I have never seen it suggested in any Muslim source, I cannot refrain from pointing out that the Prophet Isaiah, who foresaw the coming of Yeshua, foresaw also the sufferings of the African and Asian Christians, and correctly predicted their outcome. In two places in the Book bearing his name, Isaiah addressed himself to this. The first such place is in Chapter 19, where the Prophet predicted dire calamity for Egypt. Afterwards, Isaiah foresaw the LORD's salvation:

> **In that day shall there be a highway out of Egypt to Assyria, and the Assyrian shall come into Egypt, and the Egyptian into Assyria, and the Egyptians shall serve with the Assyrians.**
>
> **In that day shall Israel be the third with Egypt and with Assyria, [even] a blessing in the midst of the land:**
>
> **Whom the LORD of hosts shall bless, saying, Blessed [be] Egypt my people, and Assyria the work of my hands, and Israel mine inheritance.**
>
> Isaiah 19:23-25

In annotated versions of the Bible, both Jewish and Christian, these verses are quickly passed over. They cannot be made to accommodate themselves to any historical events of note in the history of either Jews or Christians. It may be that they refer to future events, perhaps in the End Times.

I note, however, that these passages can be reconciled readily with the events shortly following the death of the Prophet Muḥammad, whose efforts alone brought about the enduring legacy of the proper worship of the God of Abraham, through Islam, in the Arab nations. We have seen that the centers of Christian dissent—later dubbed "heresy"—were Alexandria and Antioch. Alexandria is in Egypt, and, in the days of Isaiah, the nation in which Antioch is located was called Assyria. Both these lands succumbed in the first wave of Muslim conquests of the 8th century.

There is a problem, however. Although Israel was part of the post-Muhammadan Muslim empire which swept up Egypt and Assyria, it has never been abandoned by either Jews or Christians. Certainly at the present time, Israel is not "third" with them, but remains wracked by war. Therefore, the prophecy is still evolving.

The establishment of proper—*i.e.* non-idolatrous—worship of God in Egypt, and in the nations of the Middle East, is such an obvious reference to Islam that I cannot help but marvel that no commentary, not even one of Muslim origin, has seen fit to mention it.

What about Israel being "third"? It is not obvious how this shall come about. But when it does, it will complete the fulfillment of the prophecy. Perhaps this is described by Isaiah in Chapter 27 of his Book. There he said:

> **And it shall come to pass in that day, [that] the great trumpet shall be blown, and they shall come which were ready to perish in the land of Assyria, and the outcasts in the land of Egypt, and shall worship the LORD in the holy mount at Jerusalem.**
>
> Isaiah 27:13

The modern 1948 State of Israel could be the beginning of the fulfillment of this prophecy, but it needn't be. As long as the children of Isaac continue to call Ishmael a "wild ass", and as along as the children of Ishmael call Judaism a "dead religion", the war will continue.

In the meantime, the Dome of the Rock keeps the Temple Mount holy, at least preventing it from being sold off as "luxury real estate". This Muslim mosque, built in 638 AD either directly on, or else close to, the site of the future Third Temple, may seem like an affront to Jews and Christians, but what it symbolizes was known to the prophet Isaiah one thousand years before it was built.

Chapter 8

Islam

Part III

Life of Muḥammad

Muḥammad was born in 570 A.D. in Mecca, in the nation now called Saudi Arabia. His father died before he was born. He was provided for by his grandfather, then later by an uncle.

It was his uncle who introduced him to the business of merchant caravans. Because of Muḥammad's trustworthy and honest nature he came into the employ of Khadijah, a wealthy widow 15 years older than himself. He eventually married her, thereby becoming a member of the privileged class in Mecca.

The Meccans have always regarded themselves as descendants of Abraham through Ishmael. It was Abraham and Ishmael, they believe, who built the famous cubical temple in Mecca known as the Ka'bah, home of the mysterious Black Rock. The exact details of the creation of this structure are lost literally in the sands of time—it was already ancient at the time King Solomon's Temple in Jerusalem was being built.

The Ka'bah was a place of worship of the Hebrew God, whom the Arabs have always called Allah[34]. But over the centuries, stone idols had been installed in the Ka'bah, thus violating the single most fundamental tenet of the religion of Abraham: to fear God and God only, and to renounce all forms of idolatry.

The idols in the Ka'bah depicted mythological minor deities who were regarded as "intercessors", and it had long since become the habit of Arabs to pray to these idols to "intercede" on their behalf with Allah, rather than to pray to Allah directly.

---

[34] One of the ancient Hebrew Names of God is transliterated "El" (plural "Eloheem"). Actually, the correct pronunciation is somewhere between "El" and "Ale" (like the drink). It is self-evident, to anyone who is not intellectually disabled by causeless hatred and blind rage, that the names "El" ("Ale") and "Al(lah)" are merely different regional pronunciations of the same Name.

The Arabs who opposed this form of modified idolatry were called *Hunafa*. The Hunafa fervently desired that the idols be removed from the Ka'bah and that pure worship of the One God of Abraham be restored. They were not, however, a united community, and they lacked the political power necessary to overthrow the semi-apostate ruling class.

Muḥammad became one of the Hunafa, and he adopted the practice of retiring to a cave in the desert to fast and meditate for prolonged periods of time. In or around the year 610 A.D., at the age of 40, he had the first of many visionary experiences. In that year, while meditating in the cave, he was visited by the angel Gabriel, who informed him that Allah had chosen him to be His messenger.

This vision did not come about spontaneously. Muḥammad had been fasting and praying in that cave for 40 days when it occurred.

Now, that number, 40, is a very special number. Forty was the number of days that Moses spent on top of Mt. Sinai, both the first time (Exodus 24:18) and the second time (Exodus 34:28). Forty was the number of days that Elijah spent in the wilderness before God appeared to him in a cave on Mount Horeb (I Kings 19:8). Forty was the number of days that Yeshua (Jesus) was tempted in the desert by Satan. And forty was the number of days Buddha sat under the Bodhi tree before attaining Enlightenment.

It appears, therefore, that forty are the days of purification required of a man that he may be worthy of receiving the Word of God.

It should not be presumed that a forty day fast automatically leads to enlightenment. For political hunger strikers, striving for earthly gain, a prolonged fast simply leads to death from starvation.

But Muḥammad strove for far more than earthly gain. He strove for the Word of God Himself, which came to him, and has endured in the world through fourteen subsequent centuries, spreading only farther and wider as time has marched on.

The Word, as spoken through the mouth of the Prophet, was recorded in the hearts and minds of his followers. Their recollections, compiled into a volume shortly after Muḥammad's death, constitute the book known today as the Qur'an.

As the world has "shrunk" in the 20th century, and as Jews, Christians, and Muslims have been physically thrust into face-to-face encounters in every direction in which they have turned, the time has surely come for every believing individual to consider the meaning and the message of the Qur'an, the great book of the Prophet Muḥammad.

Let us begin by considering the man himself.

The Ministry of Muḥammad

The story of Muḥammad's rise to power, which was the rise of Islam itself as we now know it, is awe-inspiring. Only a bare outline can be given here.

After his first visions, he began to preach to his family and friends, and later to the people of Mecca. On the whole, the people were offended. They liked their idols, they liked their alcohol, they liked their gambling, and they liked their political and social corruption. They *disliked* Muḥammad.

For many years, Muḥammad was largely dismissed as an annoying fool, but when he began to obtain converts from among the wealthy and influential of Mecca's inhabitants, things took a turn for the worse. Serious persecution of his followers began to occur on a regular basis.

The cruelty became so severe that Muḥammad advised those of his followers who were able, to emigrate to a safer place. The first such place was far-off Abyssinia (today called Ethiopia), a Christian nation where they were allowed to live in peace. Most, however, were not able to make the move, and the persecution continued, unabated.

Later, Muḥammad developed a sympathetic following in a relatively nearby Arabian city, Medina, which was destined to become his new home. He began to urge his followers to sell all their possessions and to move to Medina, which they did, eventually in large numbers.

By 622 AD, the situation had become critical. The clans of Mecca, in that year, agreed that it was time for Muḥammad to be murdered, and they conspired to do it cooperatively, so that no one clan could be held responsible. The possibility of him relocating to Medina only *increased* the anxiety of Mecca's leaders, because they understood that he would be even *more* of a threat to them from this new power base, where people welcomed him and eagerly awaited his arrival.

When Muḥammad correctly deduced that he would be a dead man if he spent so much as one more day in Mecca, he escaped from that city, barely avoiding the clutches of his appointed murderers, and fled to Medina. The story of Muḥammad's flight from Mecca to Medina, a journey known as the "Hijrah", occupies the same exalted position in Muslim theology as the Exodus from Egypt occupies in Jewish theology. It is so important to Muslims that they have declared the year 622 A.D. to be the first year of their own calendar.

Why Medina?

One might reasonably inquire as to why Muḥammad was so welcome in Medina, when he was so widely hated in Mecca. The answer is that Medina was a city containing a substantial number of Jews and Christians, and they, like the Jews of Jerusalem at the time of Yeshua, had been expecting the imminent arrival of a Deliverer.

The scriptural basis of the Deliverer is a rather thorny issue, because some of the Old Testament passages, which Muslims now believe to have foretold the coming of Muḥammad, are believed with equal fervency by Christians to have foretold the coming of Yeshua. One oft-quoted passage of this sort is Deuteronomy 18:15, where Moses said to the Children of Israel:

> "The Lord thy God will raise up unto thee a Prophet from the midst of thee, of thy brethren, like unto me; unto him ye shall hearken".

Other Old Testament passages held to be prophetic by Islam, such as Isaiah 42:11...

> "Let the wilderness and the cities thereof lift up their voice, the villages that *Kedar* doth inhabit; let the inhabitants of the rock sing, let them shout from the top of the mountains."

...are less controversial. Kedar was the son of Ishmael. The Muslim interpretation, namely that this passage from Isaiah foretells the coming of the word of God to the descendants of Ishmael through Muḥammad, is not particularly threatening to Christian theologians.

A somewhat more controversial passage is found in Jeremiah, Chapter II:

> Thus saith the LORD:
> What unrighteousness have your fathers found in Me,
> That they are gone far from Me? ...
> ...Wherefore I will yet plead with you, saith the LORD,
> And with your children's children will I plead.
> For pass over to the isles of the Kittites, and see,
> And <u>*send unto Kedar*</u>, and consider diligently,
> And see if there hath been such a thing.
>
> (Jeremiah 2:5-10)

It certainly sounds as if the Ishmaelite inhabitants of Kedar, at the time of Jeremiah, were more true to the ways of God than the Jews of Israel. For those Muslims who believe that God took the "Staff of Judah" away from Israel and gave it to Islam through Muḥammad, this passage would appear to provide biblical support.

But the real "kicker" in biblical prophecy as regards the Hijrah was not from the Old Testament at all. It was from the New Testament, in which was seen the promise of a unique Deliverer; one who would save the descendants of Christian Arabs from the predicament into which they had been placed by the Church of Rome.

What predicament? The Christian Councils had excommunicated their spiritual leaders, and the political leaders at home promoted idolatry. Monotheistic religion was therefore in a state of moral lapse in the Middle East. There were idols in the Ka'bah, held by Muslims to have been formerly a pure Temple of the One God of Abraham.

The Hunafa, who believed in One God, were bristling with resentment, and were eagerly awaiting a Redeemer who would restore proper worship of God to the nation. In the Book of John, from the New Testament, they found a prophecy which they saw as most explicit. In John's description of the Last Supper, Yeshua promised to send a "Comforter" (John, Chapters 14-16).

English translations of the original Greek versions of the New Testament interpret the "Comforter" as the Holy Ghost or the Spirit of Truth. But Muslims contend that the Greek word "paracletos", translated as "Comforter" (or "advocate"), is an *incorrect* word. The correct word, they say, is "periclytos", whose translation is "praised one".

The Arabic way of saying "praised one" is "aḥmad", which is also a common "nickname" or shortened form of the full name "Muḥammad". Thus, Muslims believe that Yeshua prophesied the coming of Muḥammad by name (Qur'an 61:6).

To this day, Christian readers of the Gospel of John know, in their hearts, that Yeshua promised to send them the "Comforter", the Holy Spirit. But Muslims know in *their* hearts that Yeshua promised to send them "Muḥammad". There is surely a large difference between the Christian and Muslim points of view regarding the identity of this "Comforter". Who is correct?

It is highly unlikely that we shall ever know, since all four extant Gospels were written years after the events they reported upon, in languages other than the Hebrew language spoken by Yeshua and his disciples.

If all this seems convoluted or superfluous, that is not important to history. For the fact remains that—for whatever reason—the people of Medina were firm in their conviction that Muḥammad was the Chosen One whose coming they were eagerly awaiting.

Thus, to the Arabs, and now to Muslims the world over, Muḥammad's ministry was a fulfillment of a prophecy from the mouth of Yeshua himself, that God would send a Deliverer to the Arab people.

Muhammad conquers Arabia

Ironically, when Muḥammad himself actually arrived in Medina, the Jews decided that he was *not* the Deliverer after all! The war between Islam and Judaism had begun! As you know, that war is not over yet.

But Muḥammad had many devoted followers in Medina, and he quickly rose up to become master of that city.

The subsequent history of the spread of Islam is too large a subject to be encompassed in this book. Suffice it to say that the Prophet achieved his dream when, only eight years after the Hijrah, his forces triumphantly re-entered his old home city of Mecca, having conquered the city by force, and through faith. The hated idols in the Ka'bah, those intercessors between man and God, were removed.

Muḥammad's conquest of Mecca came about against seemingly impossible odds. He was severely outnumbered in every military campaign, and he suffered several serious setbacks and defeats, any one of which might well have ended the career of a lesser man. But the Prophet, a man of immense character and faith, was indomitable.

The momentum established during the campaign against Mecca carried Islam forward with blinding speed. Within a single year after the conquest of Mecca, Muḥammad had become master of all Arabia.

Then, in the tenth year after the Hijrah, he suddenly took ill and died. He was 62 years old at the time of his unexpected death. His followers were overcome with grief, but they quickly recovered. The military campaigns were soon resumed, and his followers fought on as though the Prophet himself were leading their armies.

During the subsequent century, the world came as close as it has ever come to being totally subdued. It could only have been the hand of God Himself which stemmed the Muslim tide at either end of Europe, putting an end to the most successful[35] imperial campaign in human history.

The Qur'an

The Prophet Muḥammad had the ability to enter into visionary states, the first of which occurred in that cave in the desert in 610 AD. There were others. His sayings, which came to him during these trance-like states, were faithfully recorded later, and constitute the book known as the Qur'an.

The Qur'an is a rather large volume, encompassing, in an abbreviated sort of way, the entire essence of the Old and New Testaments. To a devout Jew or Christian, the Biblical stories sound strange or even funny. To be sure, the essential message is always there, but the dialogue seems contrived, and many of the minor details seem to have been altered.

Now, the Prophet was quite illiterate (he could neither read nor write). His rendition of the Bible was based on an oral tradition carried by word-of-mouth in the desert for centuries after the Old and New Testaments were committed to parchment. In view of this, it should perhaps not be surprising to find differences between Muḥammad's Book and the older Jewish and Christian scriptures.

It would be a serious error, however, to assume that the basic message of the Qur'an is different from the basic message of the Bible. In fact, the entire essence of Judaism and Christianity is there, and that single Book, by that single author, has sustained a huge and growing population of people for over a millennium. It is self-evident that it has successfully fulfilled all of the deepest spiritual needs of many peoples. All, that is, except one: It has not brought peace. On the contrary, the war between Islam and Judeo-Christianity is raging fiercely, and is in no way over. Something is missing.

The Message of Allah through the Prophet Muhammad

The Qur'an is a book with a single message: Fear God and God only. This message is conveyed over and over again, throughout the book. In the course of delivering the message, a comprehensive moral and ethical code, indistinguishable in most instances from that of Judeo-Christianity, is interwoven, along with certain selected elements from the history of the Arab people.

---

[35] If the success of Islam is measured only in conquered land mass, then other candidates, such as Rome, must be considered as candidates for "most successful imperial campaign". In Islam, however, we also have a longevity of 1400 years, which removes all others from contention.

With few exceptions, the revered patriarchs of the Qur'an are well known to Jews and Christians: Noah, Abraham, Moses, David and Solomon, and most of the other Old Testament prophets. In addition, we find John the Baptist and Jesus. There are only a small handful of Muslim prophets who are not known to Jews and Christians, such as Hud, Salih, and Shu'ayb. Even in those cases, there is usually a genealogy which traces them to well-known personages of the Bible.

It therefore does not seem likely that the 1400-year old war between Jews, Christians and Muslims can be based on the relatively minor differences between the Bible and the Qur'an. What else, then, can it be based upon?

What does the Qur'an say about Yeshua (Jesus)?

I have stated previously that Yeshua was the central figure in world history, whether through reverence or rejection. The very existence of the Qur'an proves this to be true. The thing which makes the Qur'an utterly unacceptable to Jews is that it accepts Yeshua as a Hebrew Prophet. The thing which makes the Qur'an utterly unacceptable to Christians is, ironically, the same thing: that it accepts Yeshua as a Hebrew Prophet.

The Book emphatically declares that Yeshua is a *man*, NOT a God, and NOT a "Son of God". To the politicians of these respective religions, these differences of opinion about the "nature of Christ" absolutely mandate a state of continuous warfare until the "enemies of the faith" are all dead.

Actually, the Gospel according to Muḥammad is quite familiar in all its essential details. In the Qur'an, Yeshua is described as the product of a virgin birth (Qur'an, 3:47). Mary is advised, by an unnamed angel of God who appears to her in the form of a man, that she will bear a holy son, although "no man has touched [her]". The wording of this passage may seem, at first glance, to suggest that the angel is the father, but this is not explicitly stated anywhere. On the contrary, the nature of the Virgin Birth is left unexplained. Like Adam, the Qur'an says (3:59), God made the Messiah from "dust".

Yeshua is described by the Qur'an as healing the sick, raising the dead, and coming to affirm the [Jewish] Law (3:49-50).

With respect to Yeshua's own death and resurrection, we have a 1400 year-old sore point between Christians and Muslims. Rather than speculating on the meaning of the Qur'an's report, let us read it directly:

> ... they said, "We killed Christ Jesus the son of Mary, The Messenger of Allah" — But they killed him not, nor crucified him, *but so it was made to*

> *appear to them......* **Nay, Allah raised him up unto Himself; and Allah is Exalted in Power, Wise...**
>
> **... And on the Day of Judgment he will be a witness against them.**
>
> (Qur'an 4:157-159)

Evangelical Christians, in order to discredit the Qur'an, quote this passage as evidence that Muslims consider the crucifixion to have been a hoax. But the Qur'an does not say this. It says he died according to our human criteria for the determination of life and death, but that through it all the LORD actually preserved him and took him up.

Since the prophet Isaiah said, concerning the Messiah, that ...

> **He was taken from prison and from judgment ...he was cut off out of the land of the living...he made his grave with the wicked, and with the rich in his death...**
>
> Isaiah 53:8-9

...we have here a fine line between what "appears" to be death, and what "really" constitutes death. I cannot cross this line. If he is alive today, in the Kingdom of Heaven, what would it mean in the first place to say he "died"? Yet if he didn't die, what would it mean to say he was "cut off out of the land of the living"? No one can answer such questions.

The Qur'an says that Yeshua was *translated directly to Heaven*, where he remains today, alive, and ready to execute Judgment on the Last Day. Indeed, his Second Coming before the Last Judgment is prophesied in that book (Qur'an 43:61).

According to the point of view I have expressed above, the Gospel of Muhammad does not differ very much from the traditional Christian Gospels. The real difference between the Qur'an and the New Testament is that the Book of Muhammad totally excludes the Acts of the Apostles and the Epistles of Paul and others, from which are derived the theories of Christ as literal Son of God, and as second person of the Holy Trinity. The position of the Qur'an is sharply to the contrary. In each of the numerous instances in which Yeshua's name comes up, it is emphatically stated that he was a *man*, not God. The idea that Allah, who is God, would deign to have a son, is utterly rejected as outrageous blasphemy. "He has no son!", is the essential message of the Qur'an, paraphrased repeatedly throughout the book.

It should be clear, to anyone who has thoughtfully considered the Christian councils where modern Christian doctrine was forced upon the world, that *Islam is the inevitable reaction to the excommunication of key Arab and African religious leaders by Rome*, two centuries before Muḥammad.

If so, then we may ask: "Whose view of the nature of Christ was correct—Rome's or Mecca's?".

Throughout history, desperate mortals have sought after the answer to this question, as if their lives depended upon it. As we saw in Chapter 5 of this book, however, the LORD God will not give us the simple answer that we seek. The Biblical passages which touch on the subject can be interpreted either way.

Was the Qur'an intended to stand alone?

The Muslims of today have vehemently rejected the Bible, both Old and New Testaments. They say these books are "corrupt", and that the only pure and unadulterated Word of God is Qur'an. Was this the Prophet's intention? Let's look at the Qur'an itself and see.

At innumerable sites within his Book, Muḥammad exhorts his readers to "remember" various historical episodes, usually Biblical episodes from the Old or New Testaments. The following is a sampling of such exhortations:

> "And *remember* that Abraham was tried by his Lord with certain commands, which he fulfilled." (Qur'an 2:124).

> "O Children of Israel...*remember*, we delivered you from the people of Pharaoh...and *remember* we divided the sea for you...and *remember* we appointed forty nights for Moses...and *remember* we gave Moses the Scripture and the Criterion..." (Qur'an 2:47-53)

> "And *remember* David and Solomon, when they gave judgment in the matter of the field..." (Qur'an 21:78)

> "And *remember* Zakariya [father of John the Baptist], when he cried to his Lord: 'O my Lord! Leave me not without offspring'...". (Qur'an 21:89)

> "And *remember* Jesus, the son of Mary, said: "O Children of Israel! I am the messenger of Allah sent to you, confirming the Law which came before me..." (Qur'an 61:6).

Since copies of Old and New Testament scrolls were not in plentiful supply in ancient Arabia, we may surmise that it was the oral tradition of the desert which he was exhorting them to remember.

Since it is nowhere stated in the Qur'an that the Bible is either corrupt, altered, or otherwise unreliable, we may surmise that the oral tradition of the desert was not *preferred* over the written tradition of the Bible, but was merely more available.

Thus, it cannot be maintained that Muhammad's exhortations to his followers to "remember" the ancient traditions were instructions to reject the Bible, but rather to *learn* it. *If it had been physically possible, it is certain that the Prophet would have distributed written copies of the Old and New Testaments to every Arab, and required that their contents be mastered along with the Qur'an.*

That was impossible, however, because there were no printing presses, and besides, the people were almost 100% illiterate.

The conclusion is inescapable, however, that Muhammad himself understood the entire substance of the Qur'an to be an *exposition*, from God Himself, of the deeper meaning of the main events of religious history, and not a substitute for the history itself.

Exactly how and when post-Muhammadan Islamic leaders succeeded in deceiving the people into believing that the Bible was corrupt, unreliable, and worthy of rejection is not clear to me, but the man through whose mouth the Qur'an came forth was *not* the man who did this.

As to *why* the Bible came to be rejected by Islam, that is easier to understand. First and foremost, there is the "wild ass" subterfuge which we exposed in Chapter 2 of this book. Additionally, there are a number of passages in the Qur'an which seem to disagree with corresponding passages in the Bible. None of these disagreements are of any substance whatsoever, and yet there are certain people who will insist that one Book be deemed "correct", and the other to be "in error". Since the Bible is the older Book, early Islamic leaders must have feared that the Bible would be favored by the majority of such people.

To avoid this potential embarrassment, these leaders simple dispensed with the Bible altogether. Having thus concealed certain disturbing truths, they were able to teach their children that Muhammad was "perfect", the Qur'an was "perfect", the Prophets of old were "perfect", and, by analogy, the Arabs were "perfect" also (as long as they followed the Muhammadan precepts, of course).

These, however, are all lies. Muhammad was a man, and he pounded that fact into the ears of his followers—apparently to no avail. But no man is perfect. No book, written by the hands of men, can ever be perfect. The Prophets of old were not perfect—some of them behaved contemptibly on occasion. And the Arabs, therefore, following in this grand tradition of imperfection, are far from perfect themselves.

Now consider this: Today's devout Muslim, who had pared his religious reading down to a single book and its associated commentaries, will daily be reading passages which exhort him to "remember this" and "remember that"...but what is it that he is now remembering? The only scripture he has been taught to respect is the Qur'an itself. But the starting point of the Qur'an is the assumption that biblical tradition is already known. If the Qur'an itself has *become* the biblical tradition, then what is left to "remember"?

The modern-day Muslim, who rejects the Old Testament, rejects the New Testament, rejects Original Sin, and considers himself to be perfected merely by reading the Qur'an, is in error. This error can begin to be corrected by reading the Bible.

There may be one or two spots in the Bible which seem insulting to Muslims, but there are a lot more than one or two spots in the Qur'an which are insulting to Jews and Christians. And yet every militant Muslim fanatic expects the whole world to read the Qur'an, and to quietly bear his insult. Is that same Muslim prepared to read the Bible, and to bear *his own* insult? How else can he obey the Prophet's command to "remember"?

Muslims claim to have deep reverence for the history of the Jewish and Christian people. In fact, they consider *themselves* to be the true heirs of the Judeo-Christian tradition. Therefore, the events of Biblical history are *their* history.

The Old Testament, in particular, is the only reliable written source of information about the greater part of Islamic history prior to the life of the Prophet Muḥammad.

It is almost impossible for me to imagine that a devout believer in the Qur'an would not have a burning desire to read the Bible, so as to learn his *own* history. Yet there seems to be no such desire on the part of the majority of Muslims. If there is anything wrong with Islam, this is it.

There is a way for the three scriptures of the Western monotheistic world (Old Testament, New Testament, and Qur'an) to be seen as parts of a larger whole, rather than as manifestos of conflicting theologies, doomed to a state of eternal warfare. But before considering this further, we must address the delicate issue of "jihad".

Chapter 9

Islam

Part IV

"Jihad"

Self-appointed Qur'an commentators have done a masterful job of persuading the world that they are under a binding commandment from the prophet Muḥammad to murder all non-Muslims, and to proclaim Islam to be the sole lawful religion of the planet Earth.

They refer to this as "jihad", an Arabic word interpreted to mean "holy war". The enemies in this "holy war" are said to be Jews and Christians primarily, but Hindus, Buddhists and others may be included. Some self-appointed commentators even go *beyond* religion in identifying their perceived "enemies", and include Caucasians generally, implying that Islam is somehow a religion of the "colored" races.

The entire "jihad" story is an elaborate work of fiction. It is publicized continuously by world banking interests, whose object is the destruction of all religion, including Islam, and the replacement of the fear of God by the fear of money. *Their* money.

Is there a commandment for "holy war"? Yes, there is. But, like monotheism in general, it did not originate in the Qur'an, and was not changed by it in any important way.

The commandment for holy war was promulgated by Moses, and was defined quite satisfactorily in the Torah. The commandment was given repeatedly, beginning at the time of the Exodus itself and continuing up to the actual invasion of the Holy Land by the Israelites 40 years later.

That there would be such war was pre-ordained in the days of Abraham, during his sojourn in Israel, about 600 years before the Exodus. In the Book of Genesis, God announced his Covenant with Abraham, saying at that time:

> "Unto thy seed have I given this land, from the river of Egypt unto the great river, the river Euphrates; the Kenite, and the Kenizzite, and the Kadmonite, and the Hittite, and the Perizzite, and the Rephaim, and the Amorite, and the Canaanite, and the Girgashite, and the Jebusite".
>
> **Genesis 15:18-20**

The names are the names of the ancient tribes who occupied Israel before the Exodus. It is not explicitly stated that they are to be removed, or that a war would be involved.

Nor was the inevitability of war necessarily clear to Moses in his first encounter with God, at the Burning Bush. There God said, concerning the Children of Israel:

> "I am come down to deliver them out of the hands of the Egyptians, and to bring them up out of that land unto a good land and a large, unto a land flowing with milk and honey; unto the place of the Canaanite, and the Hittite, and the Amorite, and the Perizzite, and the Hivite, and the Jebusite."
>
> **Exodus 3:8**

Couldn't this have meant "peaceful coexistence"? Theoretically, perhaps. But when God later gave Moses the Ten Commandments and the Law on Mount Sinai, the painful nature of what was about to happen began to emerge:

> Behold, I send an angel before thee, to keep thee by the way, and to bring thee into the place which I have prepared. Take heed of him, and hearken unto his voice; be not rebellious against him; for he will not pardon your transgression; for My name is in him.
>
> But if thou shalt indeed hearken unto his voice, and do all that I speak; then I will be an enemy unto thine enemies, and an adversary unto thine adversaries. For Mine angel shall go before thee, and bring thee in unto the Amorite, and the Hittite, and the Perizzite, and the Canaanite, the Hivite, and the Jebusite; <u>and I will cut them off</u>.
>
> Thou shalt not bow down to their gods, nor serve them, nor do after their doings; but thou shalt utterly overthrow them, and break in pieces their pillars. And ye shall serve the LORD your God, and He will bless thy bread, and thy water; and I will take sickness away from the midst of thee. None shall miscarry, nor be barren, in thy land; the number of thy days I will fulfil.
>
> I will send My terror before thee, and will discomfit all the people to whom thou shalt come, and I will make all thine enemies turn their backs unto thee. And I will send the hornet before thee, which shall drive out the Hivite, the Canaanite, and the Hittite, from before thee.

> I will not drive them out from before thee in one year, lest the land become desolate, and the beasts of the field multiply against thee. By little and little I will drive them out from before thee, until thou be increased, and inherit the land.
>
> And I will set thy border from the Red Sea even unto the sea of the Philistines, and from the wilderness unto the River [*i.e.* Euphrates]; for I will deliver the inhabitants of the land into your hand; and thou shalt drive them out before thee.
>
> Thou shalt make no covenant with them, nor with their gods. They shall not dwell in thy land—lest they make thee sin against Me, for thou wilt serve their gods—for they will be a snare unto thee.
>
> Exodus 23:20-33

The full horror of the holy war commanded by God was finally spelled out, in detail, in Moses' final discourses in the Book of Deuteronomy:

> When the LORD thy God shall bring thee into the land whither thou goest to possess it, and shall cast out many nations before thee, the Hittite, and the Girgashite, and the Amorite, and the Canaanite, and the Perizzite, and the Hivite, and the Jebusite, seven nations greater and mightier than thou; and when the LORD thy God shall deliver them up before thee, and thou shalt smite them; then thou shalt utterly destroy them.
>
> Thou shalt make no covenant with them, nor show mercy unto them; neither shalt thou make marriages with them: thy daughter thou shalt not give unto his son, nor his daughter shalt thou take unto thy son. For he will turn away thy son from following Me, that they may serve other gods; *so will the anger of the LORD be kindled against you, and He will destroy thee quickly*.
>
> But thus shall ye deal with them: ye shall break down their altars, and dash in pieces their pillars, and hew down their Asherim, and burn their graven images with fire. For thou art a holy people unto the LORD thy God: the LORD thy God hath chosen thee to be His own treasure, out of all peoples that are upon the face of the earth.
>
> Deuteronomy 7:1-6

Did you catch the threat? Not only were the Children of Israel commanded to practice what nowadays is called "ethnic cleansing", but they were told explicitly that if they failed to obey this command, then "the anger of the LORD" would be kindled against *them*, and He would destroy *them* quickly!

Why did the LORD order this holy war? Was it because the Children of Israel were "good", and the other nations "bad"? Not exactly:

> Speak not thou in thy heart, after that the LORD thy God hath thrust them out from before thee, saying: 'For my righteousness the LORD hath brought

> me in to possess this land'; whereas for the wickedness of these nations the LORD doth drive them out from before thee.
>
> <u>Not</u> for thy righteousness, or for the uprightness of thy heart, dost thou go in to possess their land; but <u>for the wickedness</u> of these nations the LORD thy God doth drive them out from before thee, and that He may establish the word which the LORD swore unto thy fathers, to Abraham, to Isaac, and to Jacob.
>
> Know therefore that it is not for thy righteousness that the LORD thy God giveth thee this good land to possess it; for thou are a stiffnecked people.
>
> **Deuteronomy 9:4-6**

The threat of heavenly reprisal for failure to drive out the inhabitants of the land was given very explicitly in the Book of Numbers:

> "Speak unto the Children of Israel, and say unto them: When ye pass over the Jordan into the land of Canaan, then ye shall drive out all the inhabitants of the land from before you, and destroy all their figured stones, and destroy all their molten images, and demolish all their high places. And ye shall drive out the inhabitants of the land, and dwell therein...
>
> ...But if ye will not drive out the inhabitants of the land from before you, then shall those that ye let remain of them be as thorns in your eyes, and as pricks in your sides, and they shall harass you in the land wherein ye dwell.
>
> *<u>And it shall come to pass, that as I thought to do unto them, so will I do unto you</u>*."
>
> **Numbers 33:51-56**

What were the Israelites instructed to do with the enemies in this Holy War? In Deuteronomy, Chapter 20, we learn this concerning the fate of the enemy cities against whom Israel would war:

1. If a city surrendered, all the people were to be made "tributary", to serve Israel.

2. If the city chose to fight, it was to be besieged until it surrendered.

It was presumed, in the giving of the second instruction, that the city would eventually surrender. The subsequent disposition was to be determined by its location. It the city was far away, all the males were to be killed. The women, children, cattle and wealth, however, were to be taken as spoil.

"Jihad"

If, however, the city was within the precincts of the Holy Land, then the instructions were downright chilling:

> **Howbeit of the cities of these peoples, that the L**ORD **thy God giveth thee for an inheritance, <u>THOU SHALT SAVE ALIVE NOTHING THAT BREATHETH</u>, but thou shalt utterly destroy them: the Hittite, and the Amorite, the Canaanite, and the Perizzite, the Hivite, and the Jebusite; as the L**ORD **thy God hath commanded thee; that they teach you not to do after all their abominations, which they have done unto their gods, and so ye sin against the L**ORD **your God.**
>
> **Deuteronomy 20:16-18**

Men, women, and children were to be destroyed. Even animals were not to be spared. How seriously were these commands taken? Since the Holy Wars of Israel went on for many years, the subject was raised repeatedly throughout the Old Testament, and the seriousness of it was amply illustrated therein.

One good example may be found in I Samuel chapter 15. There we learn that Saul, the first King of Israel, lost the support of the High Priest Samuel, and eventually the throne itself, simply because he took sheep and cattle as spoil in a Holy War with the Amalekites.

In the Book of Joshua, Moses' successor, we find an even more extraordinary example. Therein is described the bloody conclusion of the famous "Battle Of Jericho" (Joshua, chapters 7 & 8). God commanded this to be a major Holy War. Every man, woman, child, and animal was ordered killed (with the exception of the prostitute Rahab, who had become a spy for Israel). The city itself was to be totally burned to the ground. No spoil was to be saved, except that any gold and silver found was to be given over to the Tabernacle of the LORD. But an Israeli man named Achan had an opportunity to seize a few bars of Jericho's gold and silver for himself. When he was discovered, Joshua ordered him stoned, along with his wife, his children, his animals, and all his worldly possessions. Then their dead bodies were burned, along with the expropriated gold and silver. How serious was Joshua about Holy War? Serious enough to *burn gold and silver!*

"Jihad" explained from a modern perspective

How can we make sense of this sort of violence now, in a world obsessed with the twin concepts of peace and racial/ethnic equality?

We can. But we must make an effort to do so, and we must not be presumptuous about our own "righteousness".

This discussion must, by necessity, be limited to a western perspective. Here in the west, all major religions purport to be the sole legitimate heirs of the Revelation on Mount Sinai, *i.e.* the Ten Commandments and the Law of Moses. Jews claim to be so through Torah, Christians through the New Covenant, and Muslims through Qur'an. Therefore, it can be forcefully argued that if not for the Revelation on Sinai, none of our ideas about "peace" or "racial/ethnic equality" would even exist.

I would so argue.

This means that before the Revelation on Sinai, the sort of violence which characterized "jihad", or "holy war", was routine. I shouldn't have to tell you that. You've seen enough epic movies with "casts of thousands" to know that the ancient world was characterized by war, murder, racial and ethnic exterminations, expropriation of goods and lands, and by a general mentality of duplicitousness and treachery. No one thought there was anything wrong with it—just as long as *they* won the damned war.

Whether the Law of Moses was the first morally correct law or not is a point which many would love to argue, but it matters not whether it was first. It stuck, and the others didn't. There's nothing left to argue.

It was the Law of Moses, and its Christian and Muslim ramifications, which became the foundation of all secular law, and which led to a world in which the idea of "peace on earth, and goodwill to men" became even thinkable.

If you consider "peace on earth, and goodwill to men" to be desirable, then you are implicitly endorsing the Holy Wars of ancient Israel, since, if not for them, you would still be a member of a warring nation doing its best to murder its neighbors, rape their wives, enslave their children, and steal their property.

(Even with religion, mankind still does these things. At least now, however, we cannot claim innocence when caught).

Therefore, the first thing you must do, if you wish to logically comprehend the meaning of "jihad" in the modern world, is to recognize that the original Holy Wars of Israel *had* to be fought, or you would not be of sufficient moral stature now to question them from your "modern" self-righteous perspective.

And what was the stated object of the Holy Wars of ancient Israel? First and foremost, the object was the absolute destruction of idolatry. The bowing down to, and worshipping of idols was the primary activity which Holy War sought to root out.

Yeshua (Jesus) said "they that be whole need not a doctor, but they that are sick" (Matthew 9:12). If you don't believe in God or Enlightenment, I'm going to diagnose you as being "sick", and I propose to be a physician to you. Since you can't, or won't, believe in God, I'm now going to explain "jihad" ("holy war") to you in worldly terms.

The historical significance of the Law of Moses rests wholly upon the belief that it came directly from God. If God was indeed the force behind it, then Fear of Him was the basis of the enforcement of it. It follows that in the absence of the Fear of God, none of the Law was in any way enforceable except through violence; either legally-sanctioned violence, or old-fashioned brute force.

But in the long run, violence—in the absence of faith—does not work. There's an old saying, "you can't legislate morality". Either the Law comes from God, or, in the final analysis, it's essentially unenforceable.

Therefore, the obsessive drive of many to promote worship of the One God may be likened to the keel of a boat, working in the background to provide direction in the world of otherwise continuously-drifting secular law. Take away God, and all that remains is the power of public opinion, often referred to as "mob-rule democracy". As Socrates pointed out in *The Republic*, the power of mob-rule democracy eventually destroys a nation, as a succession of individuals and groups seize power, each in turn attempting to subvert all which came before, in favor of their own pre-conceived, ignorant notions.

The second great Law of religion, after the commandment to worship the One God, is the "Golden Rule", recognized throughout the world, and throughout history, as being the primary rule of human behavior upon which all else is based. Hillel, the greatest of the ancient Israeli Torah commentators, said of the Golden Rule that it was, in effect, a one-line summary of the entire Torah; the rest being merely "commentary". Likewise, Yeshua (Jesus) said, in the Sermon on the Mount, "all things whatsoever ye would that men do unto you, do them even so to others, for **this *is* the Law and the Prophets**".

The Old Testament has a commandment which is considered to be a corollary, or re-statement of the Golden Rule: **"Love your neighbor as yourself"**.

Before the Revelation on Sinai, no nation taught anyone to "love their neighbor". On the contrary, the Old Law was "kill your neighbor and steal his money".

Are you still sorry that the ancient Israelites carried out a series of Holy Wars? Would it be better for you if that had never happened, and if today the world remained a collection of petty nations, each openly proclaiming to have the sole right to destroy all the others?

There are many, many other aspects of the Law of Moses which form a basis for any moral society. These include:

1. The prohibition against "sacrificing" children to the gods.
2. The prohibition against all other 1st-degree murder.
3. The prohibition against stealing.
4. The prohibition against adultery and other forms of troublesome sex.
5. The prohibition against failing to help the needy.
6. The prohibition against interest on loans to one's fellow citizens.
7. The prohibition against failing to provide for one's family.

Jews perceive there to be 613 Laws in the Bible; we shall not list them all.

It was the Holy Wars of Moses which established that there can be a world *without* Holy Wars. Collectively, therefore, they were the original "War To End All Wars". The trouble is, the War is not over.

"Jihad". What does it mean today?

To understand the meaning of "holy war"— *i.e.,* "jihad"—in the modern world, all that is necessary is to keep clearly in mind what the original purpose was, since it's the same now.

The primary purpose of holy war was—and is—to rid the land of idolatry. Some might opine that this has already been accomplished. Have you seen anyone falling on his face in front of a statue lately? I didn't think so.

In the Bible, however, the activity we now call "idolatry" is more broadly defined, consisting of absolutely any form of worship other than worship of God. This includes the worship of trees, animals and celestial objects.

Don't think for a moment, therefore, that there aren't people in the world today who worship the forbidden things. It's hardly a secret that there are worshippers of the Sun, the Moon, "Mother Earth", nature in general, and Satan himself. They rarely practice their abominations in plain public view, although they often belong to organizations which promote themselves openly. It is a shortcoming of the legal doctrine of "freedom of speech" that these practices cannot be removed by process of civil law.

In Israel, there is, in principle, an ongoing biblical prohibition against idolatry. If any man, woman or child in Israel were to fall before a statue and worship it, that person should be liable for the death penalty.

Of course, modern Israeli law has no provision for capital punishment for idolatry. That is why the modern nation of Israel is fighting for its life. It isn't what it purports to be.

If it is not proper to regard idolatry as a capital offense—punishable by death—in Israel today, then why was it a capital offense in ancient Israel? Conversely, if it was *improper* to regard idolatry as a capital offense, even in ancient Israel, then how can the Law of Moses have come from God? No god would promulgate a law which was "improper".

And if none of the Laws taught by Moses actually came from God, then what right do Jews have to inhabit Israel today, seeing that they have displaced other peoples who lived there before 1948? Is it merely that "might makes right", and that they won a war?

There's another war going on now. The Jews may lose. If so, then will "might make right" in that war also?

Sooner or later every right-thinking person begins to understand that unless the Revelation on Sinai is accepted as having come from God, then there never really was any true Jewish religion at all. Or, by logical extension, any Christian or Muslim religion. If that's true, then all we've ever really had has been chaos, which is Hell, because when every man does what's right in his own eyes, the world is destroyed.

The price for believing in God is that His Laws must be obeyed. One of these laws is that idolaters in Israel must be totally, ruthlessly destroyed. This law is therefore not dated. It is current—whether the government chooses to enforce it or not.

Outside of Israel, the Law specifies that idolaters must be dealt with as effectively as possible, but the rule of total extermination remains legally binding within Israel, right up to the present minute—*if*, that is, Israel is to be accepted as being the living embodiment and manifestation of the Torah, which it purports to be.

Of course, no one in this day and age falls on his face before an idol. But there is another, more insidious form of idolatry which is rampant in the world. If we define "religion" as being...

{That which has the highest priority, overriding all else in importance}

... then there's the matter of *money*. In this world, "money talks". The majority of human beings in the world today "take care of the money" before *anything* else, and before *everything* else.

"Everything else" includes God.

When Moses came down from the Mount with the Ten Commandments, he found the Children of Israel groveling before a statue of a calf. The calf was, of course, a *golden* calf. And so it's been ever since—the highest priority has *always* been gold, *i.e.,* money. And that ordering of priorities, with gold at the top, has always been the established order both within and without Israel.

So idolatry, in the form of worship of nature, or of gold, or of anything else under the sun except God, is, in actuality, *rampant* in the world today. Therefore, **there's going to be "jihad".**

But, in a world in which everyone publicly shuns idols, and in which all churches claim to be the "one true religion of God", how can idolaters be identified? In other words, "Who is the enemy?".

Qur'anic definition of "the enemy"

At the time these words are being written, the acts of self-proclaimed "Muslim terrorists" are dominating the news.

If you believe everything you read in the papers, then you will live in ignorance for the rest of your life. The news media all report exactly what the so-called "Muslim terrorists" say, word-for-word. They do so because they hate *all* religion, and have a deep longing to live in a world of atheistic corruption. No, it's not because they like corruption. It's because they are currently *benefiting* from it, and they think their reign will never end.

It has been widely reported, by the news media, that Muslim terrorists the world over are involved in some sort of a "holy war", or "jihad", against, well, just about everybody. The acts of terror are real, but is this really a "holy war"?

We have seen that the concept of "holy war" did not arise in the Qur'an at all. It arose in the Old Testament. It surely did not end in the New Testament. There Yeshua (Jesus) said

> **"Think not that I have come to send peace on earth: I came not to send peace, but a sword".**
> **(Matthew 10:34).**

Neither the Old Testament Book of Daniel, nor its New Testament sequel, the book of Revelation, contain any prophecies of "love and peace" in our immediate futures.

So if, in mankind's further revelation, the Qur'an, we read of "holy war", think not that Muḥammad made it up in his own mind. Our God did indeed command war against idolatry in all forms.

Therefore, all that remains to understand modern Islamic "fundamentalism" is to read what the Qur'an says about *who* the idolaters are, and *where* they are to be found.

All right. Who are the idolaters? Are they "the Jews"? Are they "the Christians"?

Here's what Muḥammad actually said about Jews and Christians:

> **Those who believe in the Qur'an,**
> **And those who are Jews,**
> **And the Christians ...**
> **Any who believe in Allah and the Last Day,**
> **And work righteousness,**
> **Shall have their <u>reward</u> with their Lord;**
> **On them shall be <u>no fear</u>, nor shall they grieve.**
>
> Qur'an 2:62

What's this? *"Reward"? "No fear"?* What sort of "holy war" is this? It sounds more like a blessing!

The above quotation from the Qur'an was neither a mistake nor a casual remark. Just to make sure that the point got across, the Prophet repeated the passage, almost verbatim, in a later Chapter (5:69).

Obviously, there is something dreadfully wrong with the way Islam is depicted on television.

Islam has never failed to acknowledge the prophets of the Jewish and Christian religions, but, if its television spokespeople are to be believed, all those prophets pale in comparison with Muḥammad, who—they say—was the "greatest" of all of them. But is this what *he* said? You decide. Here's what the Qur'an says about who the "greatest" prophet is:

> **We believe in Allah, and the revelation given to us, and to Abraham, Ismail, Isaac, Jacob, and the Tribes, and that given to Moses and Jesus, and that given to all Prophets from their Lord:** *We make no difference between one and another of them...*
>
> Qur'an 2:136

This message is repeated so many times in the Qur'an that it's impossible to deny the full implication of it. Muḥammad certainly did not regard himself as the "greatest" of the prophets, because he did not acknowledge that such a thing existed.

Doesn't reading and following the Qur'an make a Muslim "morally superior" to Jews and Christians, and mustn't these older religions therefore be ruthlessly suppressed? This is a slightly more subtle point. In Muḥammad's day, Jews and Christians frequently supported the war of resistance against the rising power of Islam. Since, as we have already seen, the Prophet had nothing but respect for the Jewish and Christian religions, he regarded the people involved in this resistance as "Jews" and "Christians" in name only. But he referred to them as "hypocrites". The formal term for Jewish and Christian hypocrites was *"People of the Book"*, the "Book" being, of course, the Bible.

It is known that Muḥammad often lamented the fact that his people, the Arabs, did not have a "Book" of their own, like the Torah or the New Testament. That notwithstanding, he believed that those Books, by themselves, were not sufficient to save his people from their sins, and he constantly criticized any who purported themselves to be "perfected" simply by virtue of the fact that their religion had a Bible (a "Book"). Here is a passage which illustrates Muḥammad's point of view:

> **...That the People of the Book may know that they have *no power whatever* over the Grace of Allah, that His Grace is entirely in His Hand, to bestow it on whomsoever He wills.**
>
> **Qur'an 57:29**

If there is to be "peace on earth", both Muslims and non-Muslims must keep one subtle point firmly in mind at all times. Since the death of Muḥammad, at which time his sayings were quickly compiled as the **Qur'an**, the Muslims themselves have had a "Book" also! **Thus, they are now *also* "People of the Book", and have been for 1400 years.** Therefore, the above admonition of the Prophet Muḥammad also applies to *them*, and they should bear in mind that the mere reading of praises for the names of Allah and his Prophet Muḥammad will not, by themselves, force the hand of Allah to bestow grace upon them.

We are now ready to consider the Qur'anic meaning of the word "jihad". Although most readers cannot read Arabic, we shall include the Arabic words we need to consider to learn the truth, alongside their English transliterations and translations.

"Jihad"

The word "jihad"

I am well-aware that most readers of this book cannot read Arabic. That's all right. I'm still going to show you some Arabic words, along with English transliterations and translations. Hang in there—what you're about to learn is important.

The word "jihad" is derived from the Arabic verb...

جَاهَدَ

... pronounced "ja-ha-da" in English. Ja-ha-da means[36] "to strive, to fight, to struggle, to battle, to wage holy war or jihad".

The word "ja-ha-da" is used interchangeably in the Qur'an with the word...

قَاتَلَ

... pronounced "ka-ta-la". It means "to fight, combat, battle against".

If one wishes to be a follower of the Prophet Muḥammad, *who* exactly is it whom one will be "battling against"?

If we seek the answer to this question in the Qur'an, we find that the obligation to fight against unbelief is an oft-recurring theme throughout the Book. Nevertheless, the fine nuances of the commandment for "jihad" are most elaborately developed in Surah (*i.e.,* chapter) 9, usually entitled "The Repentance" in English translations. There we find a comprehensive listing of the "enemies" against whom "jihad" is to be waged. They are, in order of their appearances,

(1) اَلْمُشْرِكِيْنَ

(2) اَلْكٰفِرُوْنَ

(3) اَلْمُنٰفِقُوْنَ

I know you can't read Arabic. These words, in English transliteration and definition, are:

---

[36] All Arabic definitions are from Al-Mawrid, a comprehensive and widely-respected Arabic-English dictionary.

(1) *Al moosh-ree-kee-na,* **"the polytheists"** (or "idolaters", or "pagans").

(2) *Al ka-fee-roo-na,* **"the unbelievers"**

(3) *Al moo-na-fee-koo-na,* **"the hypocrites"**.

This, then, is the Muslim "enemies list". Who are the "polytheists"? The "unbelievers"? The "hypocrites"?

<u>The "enemy" identified</u>

<u>1. Polytheists</u>

"Polytheist" means the same thing today that it did in Moses' day. Polytheism is almost gone from the world, at least insofar as open worship is concerned. True; enemies of Christianity love to accuse Christians of "polytheism" because of the doctrine of the Father, the Son, and the Holy Ghost, but it is clear that Christians regard these as different manifestations of the One God.

Similarly, Hindus, through the millennia, have maintained their pantheon of gods and goddesses, but it has been explicitly understood, since the days of the Bhagavad Gita, that these are all different manifestations of the One God, whom they know by the name Krishna.

We have seen that the ban on polytheism was commanded by Moses, and that the commandment is still binding today; binding upon believers, at least.

If the commandment is still binding today, then it was surely still binding in the days of Muḥammad. Therefore the Quranic ban on polytheism was not original with Muḥammad, but was simply a continuation of a Commandment originally given by God to Moses.

<u>2. Unbelievers</u>

The word "unbelievers", or the phrase "those who do not believe", are found innumerable times in the Qur'an. What's an "unbeliever"? Simply a person who does not believe in Allah and His Prophet.

This clearly includes "polytheists" and "idolaters", and therefore, to a large extent, "polytheist" and "unbeliever" mean the same thing. But what about Jews and Christians? They are, by Islam's own definition, believers in Allah, but they may not believe in His Prophet. Does that make them "unbelievers"?

Certainly not. We have seen already that *believing* Jews and Christians are specifically excluded from the "enemies" list, since, by the repeated word of the Prophet himself, *believing* Jews and Christians...

> **Shall have their <u>reward</u> with their Lord;**
> **On them shall be <u>no fear</u>, nor shall they grieve.**
>
> **Qur'an 2:62** (and elsewhere)

Should they, upon whom God commanded that there should be "no fear", then be terrorized and murdered in the name of the same God? I think not.

All right. What about *non*-believing Jews and Christians?

3. Hypocrites

We now come to the crux of the matter. Just what exactly *is* a "Jew", or a "Christian", or, for that matter, a "Muslim"? Is it sufficient to merely possess a certificate showing that one's dues have been paid-up at the temple?

Very few would accept such a thin definition. But if an exact, scientifically-precise definition of any religion is sought, it recedes, like a mirage in the heat. It simply cannot be pinned down.

It is almost universally accepted that, buried within the masses of followers of any religion, there lie people—probably *many* people—who *don't* believe, and who "hang on" because of real or imagined material benefit of some sort.

There is nothing new about this. When the Children of Israel were led up out of Egypt, they were accompanied by a "mixed multitude"[37] (Exodus 12:38). This is understood as having been a large mass of non-believers who took it upon themselves to come along, either because they hated or feared the Egyptians, or because they believed that there was some sort of material benefit in hanging onto the Jews.

---

[37] The two terms for "mixed multitude", which may be transliterated "erev rav" and "asafsoof" respectively, each occur only once in Torah, and their meanings are somewhat obscure. Nevertheless, all translators, both Jewish and Christian, accept the translation "mixed multitude" for these words.

The "mixed multitude" was trouble. They were cited as having been the cause of at least one rebellion against Moses (Numbers 11:4), and they undoubtedly contributed greatly to all the unrest which accompanied Israel on it journey of 40 years through the wilderness. They were the "hypocrites" of the Exodus, although many Israelites undoubtedly shared in their unbelief.

In the New Testament, the concept of a "hypocrite" among the believers, like a weed in the garden, was more highly developed. Yeshua (Jesus) used the word "hypocrite", as a form of denunciation, 15 times in the Gospel of Matthew alone.

Therefore, when Muḥammad railed against the "hypocrites", he was, once again, speaking firmly in the Judeo-Christian tradition, and promulgating no new doctrine.

How did Muḥammad determine what lay in the minds of Jews and Christians, to know which ones "really" believed, and which ones were actually "hypocrites"?

He didn't. His definition of "hypocrite" was based *not* on what a man said, but what the man actually did. Those who fought against Islam and its Prophet were deemed the enemy, and Muslims were instructed to neutralize them by any and every means necessary. Killing was most assuredly not excluded from the methods to be employed. However...*starting* the fight was *prohibited* (Qur'an 2:190).

There is no doubt that the directive of the Qur'an was to leave unmolested those who, while refusing to follow Islam and its Prophet, nevertheless chose to coexist peacefully with the new order.

Did Muḥammad have the "right" to decide who was, and who wasn't a "hypocrite"? If the LORD really did appear to him, then he had the right, for then anyone who was against him was against God. As far as the record shows, all the things he stood firmly against, such as idol worship, drunkenness, and sexual immorality, were also forbidden by Judaism and Christianity. So what was it that drove certain people to physically oppose him? It could only have been—he reasoned—that they were not sincere Jews and Christians, but "hypocrites".

On September 11, 2001, Arab terrorists, purportedly Muslim, launched a suicide air strike against a civilian target, the twin towers of the World Trade Center in New York. Were the 2,000-3,000 people slain in this attack among those known to be actively fighting against Islam or its Prophet? The idea is ludicrous.

Could there have been "hypocrites" among the thousands slain; people who were openly or secretly opposing the teachings of the Prophet? Certainly. Among thousands of people, one is likely to find examples of anything.

"Jihad"

But is it lawful, under the Qur'an, to kill a mass of people in order to eliminate a few guilty parties?

You know the answer to that without being told. Of course the answer is "no". But where in the Qur'an may we find the Word of God on this matter?

Indiscriminate killing prohibited

In the 48th Surah of the Qur'an, entitled "The Victory", we find the Word of God on this matter. This Surah was revealed to Muḥammad during his return from the Holy City of Mecca in the sixth year of his reign at Medina. Mecca, at that time, was still in the hands of hostile pagans. Muḥammad and 1400 followers had attempted to make the Pilgrimage to Mecca over the objections of the rulers of that city. When the Prophet and his forces reached the outskirts of the city, there were some hostile encounters, which led the Muslims to take an oath, at a place called Al-ḥudaybiyah, to either all stand or all fall together in battle. However, as things developed, there was no battle, but rather a 10-year peace treaty.

There was much disappointment among some of the Muslims about this treaty, since it seemed to give too much to the enemy, and nothing to them. At this point, Muḥammad received a revelation from Allah, saying that He Himself had held them back from fighting. The reason? Because there were a number of sincere Muslims living in Mecca, in addition to the idolaters, and if war had broken out, the forces of Muḥammad would have inadvertently killed Muslims along with idolaters, and thereby incurred guilt. This revelation from Allah stated further that *if* the Muslims and idolaters of the City of Mecca could have been separated, then the Unbelievers surely would have been punished by Him with a grievous punishment (Qur'an 48:25).

The God Who spoke thusly may well have been a God of war, but He was certainly not a God of indiscriminate killing; the sort which results when a terrorist blows up himself along with numerous other people he does not know.

Must Islam "prevail"?

You can perhaps see that the Qur'an, so far as we have looked into it, does not call for "jihad" the way the news media imply. In effect, the Qur'an simple re-states, from an Arabian perspective, the Law of Moses, which demands absolute suppression of idolatry.

However, there is a Quranic verse which, if taken out of context, seems to suggest that there is indeed a Divine Commandment to wage war against all non-Muslim religions until they are destroyed. This verse occurs in the 9th Surah (Qur'an 9:33). It is so important that it is repeated, almost verbatim, in two subsequent chapters (48:28, 61:9). Clearly, we'd better take a look at this verse. One very popular English translation of the Qur'an renders this verse:

> **It is He** [*i.e.,* Allah] **Who has sent His Messenger with guidance and the religion of truth, to *proclaim* it over all religion, even though the pagans may hate it.**

That phrase, "to proclaim it over all religion", is a problem. It seems to suggest that Islam must, in some way, overwhelm everything else. This could mean jihad. But does it? Let's see how other translators render the phrase. In another version of the Qur'an, the same passage states that Allah will...

> **...cause it** [*i.e.,* Islam] **to *prevail* over all religion....**

... which is even more threatening. That means war, because the other religions are not just going to quit without a fight. A third Qur'an version states that Allah has sent His Messenger—with the religion of truth—

> **...to make it *superior* to other systems of belief...**

This is a little less threatening, but not entirely so. If the followers of one religion are *superior* to followers of all others, then that can be seized upon as an excuse to kill the others.

If there is really a Divine Commandment to cause Islam to prevail over all else, then bloodshed cannot be averted. So, since lives are at stake, we are going to have to read this verse in Arabic. I know you can't read Arabic, but try to hold on, because I'm going to show you what the Qur'an really says:

لِيُظْهِرَهُ عَلَى الدِّيْنِ كُلِّه

These are the four Arabic words which are translated **"to cause it** (*i.e.,* Islam) **to prevail over all religion"**. They are transliterated as follows:

"Jihad"

Lee-yooz-hee-ra-hoo â-la dee-nee kool-leeh[38]

The first 2 of these words, "lee-yooz-hee-ra-hoo â-la", are the words whose meanings we must determine. The last 2 words, "dee-nee kool-leeh" are non-controvesial, meaning "all religion". What is to be done to "all religion"? Destroy it?

The answer lies in the first two words. The first, "lee-yooz-hee-ra-hoo", is in the passive subjunctive tense (please keep this in mind; the verb tense here is of critical importance)[39]. It is derived from the Arabic verb "za-ha-ra":

...which, according to the Al-Mawrid dictionary, means: **"To appear, come out, come to light, show, emerge, arise, manifest itself, reveal itself; to be or become apparent, visible, manifest, evident, clear, plain, known** (etc.)**"**.

This word is quite analogous to the Hebrew word "za-har", which means **"to be enlightened, taught"**. Thus, according to the dictionary definitions, the Arabic phrase usually translated

"...**to cause it** [*i.e.,* Islam] **to prevail over all religion...**"

...would be more accurately translated

"...**to cause it** [*i.e.,* Islam] **to become known to all religion...**"

This, then, is not a call to war; but rather a call to education.

Ah, but it's not so simple. You see, there are idioms in Arabic, just as in every other language. In our phrase...

---

[38] Two notes on pronunciation are in order: (1) The pronunciation shown is for the words when read separately. When Arabic words are strung together into sentences, the pronunciations may change slightly. (2) The first "â" in the word "âla" is not equivalent to an English "a", but is a guttural sound not found in the English language.

[39] I am indebted to my son, Timothy Joseph Biegeleisen, for the discussion of the grammar of "Lee-yooz-hee-ra-hoo". Although I intended to do the grammatical analysis myself, he borrowed my copy of W. Wright's Arabic Grammar (Oxford, 1859), read the whole book in less time than it had taken me to read the first three chapters, and never returned it! Since then, he has been my Arabic grammar consultant.

Lee-yooz-hee-ra-hoo â-la dee-nee kool-leeh

... the conjugated verb za-ha-ra is followed by the word â-la. This combination is a distinct Arabic idiom. In Arabic, with the pronoun and adverb stripped from the verb, it is spelled...

(za-ha-ra â-la)

...which has two very different meanings in the Al-Mawrid dictionary:

1) **Za-ha-ra âla**: To get the better of, overcome, overwhelm, overpower, conquer, vanquish.

2) **Za-ha-ra âla**: To know (of); to be or become aware of, acquainted with; to learn (about), come to know (about).

Can we figure out which is the correct one? You be the judge. As mentioned above, the verb za-ha-ra, in the form in which it appears in the Qur'an, is in the *passive subjunctive tense.* This means that the verb "to overcome" becomes *"to be overcome"*, and the verb "to know" becomes *"to cause to be known"*. Here are the two possible literal interpretations of Qur'an 9:33, based upon the ordinary principles of Arabic grammar:

1. It is He [Allah] **Who has sent His Messenger with guidance and the religion of truth, to have it be** *overcome* **(overwhelmed, overpowered, etc.) by all other religion...**

2. It is He [Allah] **Who has sent His Messenger with guidance and the religion of truth, to cause all other religions to know about it...**

No matter which one you select, there's no commandment here for "jihad". Many hate-filled Jews and Christians would undoubtedly prefer (1), which would render Islam a laughing-stock in the eyes of the world. Therefore, the correct interpretation is, of course, (2), namely that the Messenger was sent to cause Allah's Religion *to be known to all others.*

There is therefore no "jihad", insofar as the word is used by our lying press to describe the daily murders in the Middle East. Islam only commands death to idolaters, and the commandment was originally pronounced by Moses. Any idolater deserving to die under Islamic Law also deserves to die under Jewish Law. By a process of logical argument which I shall not bore you with, such also deserve death under Christian Law, even though the ranks of Christianity include many who have forgotten that Yeshua (Jesus) said:

> **"Think not that I have come to send peace on earth: I came not to send peace, but a sword".** (Matthew 10:34).

If Muḥammad found there to be many among the Jews and Christians who were hypocrites, he still did not condemn anyone for being a "Jew" or a "Christian", but only for being a *hypocrite,* a person bent on mischief, hoping to be excused by claiming "membership" in a religious organization allegedly exempt from all judgment.

There is no religious organization which will grant any man or woman exemption from judgment. And that most assuredly includes Islam, history's most recent addition to the group called, in the Qur'an, "People Of The Book".

Chapter 10

The Question of Race

The great enemies of peace are religious and racial intolerance. We have dealt, thus far, only with the former. Let us now examine the facts concerning race. Is there a "master race"? Are certain races "inferior"?

Currently the most despised people on earth are those with dark skin color. Without a doubt, the most pervasive form of racism is the hatred borne by those with relatively light-colored skin, for anyone and everyone whom they perceive to be darker than they are. Thus, northern Italians hate southern Italians, northern Indians hate southern Indians, and, generally speaking, all "whites" hate all "blacks".

We shall look, therefore, at the plight of black people, because if we can solve that problem, the other problems of race ought to fall quickly into line.

And when we look into the matter, we find, to our surprise, that the seemingly low educational, scientific and cultural status of the black races is not "forever", but is strictly a phenomenon of the present time. If we turn the clock back to the middle ages, we find that it was the white races which were inferior. Impossible? You'll have to decide for yourself.

For those who believe in God, the truth will come as no surprise at all. For the truth is that God raises up whomsoever He wills to be raised up, and for as many centuries as whites have recently prevailed in the world, there were as many centuries before that during which the world's centers of culture and learning were in Africa and Asia.

The Biblical basis of black slavery

The Bible not only condones slavery, but gives exact rules to regulate it. But there is no racial aspect. The idea that dark-skinned people are merely "animals", to be used for forced labor, is relatively recent.

The so-called "justification" for black slavery is partly Biblical, being based on Genesis 9:20-27. In this episode, Noah curses his son Ham, proclaiming that

Ham's son Canaan will be a "servant of servants" to his brethren. Biblical genealogists consider Canaan to be the "father" of the black races (and Shem and Japheth to be the "fathers" of the Caucasian and Oriental races, respectively). Let us examine the Biblical excerpt directly:

> "And Noah began to be an husbandman, and he planted a vineyard.
>
> And he drank of the wine, and was drunken; and he *was uncovered* within his tent.
>
> And Ham, the father of Canaan, *saw the nakedness of his father*, and told his two brethren without.
>
> And Shem and Japheth took a garment, and laid it upon both their shoulders, and went backward, and covered the nakedness of their father; and their faces were backward, and they saw not their father's nakedness.
>
> And Noah awoke from his wine, and knew what his younger son had done unto him.
>
> And he said, *Cursed be Canaan; a servant of servants shall he be unto his brethren.*
>
> And he said, Blessed be the Lord God of Shem; and Canaan shall be his servant.
>
> God shall enlarge Japheth, and he shall dwell in the tents of Shem; and Canaan shall be his servant."

The meanings of the phrases "was uncovered" and "saw the nakedness of his father" are so obscure that it would be futile to speculate about them. It would be equally futile to speculate as to why it was *Canaan* was specifically cursed, when it was his *father*, Ham, who was the wrongdoer! But regardless of what these verses do or don't mean, one should note that the "curse" upon Canaan, the Biblical father of the black races, is a curse which was pronounced by Noah. Did Noah have the right to levy curses? That is, isn't there a difference between Noah saying "Thus says *The Lord:* cursed be Canaan..." and the actual Biblical quote, which is closer to "Thus says *Noah:* cursed be Canaan...". To be sure, Noah was a Prophet. But does a Prophet have the power to enforce his *own* curses?

Let us, however, play the "Devil's Advocate" (and rest assured, the Devil is at work here). Let us suppose that Noah's curse *was* from God, and was therefore binding. What is the *term* of a curse from God?

This question was answered on Mt. Sinai. When God gave Moses the Ten Commandments, He succinctly defined the hereditary length of a Divine curse:

> "I the Lord thy God am a jealous God, visiting the iniquity of the fathers upon the children unto the third and fourth generation of them that hate me" (Exodus 20:5).

Are we to regard the phrase "third and fourth generation" as being a figure of speech, meaning "countless generations"? I think not. Even in Biblical times, everyone could count to ten, and there is not a reason in the world to doubt that "third and fourth generation" means exactly what it says[40].

Besides, any doubt about the hereditary length of a Divine curse must be dispelled by the prophecies of the Prophet Ezekiel. According to Ezekiel, the word of God is this:

> "...say ye...'Doth not the son bear the iniquity of the father?' When the son hath done that which is lawful and right, and hath kept all my statues, and hath done them...the son shall *not* bear the iniquity of the father, neither shall the father bear the iniquity of the son: the righteousness of the righteous shall be upon him, and the wickedness of the wicked shall be upon him".
>
> Ezekiel 18:19-20

What this means is that any Biblical license for black slavery expired during Noah's era, about 5,000 years ago.

That didn't stop it. But slavery, historically, has not been limited to black slavery. Throughout history, any race which could discern a difference between themselves and a neighbor of any color whatsoever would endeavor mightily to enslave that neighbor. In the Middle Ages, blacks enslaved whites. *It is entirely possible that the circumstances prevailing at that time could come about again.* For those whites who thought that the only important question about blacks was whether they should be merely socially oppressed, or rather returned to full slavery or burnt in mass-genocide ovens, the realization that *blacks* used to enslave *whites* ought to be thought-provoking. If you're white, and if you don't believe it, then read on. There's more to learn.

---

[40] Some support for a longer term can be claimed from the opening of Deuteronomy, Chapter 23, which reads: "A *mamzer* shall not enter into the congregation of the LORD; even to his tenth generation shall he not enter into the congregation of the LORD. An Ammonite or Moabite shall not enter into the congregation of the LORD; even to their tenth generation shall they not enter into the congregation of the LORD for ever."

Mamzer, according to the Rabbis, means specifically a child of incest or adultery, although the King James Bible translates the word as "bastard", a more common form of out-of-wedlock child. These two verses, taken together, may suggest that "ten generations" and "forever" mean the same thing in Hebrew. Who can say? In any event, "ten" is six generations more than "four", and, if nothing else, this proves that a Jew could, at that time, count at least to 10.

The "Dark Ages"

When white people are taught history, the period called the "Middle Ages" is often referred to as the "Dark Ages". It is portrayed, in white history books, as a period during which civilization in general, and the arts and sciences in particular, lay fallow.

That was true for whites, but not for coloreds.

In reality—a painful reality that whites cannot bear to face up to—the truth is that during the Middle Ages the great empires of the world were *colored* empires, and the educational and cultural centers of the world were African and Asian. *White* people were the lawless barbarians during that period.

How could a thing of such magnitude be kept secret? There is no shortage of volumes covering the history of Spain under the Moors, and covering the history of the great African Jewish and Islamic Kingdoms of the Middle Ages, but these volumes are simply not read, discussed, or taught in schools. But it's really not a secret. Like much of the world's truly important knowledge, it's lying there for all to see. The trouble is that no one looks.

The information in the following pages was drawn principally from two sources: *From Babylon to Timbuktu* by Rudolph R. Windsor[41], and *World's Great Men of Color*, Vol. 1, by J.A. Rogers[42]. Without a doubt, these authors are prejudiced. They are both black, and they both present black history in the most favorable of lights. The facts I have selected to report upon, however, can all be readily confirmed—minus the enthusiasm, of course—in "white" sources such as, for example, the Encyclopedia Britannica.

The Moorish Empire

By the end of the seventh century the Muhammadans, having already conquered the entire Middle East, had swept across Africa, poised at either end of Europe and ready for further conquests.

---

[41] *From Babylon to Timbuktu.* By Rudolph R. Windsor. Windsor's Golden Series Publications, 1988. This book is only readily found in stores or street vendors which cater to black-oriented literature. It may be ordered direct from : Windsor Golden Series, PO Box 310393, Atlanta, GA 30331 (tel 404-349-6684).
[42] *World's Great Men of Color*, Volume I. By J.A. Rogers. Macmillan Publishing Company, 1972.

Spain at that time was inhabited by the Goths; Arian Christians of Germanic origin. We have already seen (Chapter 7) that the Arian view of the "nature of Christ" was closer to the Islamic view than to that of the Catholic Church, which by that time had grown to be the undisputed reigning Christian power in Europe. That, however, hardly made the white Goths eager to be overrun by dark-skinned invaders from Africa.

Spain also harbored a substantial Jewish population, which, it seems, originally migrated up from North Africa. The Jews of Spain were relatively dark-skinned, and it is evident that some of them were, quite frankly, Negro. By the time of the Muslim conquests, the Jewish community of Spain had come under persecution by the Christians of the nation. Many fled back to Africa, settling in relatively large numbers in Morocco. Thereafter, they were the allies of the Moroccan Muslims, both there and in Spain.

As soon as the Islamic conquest of North Africa was complete, Islam turned its eyes north toward Europe. The Muslims of Morocco, with Jewish support, planned an invasion of Spain. The first attempt failed, but in 711 AD, a Moorish army under a general named Tariq ibn Ziyad launched a successful amphibious landing on the Spanish side of the Pillars of Hercules.

Tariq was a devout Muslim, consumed by the desire to spread the religion of Muḥammad to the European continent[43]. Therefore, when his fleet arrived in Spain, he ordered that all the boats be burned! He made up his mind that if he could not glorify God by seizing Spain for Islam, then he and his army would never return home, but die fighting.

But he did not perish. His amphibious landing was a success, and within a very short time Muslim forces had conquered the entire Iberian peninsula.

In remembrance of Tariq's achievements, the European side of the Pillars of Hercules came to be known as the "Mountain of Tariq". In Arabic, this is "Jabal al Tarik", which in English later evolved into the current name "Gibraltar". This was the beginning of the Moorish period of Spanish history, which lasted exactly from 711 to 1492.

Moorish Spain as Europe's cultural center

Although the white Christians of Spain deeply desired, during this entire period, to expel the "Blackamoors" from their country, it is nevertheless an undisputed historical fact that medieval Spain was the educational, scientific and cultural center of Europe. The Moorish Kings lived in castles of highly polished marble,

---

[43] A good and entertaining source of information about this, and other aspects of the history of Spain under the Moors, was the great (white) American writer Washington Irving. His works, *Legends of the Conquest of Spain* and *The Alhambra,* are mentioned further below.

with elaborately carved walls and beautiful mosaic floors, while European Kings lived in cold, damp castles of unfinished stone; crude by comparison. The streets of Spain's capital city, Cordova, were well-paved and completely illuminated by public lights, at a time when the streets of London were dark and covered with mud.

The Moors possessed all the knowledge of ancient Greece, which was lost to Europe until the Renaissance. They made important contributions to philosophy, medicine, mathematics, chemistry, astronomy, and botany. There were academies for the rich, free schools for the poor, and libraries containing books from all over the world.

The Jews of medieval Spain coexisted peacefully with the Muslims, and for them, the sojourn in that nation is remembered as being the second most glorious period in their history, exceeded only by the glory of the reigns of David and Solomon in ancient Israel. Medieval Spain was the birthplace of Maimonides and other great Old Testament scholars whose works constitute the foundations of modern Jewish thought.

Throughout the Middle Ages, the white Christians of Spain endeavored to thrust out the Moors. It took them until 1492 to do that. When Isabella and Ferdinand finally defeated the last Moorish King in Granada (in the same year that they financed Columbus' trip to America), they immediately expelled all Jews who refused to accept Christianity. This is not at all surprising. Since the Jews had actively supported the Moorish conquests, the Christians were not about to take any chances on losing what had taken them 800 years to regain.

The day the last Moors and Jews were expelled from Spain was counted as a great day in Spanish history. But was it? It is true that Spain, largely through the strength of its navy, had achieved the status of a world power. But in less than a century, the Spanish Armada was defeated by England, and the nation went into a great decline.

Who was responsible for the glory of medieval Spain?

It is an historically undisputed fact that Spain, during the "Dark Ages", was the greatest nation in Europe, a status it has never regained. Two questions come to mind: (1) "Who gets the credit?", and (2) "Were the rulers of Spain *really* Negro, or were they Arabs, midway in color between 'white' and 'black'?"

The answer to the first question is this: Since medieval Spain was a nation of Muslims, Jews, and Christians, it would be impossible to identify a single ethnic or religious group to whom all credit should go. The credit goes to everyone involved. However, there can be no doubt about the nature of the "driving force" behind the establishment of that nation. It was Islam, and nothing else.

It is inevitable that whites will ask the second question. Were the rulers of Spain *really* black? The answer is that Islam has always been a color-blind religion, whose followers were drawn from all races, including Caucasian. It is therefore highly probable that many of Spain's Moorish Kings were ethnically "Arab", but in the case of at least two dynasties of Moorish Kings, the blackness is beyond dispute.

The Almoravids

By the eleventh century, the Moroccan Islamic rulers of Spain had become decadent and soft, and they were conquered by the "Almoravids", a dynasty of Muslim sultans whose original home was Senegal, in the heart of western Africa, thousands of miles from Spain. These people were black—very black. Their rise to power began when a pilgrim named Yaḥya (the Muslim name for John, *i.e.* John the Baptist) returned home from Mecca and founded a new religious sect. In the Muslim tradition, this new religious view quickly developed into a new military campaign, and the sect burst forth from Senegal to become master of all of northwest Africa. This all took place within the space of 50 years.

Across the Strait of Gibraltar, trouble was brewing in Spain. Initially, Spain had been a province of the "Umayyad" government, the world-wide Islamic government which ruled from the Middle East. The Umayyad Court was originally in Mecca itself; later it was moved to Damascus. For three centuries, an Umayyad Caliph, loyal to Damascus, had governed Spain from the city of Córdoba.

In the course of time, the Umayyad government in the Middle East was overthrown. Not long afterwards, civil war broke out in Spain, and the Umayyad Caliphate was replaced by "Taifa"—petty Kings who each ruled small regions of Spain from their own regional courts. There were at least 23 such petty Kingdoms before the Almoravid conquest.

The Taifa Kings had ushered in an age of brilliant Islamic cultural revival, promoting poetry, philosophy, natural science and mathematics. But they were politically incompetent. The various Islamic states were constantly at war with each other. They unhesitatingly turned to Christians for support against rival Muslim Kings. This lack of unity and inconsistency made them targets for the growing forces of the Christian re-conquest of Spain.

By 1085, the situation had become critical. The Christian King Alfonso VI had won so many military victories, and was collecting tribute from so many Muslim

Kings, that it appeared that Islamic government in the Iberian peninsula was about to expire.

In that year, Alfonso had captured the important Muslim city of Toledo. The Taifa Kings were desperate. They swallowed their pride, and turned to the Almoravids for help.

Yusuf ibn Tashfin

The greatest of the Almoravid leaders was Yusuf ibn Tashfin, who conquered an Empire encompassing all of Northwest Africa, and ultimately Spain. It was Yusuf who defeated El Cid, one of Spain's most renowned and legendary folk heroes.

Yusuf was called to Spain by the Taifa King, Motamid. Motamid was quite aware that Yusuf might usurp his own throne if he was successful, but he had no choice. The Muslims of Spain were in *big* trouble. Alphonso VI had beaten them so severely that he was literally on the verge of driving the Muslims back into the Mediterranean Sea.

Yusuf was nearly 80 years old when he came to Spain, but it is said that he still had all the powers of a young man. Although he was outnumbered by the Christians three-to-one, his indomitable spirit prevailed, and he miraculously defeated King Alfonso at the Battle of Zalacca. At that famous battle, 70,000 Christian soldiers were routed by Yusuf's army of 25,000 Muslims.

Yusuf, in accordance with a promise he had made at the outset, returned to Africa. The local Taifa Kings heaved a sigh of relief. They had been saved, and their thrones remained intact. At least for the time being.

The relief did not last long, however. Within the space of two years, the Christians had rallied, and Yusuf had to be called back. This time he stayed. One by one, he defeated the Christian generals. El Cid was the last to fall, and when he did, virtually the entire Iberian peninsula was under Yusuf's control. Muslim rule in Spain had been restored.

Yusuf thus became King of an Empire that encompassed a large part of Africa, and most of Spain. There is no doubt about his skin color. He was black—very black.

The Almohads

Muslims consider the greatest of all the medieval Kings of Spain to have been Yakub ibn Yusuf (1149-1199 AD). He was known as "Al-Mansur", which means "the invincible". It is said that he never lost a battle. His Empire was immense, stretching to the border of Egypt. At the time of his death, at the early age of 50, he was contemplating an invasion of Egypt as well, which would have made him master of half the continent of Africa.

He began as the leader of a coalition of tribes known as the "Almohads". These were strictly puritanical and fanatically monotheistic Muslims from the Atlas Mountains of Morocco. The name "Almohad" is easy to confuse with "Almoravids", but they were two different groups. In fact, the Almohads *overthrew* the Almoravids in Africa, then went on to establish yet a third Moorish Dynasty in Spain.

Al-Mansur's father was of mixed race, and his mother was a full-blooded Negro slave woman, from Senegal or Timbuktu. Thus, Al-Mansur was at least 75% Negro. It would be hard to find a black American who was "more Negro" than that. But this black man ruled Spain during its most glorious period.

Al-Mansur came to power, in Africa, during a period when the Christian re-conquest of Spain had once again gained tremendous momentum. The Almoravids, like the Umayyads before them, had become soft and decadent. The *Almohads* overthrew them, first in Africa, then in Spain. Al-Mansur thus conquered and began expanding the empire first established by the great Almoravid leader, Yusuf ibn Tashfin.

As in the past, however, the internal strife between Muslim sects played into the hands of the Christian forces of re-conquest. There was a feeling of chaos in the air, and the Christians intended to take full advantage. Feeling that their day had come at last, they assembled a vast army of 300,000 men at Alarcos, intending to put an end to Moorish rule in Spain once and for all.

But Al-Mansur sent emissaries over his vast North African domains, calling for every able-bodied man to come to the rescue of Islam. This they did—people of all races and colors responding to the call. At Alarcos, Al-Mansur dealt the Christian forces a crushing defeat. According to Arab historians, the spoils of this battle were "beyond calculation".

Al-Mansur went on to re-take all the principle strongholds of Christian Spain. It would be nearly 300 years before the setbacks to Christianity were fully reversed, and the Moors finally expelled.

Al-Mansur was a military genius, but he was also a patron of the arts and a lover of justice. According to J.A. Rogers, when he came to power, the first thing he did was to distribute vast quantities of food to the poor. He freed all who were unjustly held in prison and reformed the laws to prevent others from being so held. He initiated a vast public works program, rebuilding the cities and erecting mosques, schools, hospitals, and aqueducts. Some of Spain's greatest Moorish architectural works, including the Alhambra, were begun during his reign.

A fourteenth century Islamic historian wrote of him that "his reign was remarkable for the tranquillity, the safety, the abundance, and the prosperity that reigned everywhere...his religion was sincere and deep; and he was a great benefactor of Islam".

Al-Mansur was known, to his subjects, as "The Black Sultan".

There can be no doubt that Spain, during at least parts of her most glorious period, was ruled by Negroes.

Racism

A very interesting question arises from a consideration of the facts we have examined above. What was it like to be a white in a nation ruled by blacks?

I have found this question to be very difficult to answer. Light-skinned Christian Americans of Spanish ancestry to whom I have addressed it have little to say. It seems that the Spanish have very effectively suppressed the memory of their Moorish background.

The books I have had access to do not address the question, except in the negative sense. That is, I have *not* seen any books which suggest that Spain, under Muslim rule, was a place of misery for whites. This is not to say that whites were not discontent. On the contrary, white discontent was widespread and deeply-felt. But it appears to have been mainly a matter of injured pride, and not a matter of the sort of horrendous discrimination against colored minorities which characterizes much of the world today.

The nineteenth century white American writer Washington Irving, best known as the author of *The Legend of Sleepy Hollow*, had a deep and abiding interest in medieval Spain. He spent several years there, including a long period during which he actually lived within the famous Alhambra palace. His experiences during those years were recorded in two books: *Tales of the Conquest of Spain*, and *The Alhambra*.

If Washington Irving's descriptions of medieval Spain were accurate, then, based on his writings, it must be said that the sojourn of the Moors in Spain was a period of an almost magical fairy-tale quality; a time of general prosperity and happiness, albeit punctuated by periodic military-political upheaval. But the evils of racism, discrimination, and crime, such as are threatening the very fabric of mixed-race nations like America today, were apparently not anywhere near the magnitude that they are now. As a white American, I am somewhat embarrassed to report this, but I have, as yet, found no evidence to the contrary.

What I am saying is that it seems to have been better to have been a white living under black rule in medieval Spain than it is to be black living under white rule in America.

Slavery

It has been the policy of military victors, since the beginning of time, to make slaves of some or all of their prisoners-of-war. Thus, it is not surprising to find that countless white Spanish Christians were taken to Africa as slaves after military encounters in which the Muslims prevailed.

I have discovered no reports of the conditions under which these white slaves lived, but I cannot imagine that it was a good life.

The only important lesson to be learned from this is that white Europeans and Americans did *not* "invent" slavery; nor did "the Jews". Black Africans were taking *white* slaves for themselves many centuries before America was even founded.

Furthermore, enslavement of *blacks* by blacks was also a routine phenomenon in medieval Africa. Like the great cities of the Greek and Roman Empires, the legendary black city of Timbuktu was entirely dependent on slave labor. Few if any of those slaves were white.

No race has a "patent" on slavery.

Timbuktu

Nowadays, the name "Timbuktu" is only used by white people as a joke. While most people have no idea where it is, it has come to embody the concept of the "farthest possible place" from civilization.

The Question of Race

There was, however, a time when Timbuktu was not the "farthest possible place" from civilization, but was the very *center* of world civilization. Since Timbuktu is in the heart of "darkest Africa", this seems categorically impossible. How can such things be? But such things *can* be—and, in fact, they were.

Jewish tribes seem to have been migrating into the heart of Africa since the dawn of recorded history. Ethiopia is mentioned in the beginning of the Biblical Book of Genesis, and there is no time in history when there were not Jews living there. From Ethiopia, they went west and south into the heart of Africa. Other Jews also migrated directly west from Egypt, entering Africa along the northern coast of the continent. This was undoubtedly the route taken by the "Lost Tribes of Israel", fleeing from the Assyrian and Babylonian invaders of the Holy Land.

The roots of what eventually evolved into the greatest of all the African empires arose in the area which now constitutes the northwest corner of Nigeria. This was the Kingdom of Ghana; not the Ghana of today, which is a small nation to the south, but a large empire corresponding to the modern nations of Mauritania and Mali.

Starting about 300 AD, the Kingdom of Ghana began to be ruled by a dynasty of Jewish Kings known as the Za Dynasty[44]. The founder of the Dynasty was a man named Za el Yemeni, who was descended from Jews of Yemen. He established his capital city at Gao on the Niger River, in what is now the nation of Mali.

This area was rich in gold and iron, the latter metal being of great value in the forging of weapons with which neighboring Kingdoms were conquered. Within the Kingdom of Ghana the first public buildings, canals, and irrigation systems in this part of the world were built.

According to the writings of Eldad the Danite, a famous Algerian Jewish author of the ninth century, Ghana was a Hebrew nation which followed the Law of Moses[45]. The people of Ghana traced their roots to Jews of the First Diaspora of

---

[44] The history of Jewish root of the Kingdom of Ghana is taken largely from the thought-provoking book *From Babylon to Timbuktu*, by Rudolph Windsor, pp. 87-94. Most of the historical details may be confirmed in such sources as the Encyclopedia Britannica or the UNESCO series General History of Africa (Vols. III & IV), although these latter sources have a strong anti-religious sentiment. They make no mention whatsoever of Judaism, and their discussions of Islam betray a powerfully secular humanist outlook.

[45] See *From Babylon to Timbuktu*, pp. 92-93. In scholarly works touching on medieval Middle Eastern or African history, the name Eldad the Danite comes up frequently as a source of information.

As is almost always the case with historical works written during either the ancient and medieval periods, the writings of Eldad are not considered to have been 100% reliable. This is bound to be a problem in the situation which prevailed during those times, when even a journey of a few hundred miles was an immense undertaking. Long journeys solely for the purpose of verifying (or disputing) things said in books were simply not practical, and therefore historians, free from the sort of strict editorial peer review they face today, virtually all had a tendency to exaggerate.

600 BC, who were forcibly expelled from the Northern Kingdom of Israel by the Assyrians. In support of this, Eldad reported that the Ghanans possessed the Torah, which was compiled *before* the Diaspora, but not the Talmud, which was compiled in Jerusalem and Babylon much later, during the early centuries of the Christian era.

In the seventh century AD, the whole of Africa north of the Sahara desert was conquered by the armies of Islam. Subsequently, an extremely lucrative trade system developed with the Sub-Saharan Kingdom of Ghana. The commodities first traded were gold and salt[46]. This led to the appearance of regular caravan routes across the Sahara Desert to various cities in Ghana. These cities became wealthy.

Shortly after the year 1000 AD, the Kings of Ghana converted to Islam. Initially, the conversions were mainly for the purpose of fostering trade with the powerful Muslim states of North Africa, and had little to do with faith. But once Islam took root in the area, its impact grew inexorably.

At about this time, the Kingdom of Ghana was invaded by the Moors, and it went into an irreversible decline. But in the middle of the 13th century, a tribe called the Mandingo, who had been subjects of Ghana, rose up and took control of the Kingdom. They expelled the Moorish invaders, and set out creating an even greater Empire. This was the Empire of Mali[47]—not the Mali of today, but a huge empire which eventually stretched from the Atlantic Ocean across Sub-Saharan Africa to Lake Chad—an area the size of Western Europe. Like their predecessors, the Mandingos traded heavily with the Muslims to the north. Their Kings, like the Kings of Ghana before them, accepted Islam as the state religion.

The Mandingos were a highly successful agricultural society, and their cities grew rich through the trading of grain with the north. Their chief cities were Gao, which was the political capital, and Timbuktu, which was destined to become one the world's leading educational and cultural centers.

Timbuktu, originally founded about 1100 AD, grew to become a city of great wealth and strategic importance. In addition to being favorably located with respect to trans-Saharan trade, it was also a major conduit for trade between Europe and the Orient. This was a period in history when Europe was a large collection of petty Kingdoms which were primitive and warlike. Travel across the European continent was dangerous, and movement of expensive goods was out of the question. Therefore, the trade route between East and West, a source of enormous financial profit, took a circuitous pathway.

---

[46] *Dictionary of the Middle Ages*, Vol. 2. Edited by J.R. Strayer. Charles Scribner's Sons, New York, 1983. See "Timbuktu", pp. 54-56.
[47] *From Babylon to Timbuktu*, pp. 95-98. For a drier rendition of history, see the Encyclopedia Britannica article on "Mali" (the ancient Kingdom; not the modern state).

Goods from the Middle East and the Orient were carried across the Sahara Desert by caravan to Timbuktu. The Africans then transported them nearly 1000 miles to their ports on the Atlantic coast. From there the goods were loaded onto ships bound for Europe.

The wealth of Mali was demonstrated by the famous pilgrimage of the Emperor Kankan Musa in 1326. He arrived in the holy city of Mecca with 60,000 mounted soldiers and 500 slaves, each one bearing a ponderous bar of gold, which he gave to the city.

It was during this time that the University of Sankore was founded at Timbuktu, and this city began to become one of the world's leading centers of academic learning. The city flowered during the period when the Empire of Mali came to be known as the Empire of Songhay (*ca.* 1470-1591).

This last, and greatest, of Sub-Saharan Empires began when a man named Sonni Ali, of the Songhay tribe, began to attack and conquer the neighboring territories. Before long, all the territories of Mali were in his hands.

Sonni was the last of the long line of formerly Hebrew Za Emperors, tracing his roots back to Za el Yemeni, the founder of the old Kingdom of Ghana. Sonni was a great military leader, but he offended the Muslim clergy by his casual and even contemptuous attitude toward religion. He was nominally Muslim, but it seems that he, and all the other Emperors of the Za Dynasty, somehow maintained a loyalty to the Jewish religion while exhibiting an outward veneer of Islam for commercial purposes. When Sonni's successor, Muḥammad Askia, seized power by force, the 1200 year-old Za Dynasty came to an end.

The greatest of the Kings of Songhay, Muḥammad Askia ("the Usurper"), seized power in a military coup in 1492—the year Columbus set sail for America. Askia is remembered as a true and great champion of Islam, and of education. Not long after assuming power, he made his own Pilgrimage to Mecca, with the intention of outdoing his predecessor Kankan Musa. He brought gifts to Mecca, Medina, and to the Caliph of Baghdad which astounded everyone. Topping the list was an offering of 300,000 pieces of gold to the Holy Cities. His gifts exceeded all others, and left an indelible impression on the Muslims of the Middle East.

Songhay came to be known as the "Mecca of the Sudan" during the reign of Askia. By about 1500, this Empire in the heart of "darkest Africa" had become the center of the Muhammadan world, at a time when the Renaissance in Europe was just getting under way.

The students of Timbuktu were sent out to the great Muslim Universities of Spain, North Africa, and Asia, and learned teachers of all races and nationalities were paid high salaries to come to Timbuktu. The commodity which came to be the most profitable object of trade in Timbuktu was not gold, or silver, or grain—but books! It is said that there were more books in the libraries of the University of Sankore than in all the libraries of Europe combined.

It is also said that the entire body of male free citizens was literate. Leadership and authority were vested mainly in the learned scholars of the city.

These facts concerning the Empires of Ghana, Mali and Songhay seem totally at odds with what modern day white people think about blacks. Aren't black people intellectually inferior? Aren't black people "innately violent"?

Apparently they didn't know that in Timbuktu.

There was a legendary fourteenth century Muslim traveler named Ibn Battuta. Western historians often liken him to Marco Polo, although his travels actually extended even farther, spanning much of the known world from the Atlantic Coasts to China. Ibn Batuta paid a visit to sub-Saharan Africa during the time of the Kingdom of Mali. This is what he had to say[48] about the people:

> "The inhabitants had a greater abhorrence of injustice than any other people. Neither the man who travels nor he who stays at home has anything to fear from robbers or men of violence."

Thus we see that Timbuktu, a black city in the heart of "darkest" Africa, became a leading cultural and educational center, attained a literacy rate of nearly 100%, and was free of crime and violence.

The driving force behind these developments was Islam, and nothing else.

End of the black empires

What destroyed the black empires? It was greed and lust for power. The Ummayad Dynasty in Spain was overthrown by the Almoravids, who were in turn overthrown by the Almohads.

---

[48] *From Babylon to Timbuktu*, p. 59. When Battuta retired from his travels, he settled in North Africa. The sultan of Fez commissioned an Andalusian scholar, Ibn Juzayy, to record Battuta's experiences while he was still alive. The resulting volume, the *Rihla,* astounded readers even in its day. The consensus of modern scholars, however, is that the *Rihla* is a reliable source of information for the history of most of the areas Battuta visited.

Many remnants of the world of Ibn Battuta survive to this day, and these became the basis for a colorful and picturesque review of his life and travels, which appeared in National Geographic Magazine (Vol. 180, no. 6, December 1991, pp. 2-49).

In Sub-Saharan Africa, the Kingdom of Ghana was overthrown by Mali, which in turn was overthrown by Songhay.

Each of these Kingdoms comprised the same general territory as its predecessor, and the only real purpose accomplished by all this internal turmoil was the gratification of the desires of the leaders for supreme power.

Finally, during the periods when the empires were not distracted by internal dissension, they attacked each other. With the rise of Christian power in Spain, and the decline of the economic power of trans-Saharan caravan trade, the Moors and Songhays went to war against each other, and wiped each other out. Thus, in the final analysis, it was black people themselves who destroyed the great medieval black empires.

It was only *after* this self-destruction that white slave traders were able to establish a foothold in Africa.

The Ark of the Covenant

For those whites, especially those driven by misreadings of the Judeo-Christian Testaments, who still cling tenaciously to the belief that blacks are inferior by nature and held in low esteem by God, there is the delicate issue of the Ark of the Covenant.

It seems that in Jerusalem after the Civil War, during the bloody reign of Manasseh (687-642 BC), the Ark was removed from the Holy of Holies in Solomon's Temple. It was replaced by a statue of the pagan deity Asherah.

The reign of Manassah and his son was the single great stain in the history of the Southern Kingdom of Judah, yet these rulers were so evil that even *after* the wrongs had been righted, God could not forgive the Jewish Nation (II Kings 23:26).

Manasseh's son Amon, who was as evil and as hated as his father, ruled for only two years. Then he was assassinated, and his own son Josiah became King. Josiah was only 8 years old when he came to the throne. Apparently, the priests had a large part in his upbringing, because in his adult years he rose to become the most devoutly Jewish, and the most highly revered of all the Kings of Judah.

King Josiah called upon the Levites to return the Ark of the Covenant to the Temple (II Chronicles, 35:3), but there is no evidence that it ever did return. In the first place, the Bible contains no references to the physical presence of the Ark in the Temple after the reign of Manassah, and secondly there *are* numerous suggestions in the Bible of its *absence*. These, and all other aspects of the Ark story, have been persuasively argued in a lengthy and detailed analysis by Graham Hancock, in his book *The Sign and the Seal* (Crown Publishers, New York, 1992). Although there is no evidence in his writings of any faith in God, Hancock's logic is nevertheless persuasive.

It is now known that there was a replica of the Temple of Solomon which was built on Elephantine Island, in the Nile River near Aswan, Egypt, around 650 BC. There is good, albeit circumstantial evidence that Jews fleeing from Manassah, who "shed innocent blood ... till he had filled Jerusalem from one end to another" (2Kings 21:16), established a new center of worship in Elephantine, and brought the Ark there.

The existence and activities of the Jewish colony at Elephantine are well documented by papyri which have been preserved. It flourished until 410 BC, when the local Egyptians apparently lost their willingness to tolerate Jews in their midst. The Egyptians destroyed the Temple and scattered the Jewish inhabitants. This date coincides with the date which Ethiopian oral tradition holds the Ark to have begun its journey up the Nile River to their country. It stopped for a time in the city of Meroe (which has only recently been excavated), and then continued southward into Ethiopia, where it resided on an Island in Lake Tana for 800 years. There it found rest in the hands of the ancient Ethiopian Hebrew community.

When, in the 4th century AD, Ethiopia converted to Christianity, there quickly came a time when the Jews were overwhelmed by Christian military force. The Ark was seized and brought to the ancient capital city of Axum, where it remains to this day, in the hands of the Ethiopian Coptic Christian Church.

Anyone not familiar with the beliefs and rituals of the Ethiopian Coptic Church cannot imagine the depth of conviction associated with their belief that the object in their possession for these last two millennia is the Ark of the Covenant. Indeed, it is the entire focus of the nation's Christianity. Every Ethiopian Coptic church has a replica of the Ark in it, and awareness of the importance of the original in Axum permeates their very consciousness at all times.

There is a "Guardian of the Ark", a man who is selected upon the death of the previous Guardian. His entire life is spent in the rock church in which the Ark is kept. He lives a life of prayer, fasting, and meditation, never leaving the church unless the Ark goes out, in which case he accompanies it. It is not at all clear, however, that the Ark *ever* actually goes out; it may well be that "Timkat" (Epiphany), the once-a-year ceremony in which the Ark is thought to be seen being carried jubilantly through the streets of Axum, involves a replica.

The earliest known attempt to recover the Ark from Ethiopia was made by the so-called "Poor Knights of Christ and of the Temple of Solomon", more often referred to as the "Knights Templer", or simply the "Templers". This group emerged as the ruling power of Israel (and nearly of all Europe as well) after the Crusader conquest of Jerusalem in 1099. There was nothing "poor" about them. On the contrary, they were an extremely wealthy and influential order. They dug for the Ark unsuccessfully under the Temple Mount in Jerusalem for 7 years (1119-1126 AD). They were in complete control of this excavation. There was no one to answer to, and no one to inhibit the scope or extent of their work. That notwithstanding, they did not find the sacred relic.

When word came to them of the legend that the Ark had been taken to Ethiopia, they went there. But their attempts to seize it, by force or by guile, failed.

Graham Hancock's logic and scholarship are persuasive, and one is driven forcefully to the conclusion that the Ark is, in fact, in Ethiopia, no matter how unpleasant this may seem to whites in general, and to Judeo-Christian whites in particular.

Most devoutly believing Jews and Christians would agree that the Ark is the most precious religious object on earth today. And yet God seems to have entrusted its care not to Jews, or to white Christians, but to black Ethiopians. This single fact, even more so than the facts concerning the great black empires of the Middle Ages, renders it a certainty that God loves black people as much as white people.

As a white person, I would add "hopefully not more".

What was the "secret" of black prosperity in medieval times?

The black nations of today are, without a doubt, culturally depressed. How can we account for this?

If one examines the histories of medieval Spain and Timbuktu, one finds exactly and precisely One, and only One explanation for their prosperity: God.

The Empire of Ghana began as a *Jewish* empire, evolving in the course of time into the Islamic empires of Ghana, Mali, and Songhay. Moorish Spain was Islamic from the start.

It was a love of God, and a fear of God, which lay behind all the heroic exploits and cultural achievements of these Empires. It is absolutely impossible to explain these things in any other way.

The black men and women who created the great empires of the "Dark Ages" were devout Jews and Muslims, often fanatically so. They feared God. This, and this alone, is what is missing in the western world today.

When people of all colors turn back to God, through the Torah, and through Yeshua (Jesus), and through Islam, then the world can conceivably become the paradise which we have all dreamed of. This is our only hope for peace and tranquility.

Should medieval history be read as a warning?

Before leaving the subject of skin color, one further point must be made. The period of colored dominance in the western world, fueled by Jewish-Islamic fervor, was fully established between the years 700-800 A.D. It was dealt its first major blows during the years 1100-1200, the first century of the Crusades. It lingered for centuries more after that, fading gradually, but not dying out fully until the 17th century.

Therefore the period of unchallenged "colored" greatness, before the Crusades, lasted about 400 years.

The period of *white* greatness, unknown during the entire Middle Ages, but firmly established since 1600 AD, is 400 years old. Suppose these things are cyclical? It *that's* true, then whites may already have *had* their 400 years of unchallenged supremacy, and may have already entered into another period of sickening decay and decline. Must history always repeat itself?

The lesson to be learned from the Moors and from Timbuktu is a lesson which has been taught so many times, one cannot help but wonder just how many times it needs to be taught before people will finally pay attention. The lesson is this: It is *God* who raises up people and nations, not skin color or anything else. And it is human greed and lust which brings men and nations down.

This lesson has been taught by Jews, Muslims, Christians, and Buddhists since the beginnings of their histories, but it just doesn't seem to sink in.

How can people avoid endless cycles of being dominated, being "liberated", and in turn dominating others, having learned nothing from their own miserable experiences?

The answer is through "brotherhood". But *not* the "brotherhood" of hypocritical Civil Rights legislators, whose slogans, such as "all men are brothers", are duplicitously taught to spring from pure logic and human ingenuity, without reference to God. They are lying. It is *because* secular humanism is a lie that years of vainly preaching "all men are brothers" have lead only to *more* violence, not less.

The brotherhood which will elevate humankind above racial suffering is the brotherhood spoken of by Yeshua, when he was told that his family wished to see him. He motioned to his audience and said:

> **...whosoever shall do the will of my Father which is in heaven, the same is my brother, and sister, and mother.**
>
> **(Matthew 12:30)**

Chapter 11

What is the relationship between "Enlightenment" and "God"?

> **And when [Eve] saw that the tree was good for food, and that it was a delight to the eyes, and that the tree was to be desired to make one wise, she took of the fruit thereof, and did eat; and she gave also unto her husband with her, and he did eat.**
>
> **And the eyes of them both were opened, and they knew that they were naked...**
>
> **(Genesis 3:6-7)**

In Chapter 1 of the present book, we said that the above excerpt from Genesis was the basis of Oriental religion. Is it really so? Let's find out.

The Four-fold Noble Truth

In Buddhism[49], as in Western religion, there are numerous competing sects. But, also as in Western religion, they are bound together by certain common beliefs.

In the case of Judaism, for example, the bond is the Torah. No sect which renounced the Torah could ever be construed to be "Jewish". In Christianity, the bond is the universal belief in Yeshua himself. In Buddhism, the element common to all sects is the "**Four-fold Noble Truth**".

What is the Four-fold Noble Truth? Buddha regarded the world as a place of suffering. He discovered a pathway to salvation, and taught it to the world. The

---

[49] The source of most of the information in this chapter is the book *The Teaching of Buddha*. It is the most concise and all-inclusive Buddhist reference I know of, and I strongly recommend it to all. It is published by the *Buddhist Promoting Foundation* (Bukkyo Dendo Kyokai), and may readily be obtained from: The Society for Buddhist Understanding, 16925, E. Gale Avenue, City of Industry, CA 91745. The book is free, although a contribution is appreciated. The Internet address of Bukkyo Dendo Kyokai is: http://www.bdkamerica.org/.

Four-fold Noble Truth is a succinct statement of his teachings. The four aspects of this Noble Truth are:

1. **To know the fact of suffering and its nature.**
2. **To know the source of suffering.**
3. **To know what constitutes the end of suffering.**
4. **To know the Eight-fold Noble Path which leads to the end of suffering.**

Let us now briefly examine these four pillars of Buddhism.

The first element of the Four-fold Noble Truth: "The fact of suffering and its nature"

Buddhists believe in reincarnation. This means eternal life—*not* in heaven, but on earth. One way to understand this is by way of comparison with dreams. Just as the soul, at the moment of sleep, passes instantly into a dream world—a world possessing all the attributes and appearances of "reality" for the duration of the dream—likewise, Buddha teaches, at the moment of death the soul, clothed in a new body, "transmigrates" into another world.

The nature of one's new world is entirely determined by the collective moral weight, or "karma", of one's previous life. Good deeds in this world lead to a better life in the next, whereas evil leads only to increased suffering.

This endless cycle of birth, death and rebirth can be broken by only one thing: Enlightenment. Then, and only then, one is born into Nirvana, a state of eternal peace, corresponding to the Judeo-Christian Heaven.

In this scenario of Buddhism, even small affronts can become nightmarishly large. Take school, for example. Sure, in retrospect school was bearable. But suppose you had to do it over again—a thousand times? Or a million times? Or a trillion times?

Or how about the pain of giving birth, or of losing a job, or of going through a divorce, or of a serious illness? Sure, you got through these things once. Can you stomach them one billion more times? Buddha says:

> **"If one were to pile the ashes and bones of himself burnt in this everlasting transmigration, the pile would be mountains high; if one were to collect the**

milk of mothers which he suckled during his transmigration, it would be deeper than the sea". [50]

What a thought! In this view of life, even the smallest insult becomes magnified by repetition, growing into a living hell of sorts. Thus, Buddha teaches that the world is a place of suffering—not because it is a place of unendurable *torture*, but because it is a place of *endurable* but *ceaseless unrest,* which ends neither with sleep nor even with "death", but continues, without interruption, until Enlightenment is attained.

The Buddhist view recognizes life in this world as a succession of sufferings. The following is an arbitrary grouping into six categories, which embrace many of the sufferings between birth and death:

1. <u>Birth is suffering</u>. I present this fact without argument. Even the most chauvinistic of males, rejoicing over the birth of a male child, could not possibly expect anyone to believe that the "blessed event" was fun for the child also.

2. <u>To want something you don't have is suffering</u>. For most of us, the remainder of our lives, between birth and death, is a never-ending succession of desires. We crave wealth, property, sex, power—there's no end to the list of cravings. In general, there's no such thing as "enough". In some cases, this truth is self-evident. No matter how exquisitely delicious is the food you eat, you'll always be hungry the next day. No matter how enjoyable sex is, the desire for it, once unleashed, is insatiable.

In other cases, this truth may not be self-evident. Consider the case of wealth, for example. A man who has *removed* his desire for money is happy with a nickel, but a man who desires money can never have enough. John D. Rockefeller's biographers report to us that he had a consuming fear of poverty all the days of his life, even after he became the world's first billionaire.

Therefore, who among us has everything he wants? And every unfulfilled desire is a cause of constant unrest, until it is fulfilled.

3. <u>To have something, and to be afraid of losing it, is suffering</u>! So, if you are "blessed", and if you actually acquire that fortune you craved so deeply, then what? You have to protect yourself against loss! What if someone steals your money? What if the nation's currency is devalued? What if you spend too much and you can't get any more?

In fact, neither money nor any other material "possession" brings rest. On the contrary, to "have much" only means that you "have much to *lose*".

---

[50] *The Teaching of Buddha*, section entitled "Dharma", Chapter Four, "Defilements", part I, pp. 172-4.

The biggest mistake in the world today is the fixed belief that somehow, in the end, money will "find a way". The truth is that wealth and power only increase our unrest. It is never the other way around.

4. <u>Disease is suffering</u>. I present this without argument. With the exception of those who suffer from "Munchausen's Syndrome"[51], no one enjoys being ill.

5. <u>Old age is suffering.</u>

6. <u>Death is suffering.</u>

<u>Second element of the Four-fold Noble Truth:</u>
<u>"The source of suffering"</u>

Buddha teaches that the source of suffering is *desire and attachment* to the pleasant things of the physical world.

Is it possible to live in the world and *not* develop such attachments? Perhaps. The Hindu Bhagavad Gita, for example, states that a good person can, and in fact *must* act righteously, but without ever becoming attached to the fruits of his actions. For most of us, however, life is ruled by desires and attachments.

In certain cases, the relationship of suffering and desire is obvious. In others, it is subtle indeed. Let us examine the Buddhist view of life, as outlined above, and see how it relates suffering to desire. Once again we shall, perhaps arbitrarily, divide the sufferings of life into categories. Let us look at five such categories:

1. We said that *birth* was suffering. It is not easy to see the relationship between suffering and desire in the fetus, unless one makes an effort to consider life in the womb from the fetus' point of view. All the physical needs of the developing baby are fulfilled, but it feels no gratitude for this—the womb is presumably the only "world" it knows or remembers, and the peacefulness and security are taken for granted. But the fetus surely suspects that the world is bigger than that. It hears loud sounds from the outside, and it sees brighter and darker shades of light (if you don't believe this, go into a dark room with a mirror, and put a lit flashlight into your mouth—you'll be surprised at how much light penetrates the human body).

---

[51] Munchausen's Syndrome is the name applied to a psychological disturbance which causes people to seek medical care, including major surgery, when they are *not* sick. Such people have been known to intentionally fabricate false evidence of serious disease so as to persuade surgeons to operate on them unnecessarily.

Furthermore, the fetus can move, and it soon finds out that the greater effort yields the greater movement. It wants to stretch out fully, but it can't.

Although it cannot be proven, I believe nevertheless that the fetus "desires" to be born, even though it has no idea who it is, what the womb is, or what birth is. Although the fetus "has it all" from the physical point of view, it does not appreciate what it has, and it *desires more*. It is therefore in a state of unrest, or suffering.

<u>*It may therefore be concluded that life in the world, with all the suffering which that entails, arises from the desire to be born.*</u>

This is admittedly a rather subtle point. It may seem, to the Western mind, that the processes of fetal development and birth are purely physical, and proceed mechanically without the slightest regard for the fetus' state of mind. But when one reflects upon this from the Buddhist point of view, starting from the basic premise of reincarnation, then the conclusion becomes logically inescapable.

2. At the moment of birth, the fetus experiences a shock that no living person can remember. The physical trauma of being squeezed through the birth canal must be painful, because it can cause serious and permanent injury or even death to the baby. Once outside, the child is, for the first time, plunged into coldness. With the sole exception of brain-injured babies, it is a universal fact that the newborn infant cries hysterically. The crying continues until baby is dried off, warmed up, and comforted.

Thus, it is apparent that the new-born child, no sooner having been born, immediately desires to *have back* the comforts of the womb, where oxygen, food, and temperature were in perfect balance and were obtained without effort! But there is no turning back. The child can move only forward. Since it now earnestly desires to get back what it had before, it is thus in a state of unrest, or suffering. As a child, it can do only one thing—it cries.

If the child could somehow understand and accept the realities of life in the world, it wouldn't cry. But that is impossible for a child.

<u>*It may therefore be concluded that, immediately after birth, suffering arises from the desire to regain the physical comfort and security of the womb.*</u>

3. As a human being grows and develops, it proceeds from desire to desire. With respect to the innumerable physical cravings people feel, throughout their lives, the relationship to desire seems self-evident. We are constantly in a state of unrest because we desire more power, or more money, or more sex, or more physical comfort.

Buddha teaches that human desires may all be traced to the physical instincts, which have a strong will-to-live as their basis. This will-to-live is manifested internally as a need for the gratification of the physical senses; for the slaking of the many hungers and thirsts of the physical body.

When manifested externally, this same will-to-live becomes a desire for *knowledge* about our environment. It is through such knowledge that we gain power and mastery over our surroundings, so that we can learn where, when, and how our physical desires may be better satisfied.

In a society of human beings, the ultimate manifestations of the instinctual will-to-live are the desires for wealth, power, and influence.

Yet we have seen that the physical desires are ultimately insatiable, and that the possessions of wealth only increase unrest, never the opposite. *It may therefore be concluded that suffering arises from the desires and passions of life in the physical world.*

4. The sufferings of old age and death are also readily seen to be caused by desire. The aging process involves pain and loss of physical and mental power. We desire to have our comfort restored, as well as our physical strength. As death approaches, we desire the peace of eternal life in paradise, but, with few exceptions, we all fear death. What lies beyond? No one knows for sure!

Concerning the events which befall a person after death, the wisest of people throughout history have not agreed on any part of it, except for the one universal point of agreement, which is that we don't really die. In some way, shape, or form we go on after "death". The possibility that the next world might be unpleasant fills us with fear. We have no control over this at all!

Thus, somewhat like the fetus, who desires deliverance from the confines of the womb, we desire deliverance from the sufferings of this world. But we also fear that very same deliverance, for we know not what lies beyond. This state of conflict is usually resolved in favor of a clinging to life. The predominant desire is thus to hold onto what we already have, which has taken us a lifetime to acquire. Since the aging process moves inexorably forward, however, this desire cannot be fulfilled: We cannot forever hold onto what we have. The attempt to do so only causes our unrest to increase.

It may therefore be concluded that suffering arises from the desire to live, and to avoid the common calamities of old age and death.

Disease

5. I have segregated the subject of disease from the others, because it is most difficult of all to see how the suffering of disease can be due to "desire". The suffering of birth is due to the desire for the comfort and security of the womb—that's simple enough. The suffering of life on earth is due to the desire for more and more wealth and power—that's simple enough. The suffering of death is due to a desire to live—that's simple enough.

But how can the suffering of disease be due to desire? Desire for what? Isn't the pain of disease universal, and felt the same way by all people, regardless of how many "desires" they do or don't harbor?

The answer to the above question is "No". If one examines the suffering caused by disease, one finds that it is much more complicated than it seems at first. In fact, virtually all the suffering of disease is a manifestation of the other sufferings we have already considered. For example, when we become ill, we lose money. We can't go to work, and, additionally, we acquire medical bills. So, at the very least, *part* of the suffering is the same suffering we saw earlier: the suffering caused by desire for money and fear of losing what money we have.

If the illness becomes chronic, or causes lingering disability, our money-making capacities may be permanently reduced. So a serious illness can cause a serious or permanent loss of money. That hurts.

Imagine a person in the pre-antibiotic era with tuberculosis. This disease used to be so common it was called the "white man's plague", and the world was filled with the sounds of people coughing. A chronic cough eventually leads to wracking pain in the chest, spine, and abdomen, as the ligaments and muscles get stretched and torn from the constant trauma. Each cough becomes a painful torment. How much worse it must be for the victim if, in addition to everything else, each cough is also a painful *reminder* that the illness is robbing him of money, and plunging his family into the straits of poverty!

But it's far more than simply the pain of financial loss. A serious illness may get better, or it may get worse. Ultimately, it may kill us. We have already seen that fear of death causes suffering. So part of the suffering of disease is actually the suffering caused by desire for life, and fear of death.

Furthermore, an illness may temporarily restrict our abilities to obtain such physical gratifications as food and sex. If we are students, than the illness may restrict our continuing efforts to acquire knowledge; the very knowledge we will need to gain mastery over our environment. These restrictions can become permanent if the illness is severe enough. Thus, part of the suffering of disease is actually the suffering caused by desires for food, sex, knowledge, and other worldly commodities.

What if we had none of the above desires? Would disease really be all that bad? I have approached this question by creating an imaginary parable based on the life of the American President, Franklin D. Roosevelt.

Roosevelt was one of America's most beloved Presidents, although an unbiased consideration of his acts in office reveals that he did more to destroy Christian-based American freedom than anyone who came before him, replacing it with godless socialism. Be that as it may. He makes a good example for the lesson I wish to promulgate.

As everyone knows, Roosevelt had polio, and became a cripple. Evidently, that didn't stop him. Imagine, now, that prior to his illness, he had been visited by an angel, who gave him a *choice* between two options: (1) "perfect health", or (2) polio.

An easy choice? Wait, there's more. The angel of the parable explains it to Roosevelt thusly: If he chose "perfect health", he would be granted it, but he would have to live the ordinary life of the ordinary politician, with all its ups and downs. Like most of them, he would be striving endlessly for more power and money, with the constant threat of losing an election hanging over his head continually, like a sword. His career might end in success or honor, or, depending on circumstances, it might end in scandal and disgrace.

But if Roosevelt chose "polio", the angel explains, the deal would be different. He would be stricken with polio, but he would surely recover, and the angel guarantees that the damage would be limited to his legs. Thereafter, he would be *raised up* to become a great leader. True, he wouldn't be able to walk, but there would always be people to carry him around. Is that not what the Kings of old desired?

Furthermore, although he would not be able to obtain food for himself, he would always be provided with the finest of foods that this world had to offer.

Finally, he would, from his wheelchair, command the mightiest army ever assembled, leading it to victory over Adolph Hitler, one of history's most heinous criminals; to triumph in the greatest war ever fought. In short, he would live the life of a hero, and die beloved by all. What more could one ask of life?

Now, which of these two options would Roosevelt have chosen? Surely the second. In fact, I imagine he would have shouted "bring on the polio!".

When the disease actually struck, how much suffering would he experience? Not much, I'd wager. In fact, he'd probably be smiling. Why not? His disease was now a stairway to success. With each pang, he would be one step closer to his glorious destiny. He would have everything to look forward to, and no reason to fear either death or disability.

It may therefore be concluded that the suffering of disease has little "substance" of its own, but actually arises from the other desires we have already examined, namely the desires for wealth, for physical comfort, and for life itself.

Third element of the Four-fold Noble Truth: "The end of suffering"

Buddha teaches that the end of suffering is Enlightenment, which comes about through a total renunciation of all worldly desire and passion.

It is important to emphasize that there is a large difference between not *having* anything, and not *desiring* to have anything. Buddha does not condemn money, or sex, or political office, when these things are rightly employed. He only condemns desire and attachment.

If a person, seeing the world through the eyes of Enlightenment, perceives that there is a way to remove suffering from the lives of others, and if that way involves "having" certain things of this world, then there is no harm in having those things. Thus, to spend money to relieve human suffering would be an honorable practice in Buddhism. But to stockpile money in a bank account would be regarded as a manifestation of delusional thought, if one imagined that by doing so one could somehow avoid the unavoidable sufferings of disease, old age, death, and reincarnation.

Fourth element of the Four-fold Noble Truth: "The Noble Path which leads to the end of suffering"

Buddha recognizes that people cannot simply turn off desire, as if it were a water faucet. In order to assist people in attaining Enlightenment, he has shown mankind the "Eight-fold Noble Path" which leads to the removal of desire. Without a doubt, it is a difficult path to follow, and, in any given generation, few will make it to the end. Nevertheless, it is a worthy goal to strive for.

Although there are other paths to Enlightenment known in the Orient, such as the path of extreme asceticism of Mahavira, the Path of Buddha is a "Middle Path", avoiding extremes of sensuality on the one hand, and physical self-torment on the other. It is a Path whose validity has been recognized throughout the Orient, and to a lesser extent in the West as well.

We mentioned some of the steps in this Eight-fold Noble Path earlier, in Chapter 3 of this book. If you read that chapter, you will recall that the Noble Path is very similar to the "Ten Commandments" given to Moses on Mount Sinai. If this "Pathway to Enlightenment" sounds trivial, ask yourself how many people *really* follow these Commandments. When is the last time you read a daily newspaper which didn't contain at least one report of murder? How many people do you know who don't steal, even when there's no chance of getting caught? How many people do you know who are entirely free of envy? How about greed, jealousy, anger, rage or hatred? There's nothing trivial about either the Eight-fold Path, or the Ten Commandments.

If you doubt the existence of Enlightenment because you have "followed" the Ten Commandments and remain as unenlightened as you were before, think again. Have you *really* followed these Commandments? Or are you simply "patting yourself on the back" for a job "well done", when in truth, the job is not "done" at all?

The relationship between Enlightenment and God

If you can agree with what has just been said about the relationship between worldly suffering and worldly desire, then the relationship between Enlightenment and God will now be easy to grasp.

It is widely taught, by Judeo-Christian-Muslim spokespeople, that Buddha is an avowed atheist. This is not true. Here is what Buddha says about God[52]:

> "**In this world there are three wrong viewpoints. If one clings to these viewpoints, then all things in this world are but to be denied.**
>
> "**First, some say that all human experience is based on destiny; second, some hold that everything is created by God and controlled by His will; third, some say that everything happens by chance without having any cause or condition.**
>
> "**If all has been decided by destiny, both good deeds and evil deeds are predetermined, weal and woe are predestined; nothing would exist that has not been fore-ordained. Then all human plans and efforts for improvement and progress would be in vain and humanity would be without hope.**

---

[52] *The Teaching of Buddha*, section entitled "Dharma", Chapter One, "Causation", part II, pp. 86-88.

> "The same is true of the other viewpoints, for, *if everything in the last resort is in the hands of an unknowable God, or of blind chance, what hope has humanity except in submission?* It is no wonder that people holding these conceptions lose hope and neglect efforts to act wisely and to avoid evil".

Buddha, therefore, does not deny the existence of God. He simply says that salvation through God requires "submission". Is this different from the "Western" point of view?

It is very interesting, at this point, to review the meaning of the word "Islam". The word is derived from the verb...

...pronounced *as-la-ma*. It means "to submit". Therefore, a Muslim is one who *submits* (*i.e.,* totally) to God.

Extraordinary! The Muslims; those most aggressive and warlike of monotheists, who drove Buddhists out of the Middle East with the edge of the sword...the Muslims actually *agree* with Buddha about the "nature" of God-worship! It involves complete *submission*.

Therefore, the difference between monotheists and Buddhists is not a difference in the way they perceive God. It is simply that Buddha chooses not to "submit". Why?

This question can most assuredly be answered. First of all, it is extraordinary that Buddha even acknowledged the existence of the One God, because the available history of the period shows that God was hardly known in India at that time. India was a nation of idol-worshippers, each idol representing one of a multitude of regional and petty gods.

As we mentioned in Chapter 3 of this book, the Upanishads were just starting to be written, and the Bhagavad Gita had not yet been started, around the period of Buddha's life on earth. The current Hindu concept of One God was therefore not yet known. Furthermore, word of the existence of the Western God — the God of Abraham — was also just reaching India at that time.

But it is apparent that the God of Abraham was not well-known to Buddha, since he describes God as "unknowable", whereas the Bible says that God can be *known* through prayer, and through faith.

Therefore, we may conclude that Buddha's Path to Enlightenment was not against the God of Abraham, but against the stone "gods" of ancient India. As for the true God, Buddha did not know enough about Him to proceed *against* Him. Buddha's method of attainment of Enlightenment simply proceeded without any reference to the Almighty at all.

If you still remain convinced that Buddha is the enemy of God, consider your own sin. Your Original Sin, that is. Let us review, again, the history of Original Sin:

> **And when [Eve] saw that the tree was good for food, and that it was a delight to the eyes, and that the tree was to be desired to make one wise, she took of the fruit thereof, and did eat; and she gave also unto her husband with her, and he did eat.**
>
> **And the eyes of them both were opened, and they knew that they were naked...**
>
> (Genesis 3:6-7)

What was it that drew Eve to the Tree of Knowledge of Good and Evil? What, for that matter, was the "nature" of mankind's Fall from Grace?

The above passage from the Bible says that the Tree was "good for food". That means that its fruit had a nice taste. In our review of Buddhist thought, did we not make mention of desire for food?

The Bible says the Tree was a "delight to the eyes". In our review of Buddhist thought, did we not make mention of desire for gratification of the physical senses?

Finally, the Bible says the Tree was "to be desired to make one wise". That is, it gave Eve "knowledge". In our review of Buddhist thought, we showed how the gratification of physical desires was achieved through manipulation of the external world, which requires *knowledge* of the ways of that world.

But, as living beings in this world, what *sort* of "knowledge" is it which we attain to? What, exactly, did Adam and Eve "buy into" when they ate from that Tree? And what did they "opt out of"?

It is clear, from a reading of Genesis, that Eve did not eat from the Tree specifically because she desired to be removed from the presence of God, although that *was* the result. Clearly, she ate from the Tree because she wished to gratify her *desires*; the same desires we have been considering in this chapter: desires for wealth, pleasure, power—the power which comes from worldly knowledge—and, last but hardly least, the desire for life itself. ***Not*** the eternal life promised by Yeshua (Jesus) to all those who believe, but the incarnate life of those who live in the physical world of desire, passion, and illusion.

Isn't it self-evident, then, that the following of Buddha's advice, namely to remove desire, would amount to nothing more or less than a direct reversal of Original Sin? That is, Adam and Eve did not fall from Grace because they "renounced God", but rather because they *embraced desire*. Therefore, says Buddha, "embracing God" is not the only way of returning to Grace: it may also be regained through *renouncing desire*.

Isn't it also true, therefore, that Buddha's Path to Enlightenment is not so much a "renunciation of God" than it is an *acceptance of responsibility* for what we did in the Garden of Eden, and a recognition that what we did must be *undone*?

<u>Buddha's parable of "desire" as a "poison arrow"</u>

To further understand Buddha's point of view, consider the following parable which he told[53] two-and-a-half millennia ago:

> "Suppose a man were pierced by a poisoned arrow, and his relatives and friends got together to call a surgeon to have the arrow pulled out and the wound treated.

> "If the wounded man objects, saying, 'Wait a little. Before you pull it out, I want to know who shot this arrow. Was it a man or a woman? Was it someone of noble birth, or was it a peasant? What was the bow made of? Was it a big bow, or a small bow, that shot the arrow? Was it made of wood or bamboo? What was the bow-string made of? Was it made of fiber, or of gut? Was the arrow made of rattan, or of reed? What feathers were used? Before you extract the arrow, I want to know all about these things.' Then what will happen?

> "Before all this information can be secured, no doubt, the poison will have time to circulate all through the system and the man may die. The first duty is to remove the arrow, and prevent its poison from spreading.

> "When a fire of passion is endangering the world, the composition of the universe matters little; what is the ideal form for the human community is not so important to deal with.

> "The question of whether the universe has limits or is eternal can wait until some way is found to extinguish the fires of birth, old age, sickness and death; in the presence of misery, sorrow, suffering and agony, one should

---

[53] *The Teaching of Buddha*, section entitled "The Way of Practice", Chapter Two, "The Way of Practical Attainment", part II ("Search for Truth"), pp. 296-298).

first search for a way to solve these problems and devote oneself to the practice of that way".

This parable explains Buddha's position on God and Enlightenment. Although Buddha does not specifically state that it was God who shot the "arrow of desire" at mankind, a moment's reflection reveals that desire is nothing more or less than the *flame* of the "flaming sword" which God placed at the "east of Eden" (Genesis 3:22-24). Had God allowed Adam, having become desirous, to remain in Eden, he would have "put forth his hand, and [taken] also of the Tree of Life". Therefore, there is no return to the state of Grace, called Enlightenment, until the desires which caused the Fall from Grace have been thoroughly removed. When desire has been removed, the flaming sword east of Eden will cease to exist.

Thus, desire, which surely rules mankind, was the "arrow" of this parable, and the "arrow" was surely shot by God, who rules over all, and who alone is empowered to do such things.

Yet Buddha does not inquire about the "nature" of God. He simply teaches how the arrow may be removed. It may be removed in the same way it was introduced. In the Garden of Eden, Adam and Eve "bought into" the world of desire. To return to Grace, we must *renounce* those very same desires.

We did not wish to remove ourselves from the presence of God when we ate from that Tree; we simply wished to *live*, which means to experience fulfillment of worldly desires. Our spiritual ancestors, Adam and Eve, proceeded impulsively, having no thought about the consequences of their actions: Entering into the world of desire automatically and determinedly cut us off from the Presence of God, Who does not dwell here. Therefore, simply *wishing* to be back in God's presence is surely not enough to get us there. We must first renounce the desires we "bought into" when we ate from that Tree.

Is this teaching the same as, or equivalent to "accepting Jesus Christ as one's Lord and Master"? Or is the teaching "antichrist"? Many proselytizing Christians would hastily assert the latter, without even considering the matter. You decide. Here's a clue: Yeshua said:

> **The foxes have holes, and the birds of the air have nests; but the Son of man hath not where to lay his head.**
>
> Matthew 8:20

I never said it was easy.

Here's another clue:

Not every one that saith unto me, Lord, Lord, shall enter into the kingdom of heaven; but he that doeth the will of my Father which is in heaven.

Matthew 7:21

Difference between worldly "knowledge" and Enlightenment

God planted a "Tree of Knowledge of Good and Evil" in the midst of the Garden of Eden. Man disobeyed God's order and ate from that Tree. What was the *nature* of the knowledge which we sought, and what sort of knowledge did we leave behind?

We require "knowledge" of the physical world in order to live in it. Nowadays, people get all excited when they think to themselves that space travel or DNA-based genetic engineering will make us "gods". God forbid! What a curse, that we should have to "conquer" a whole physical universe, especially one which is constantly changing, and which seems to grow much larger every time we think we have looked to its outer (*or* inner) limits!

The highest form of knowledge in this world; the form which is the most uplifting of all the sciences, is the science of knowledge of God. We call this "religion". But is this form of "knowledge" really satisfactory, or, by itself, *sufficient* for the attainment of salvation of the soul?

In the Garden of Eden, I submit to you that man had no "knowledge" of God in the sense in which we use the word "knowledge" down here. God was known to man in the Garden because He was present, we were present, and we "knew" Him through His very Presence. There were no books! There were no Bibles!

In fact, there was no "religion" at all in the Garden of Eden. Religion is for outcasts from the Garden, whose knowledge of God can only be the sort of murky "knowledge" which is acquired through the consideration of data collected by the five senses, and processed by the sluggish human mind.

Was Buddha wrong to chose to ignore such unsatisfactory sorts of knowledge in preference to his own Path to Enlightenment? Let us now consider the difference between the *true* knowledge of Enlightenment and the *worldly* knowledge with which we are more familiar in our day-to-day lives.

True knowledge may be likened to the knowledge one has about one's own leg. Now, legs are made for walking. Excepting the case of a cripple, sooner or later in a man's life he will stand up and walk. Doesn't that man, at that point, "know" his leg, in the truest sense of the word "know"? That is, does he really need to learn the Latin names for all the muscles, or the pathways of the flow of blood, or all the nerves, bones, or ligaments?

To put it differently, what would you rather have: a fully-functioning leg which you "knew" nothing about, or a crippled leg whose parts you could all name? Which is the real "knowledge", to know the leg through actually having and using it, or to be able to name all its parts?

This situation is quite analogous to "knowledge" about God. On earth, members of militant religious sects, who are inclined to murder everyone who seems different to them, would have you believe that you can have "knowledge" of God by reading *their* book, or by reading *their* Bible, or by following *their* example. They claim that by joining *their* sect, you can learn all the names of all the "parts" of God, and thereby attain salvation. But don't believe it.

The knowledge of God which we can attain to on earth is, at best, that which is described in the Bible as "looking through a glass darkly". Or, to state this position by analogy to the human leg, we, in "buying into" Original Sin, have done the spiritual equivalent of cutting off our own leg, and replacing it with a prosthesis.

In getting expelled from the Garden of Eden, we have traded in the real "leg" of the Presence of God for the "prosthetic leg" of Bible-based worldly religion. To regain a real leg, we must find a way to remove Original Sin. In the meantime, we must hobble along on the prosthesis.

This does not mean "throw away your Bible". It means that it's not enough to just own a copy, or to read it with half-a-heart. It must be read whole-heartedly, and its teachings, which are often subtle, must be welcomed and brought into that special place deep within the soul where you yourself cannot go during ordinary everyday consciousness. Perhaps Buddha can help you do this. Or perhaps not. It will depend upon your own individual makeup.

As for Buddha, he took it upon himself to remove desire so as to attain Enlightenment. In his case, it took six years. During that time he lived as a homeless monk in the wilderness. He now brings to us a Path to follow, solely so that we may, perhaps, be spared some of the sufferings he endured. If we refuse to accept his teaching, because we are afraid that God will be "mad" at us, then we will have to find our own way to remove desire. This is surely "reinventing the wheel".

The "New Covenant" of the End Times: Removal of Desire

If you still cannot see any relationship between the Oriental concept of attainment of Enlightenment by removal of worldly desire, and the attainment of Salvation by complete submission to the will of God, then consider the "New Covenant" spoken of by the Hebrew Prophets. The Prophet Jeremiah, for example, said:

> **Behold, the days come, saith the LORD, that I will make a new covenant with the house of Israel, and with the house of Judah:**
>
> **Not according to the covenant that I made with their fathers in the day [that] I took them by the hand to bring them out of the land of Egypt; which my covenant they brake, although I was an husband unto them, saith the LORD:**
>
> **But this [shall be] the covenant that I will make with the house of Israel; After those days, saith the LORD, *I will put my law in their inward parts, and write it in their hearts*; and will be their God, and they shall be my people.**
>
> **And they shall teach no more every man his neighbour, and every man his brother, saying, Know the LORD: for they shall all know me, from the least of them unto the greatest of them, saith the LORD: for I will forgive their iniquity, and I will remember their sin no more.** [Jeremiah 31:31-34}

And what does this *really* mean; to "write the law in our hearts"? It means this: You do not steal. *Not* because you're afraid you might get caught—*not* because you're afraid that you might go to Hell after you die—but because you do not even *desire* anything which belongs to another person.

To "write the law in our hearts" means to not commit adultery. *Not* because you're afraid you might get caught—*not* because you're afraid that you might go to Hell after you die—but because you do not even *desire* to have sex with your neighbor's wife. Did Yeshua not say "whosoever looketh on [another man's wife] to lust after her hath committed adultery with her already in his heart"? (Matthew 5:28).

Without a doubt, the great prophets of old had personally triumphed over worldly desire. Do you think, even for a second, that men like Moses or Yeshua could have been "bought off" with a new car, or with a fleeting sexual encounter? You *know* that they couldn't have been! Do not, therefore, reject Buddha's teachings until you have fully considered all the facts. After that, if you still cannot accept Buddha, be prepared to recreate everything he accomplished, because you will never be admitted to the Kingdom of Heaven while you cling stubbornly to worldly desires.

Chapter 12

A Symbolic Representation of the World's Religions

The world has been at war with itself since the Beginning. How can we stop killing each other?

We can start by confessing that we are rebels against the LORD, even to this day. We fell from grace in the Garden of Eden, every one of us. Once precipitated into this physical world of insatiable desires, we made gold our "god".

The LORD established a Covenant with one man, which was a milestone in our road to salvation. But we made even the Covenant with Abraham a source of strife. Who are the children of Abraham? Each of us screams *"Me!"*.

It may be seen, however, that in actuality the Covenant was made with *all* of Abraham's children; Jew, Christian and Muslim. By the process of logic[54], it might be deduced that this Covenant, at least in part, even extends to Hindu and Buddhist, which would certainly be consistent with biblical prophecy:

> **[And the LORD said unto Abraham]...I will bless them that bless thee, and curse him that curseth thee: and in thee shall ALL families of the earth be blessed.**
>
> **Genesis 12:3**

Note the blessing extends to ALL families, not just some.

We have seen that the religions of the Orient, in the forms in which they now exist, all started more or less simultaneously, and that this start coincided with the expulsion of a vast number of Jews from Israel, many of whom settled in the same nations of the Orient where the new religions arose. I have shown (Chapter 3) that such coincidences cannot be explained except as deliberate acts of God, proving mathematically that God is the Father of Oriental religion. Furthermore, I have shown you the exact verses in the Bible where Enlightenment is defined (Genesis, Chapter 3), and described the relationship between Enlightenment and God.

---

[54] See, for example, Genesis 25:6, "But unto the sons of the concubines, which Abraham had, Abraham gave gifts, and sent them away from Isaac his son, while he yet lived, eastward, unto the east country". The identity and location the "east country" is not specified.

I showed that the descendants of King David have been scattered throughout the world, and that the Messiah, the son of David, could come from anywhere, including China. Indeed, it would be hard to find a person in any country who did not have the minimum requisite genetic relatedness to David to not qualify as a lawful heir, incredible though that may seem.

We have seen that the fundamental precepts of the Christian religion are actually Jewish precepts, and that the Christian religion is the inevitable outcome of Jewish prophecy; prophecy which is still unfolding.

We have seen that disagreements about the "nature of Christ" were settled by carefully-crafted political consensus at the Christian Councils, where the predominantly Caucasian Bishops of Europe triumphed over the generally darker-skinned Bishops of the Middle East and Africa in establishing a rigid doctrine of the divinity of Christ. Subsequently all dissenters were excommunicated. Later, the various groups of dissenting Christians found a common ground in the theology of the prophet Muḥammad, coalescing to give rise to the now-unified body of Islam: the inevitable response to the extreme position taken by the European Bishops at the Councils, and a permanent "thorn in the side" to the Christian Church ever since.

Finally, we have seen that, just as no one church can properly claim to be the exclusive "Church of God", neither can any one race claim to be the "People of God". On the contrary, we reviewed the history which shows that in the past, races now considered to be "culturally inferior" were actually culturally *superior*, which can only be attributed to the hand of the LORD Himself, Who raises or lowers a race or nation according to its devotion to Him.

I will now offer a graphic representation of the relationships between the various churches which the LORD has raised up in the earth:

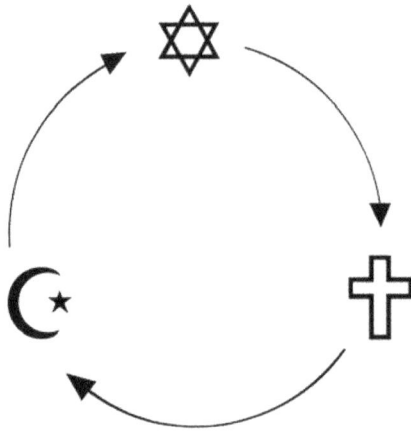

Symbolic representation of the world's religions

This diagram shows a Jewish star, a Christian cross, and an Islamic crescent moon on the same continuous circle. The critical aspect of this representation is not the mere coexistence of all three in the same figure, but the arrows, pointing continuously in a clockwise direction. What do they mean?

Christianity was the inevitable outcome of Judaism, since the prophecies which formed the original substance of Christian theology were, and remain, *Jewish* prophecies. Therefore, there is an arrow pointing from Judaism to Christianity.

Islam was the ultimate outcome of the political bullying at the Christian Councils, where those Bishops who favored the view that Yeshua was God overcame, and eventually excommunicated, those predominantly darker-skinned Bishops who favored the view that Yeshua was a man. This latter group, scattered at first, coalesced later into Islam. Since the extreme view adopted by the European Church at the Councils caused the appearance of Islam to be inevitable and unavoidable, there is therefore an arrow pointing from Christianity to Islam.

The Muslims, in the course of time, rejected the Bible—Old and New Testaments alike. Yet Islam exhorts its followers to "remember" Biblical history. They cannot possibly do this if they don't read the Bible, since the Bible is the only history of itself which exists. Therefore, it is incumbent upon all believing Muslims to study the Bible, which is, after all, the history of their own religion. This is the only way in which Islam can truly become complete. Therefore, although they have not done this, nor indicated any intention of doing it anytime soon, there is nevertheless an arrow pointing from Islam back to Judaism, completing the circle.

What lies within the circle?

In the picture above, I have depicted the inside of the circle as being empty. That is not the whole story, however.

When a human being wishes to seek God within himself, he generally turns to one of numerous paths which have been defined and described by the prophets. Each of the monotheistic faiths has a counterpart, called a "mystical" part, which can be depicted as existing *within* the circle.

In the case of Judaism, the mystical part is called "Kabbalah". This esoteric branch of Judaism is usually traced back to Simeon ben Yohai, an ascetic of the 2nd century AD. This was the period when the Rabbis were completing the final compilation of the Old Testament, and declaring religion to be "complete".

Simeon rebelled against this rigid formalism. He spent 13 years meditating in a cave, emerging in a terrible-looking physical state, covered with sores, but allegedly glowing with a spiritual light of great intensity. His teachings are said to be contained in a book called the *Zohar* (although some believe that much of this huge work was written by Moses de León (1250-1305), a Jewish mystic living in Spain under the Moors).

The essential teaching of Kabbalah is that the whole of the Torah, revealed to Moses on Mount Sinai, is a huge parable with a deeper underlying meaning. That meaning was known to Moses, but for others it was hidden until the work of the Kabbalists. To them was revealed, for the first time since the days of Moses, a means of establishing a personal relationship with the Creator.

Although many Kabbalah centers exist in the world today, no one seems to be emanating visible light anymore. Kabbalah has apparently become relatively undemanding, compared to ben Yohai's 13 year cave ordeal.

In the case of Christianity, there is no formal name for the mystical branch of that religion, but it is contained in the practices of the Christian monasteries. The monastic movement began early in the Christian era; that is, during roughly the same historical period as Simeon ben Yohai lived. Again, this was a period when religion, in this instance the New Testament, had been formalized and declared "complete".

The original goal of the first Christian mystics, such as St. Anthony of Korma in Egypt (251-356 AD), was to go into the desert, as Yeshua (Jesus) had done, and to somehow receive the Holy Spirit directly. Anthony soon attracted followers, but many of the ascetic monks who went into the desert to practice solitary meditation received demons rather than the Holy Spirit, and went mad. Clearly some sort of support system would be needed.

Monasteries, such as that of the Egyptian Coptic Christian St. Pachomius (290-346 AD), were created in which a program of balanced work and meditation could be practiced under the supervision of an abbot.

As in the case of the Kabbalah centers, there are few examples, these days, of people who emerge from monasteries physically emanating the light of the Holy Spirit. The monasteries themselves, however, can hardly be faulted, since they are vital centers of Christian charity and other good works.

The mystical branch of Islam is called Tasawwuf in Arabic. In America and Europe it is called *Sufism*. The Sufis are the "whirling dervishes" of legend, whose activities, ridiculous-looking as they may seem to Americans, are actually methods of obtaining direct personal experience of God.

Like its Jewish and Christian counterparts, Sufism began almost immediately after the "finalization" of Islam into a fixed legalistic and world-oriented way of life, *i.e.* at the end of the 7th century. The relationship between Sufism and traditional Sunni and Shiite Islam has been uneven, vacillating between acceptance and persecution.

The greatest of the Sufi writers was al-Ghazali (1058-1111) who, in the midst of a brilliant academic career, disposed of all his wealth and took up a life of poverty. He established a monastic commune where many disciples joined him. Eventually, however, he returned to academic life, at the urging of his colleagues. Having in their minds an Islamic tradition, that every century a so-called "renewer of the life of Islam" would arise, his colleagues persuaded him that for the century which was about to begin, *he*, al-Ghazali, was that renewer.

Subsequently, he produced a large quantity of literature. His greatest work, "The Revival of the Religious Sciences", achieved wide acceptance, and brought Sufism into the mainstream of Islamic thought.

Although al-Ghazali taught that theology was inferior to mystical experience, there is little evidence to suggest that the Sufis fared any better in developing a well-defined pathway to Enlightenment than did their counterparts in Kabbalah or Christian monasticism.

Our original diagram may now be modified, to show where the mystical branches of each religion lie:

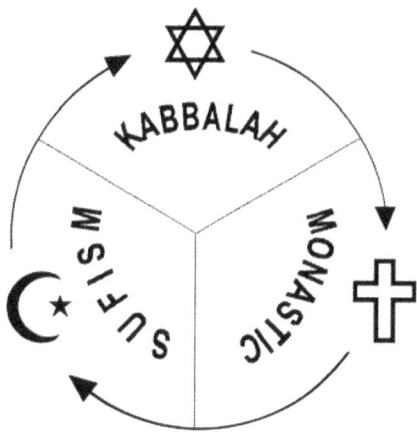

<u>Where is Oriental religion in this diagram?</u>

In the religions whose primary teaching is Enlightenment, the mystical aspects of Judaism, Christianity, and Islam become the entire focus, sometimes almost to the complete exclusion of theology. Thus, the entire inside of the circle is the province of Oriental religion:

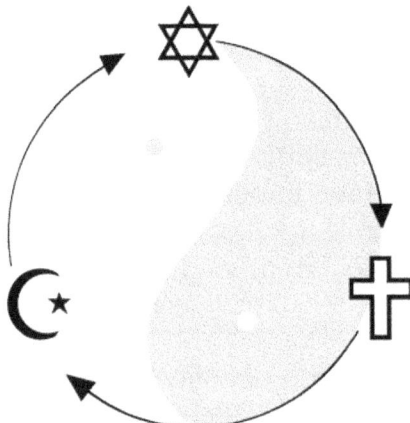

In this version of our picture, the yin-yang symbol fills the entire center of the circle. Because this symbol is so familiar to Westerners, I have arbitrarily chosen it to symbolize the whole of Eastern religion, encompassing Buddhism, Hinduism (in its mystical aspects), Taoism, and other forms of Enlightenment-seeking practice. It also encompasses Kabbalah, Christian mysticism, and Sufism.

Some years back I went through a period where I inquired, of all the Oriental religious teachers whom it had been my privilege to meet, as to whether they, or anyone they knew personally, had attained complete Buddhist Enlightenment. None of them answered in the affirmative.

One of those negative answers stuck in my mind. It was given by a devout Buddhist who was employed at the East-West Bookstore in New York City. He said that no one had obtained complete Enlightenment since the Enlightenment of Buddha himself, and that no one would until Buddha's return.

The closest anyone has come to Enlightenment, he said, was to see and experience "the Void". I understood this to mean *non-existence;* the absence of all.

The Void is neither joy nor sorrow; neither the brilliant world of Enlightenment toward which many strive, nor the dark world of ignorance in which we all live. It is simply....nothingness.

If you try to picture it in your mind, you cannot. It is exceedingly difficult for one who *exists*, to grasp the true meaning of *non-existence*.

Now Enlightenment, like God, cannot be described in words or pictures. The Void, on the other hand, can be graphically depicted, since that graphic depiction would be...nothing.

Therefore, since I cannot graphically depict Enlightenment, and since the closest I can come is a graphic depiction of the Void, I shall return to our original picture showing the relationships between Judaism, Christianity and Islam, and proclaim that the whole of Oriental religion is in the drawing by implication, since the Void, *i.e.* nothing, is contained in the center.

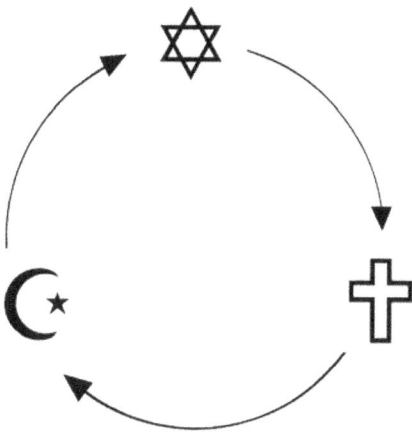

Conclusion

We have thus seen—contrary to what most of us are taught in childhood—that the religions of the world are *not* really competing ideologies at all, but rather parts of a large puzzle which cannot be completed until all its component pieces are put in their proper places.

Those who love and worship money as a "god" are working feverishly to preemptively establish the "New World Order" — a godless world banking dictatorship whose exterior is gorgeous, but whose inside is Hell. A thoughtful consideration of the principles laid out in the book you now hold in your hand suggests a totally different sort of "New World Order"—a "world order" under **God**. This "**New** 'New World Order' " is described in the next chapter.

But if the principles of peace already laid down in this book cannot be accepted, and if the people of the world are determined to continue trusting in Gold instead of **God**, and to continue to fan the flames of overbearing arrogance, hatred, and base pride, then there is no point in considering any further principles.

Chapter 13

The *New* "New World Order"

Just about everyone has heard the phrase "New World Order" at this point[55]. What is it? Although its advocates present it as a flowering paradise, in reality it is nothing more than a thinly-concealed world banking dictatorship; a modern-day feudal manor of sorts. If it succeeds according to plan, then a tiny percentage (certainly less than 5%) of the world's population will control essentially all the world's wealth, and the rest of us will be hopeless and powerless serfs, existing only for the benefit and amusement of our "leaders".

You must take heed that should this dreadful plan go to completion, there will be no place to run or hide from it. Historically, the overthrow of evil governments has revolved around resistance groups, which have usually operated from outside the oppressed country. When the world has reduced itself to one huge, miserable nation, where will your resistance group be? The Moon?

As documented in many books, this "New World Order" has decisively rejected God. Whether or not its leaders serve Satan directly is moot. They have steadily acquired power through the centuries by doubting God, while believing fully in the power of money, influence, and corruption. The Bible teaches that you can't serve God and Mammon. You've got to choose — it's either one, or the other.

The "religion", if you could call it that, of the "New World Order" is *Secular Humanism,* a godless philosophy which states that wisdom and charity spring forth "spontaneously" from the human heart and mind, which are "pure". If so, then we are already in "heaven". Do *you* feel like you're in "heaven"? All true religions teach the diametric opposite of this. True religions, whether Eastern or Western, teach that mankind has *fallen*, and needs to be raised up morally. No one was born "pure".

Clearly, the New World Order "religion" has *not* worked. The United Nations notwithstanding, the world has become more violent, more polluted, and more

---

[55] If you haven't yet read about the "New World Order", I would recommend starting with Pat Robertson's book by the same title (publisher, Thomas Nelson, 1991). Although the agenda of the One-World atheists has advanced considerably since then, Robertson's eloquence, and the timelessness of the subject matter generally, render the book as valuable today as when it was written.

depraved with each passing year. It becomes more and more evident, as time marches on, that secular humanist "compassion" is merely a cover story, to conceal the rapidly-developing dictatorship of the rich.

I shall now show how all of the ideas and concepts which we have discussed in previous chapters can be put together to form the basis for a *New* "New World Order"; one based on belief in God, and faith in the Bible as His true word. As we shall see, this will lead inevitably to the fulfillment of the promise embodied in the title of this book, "Whoever You *Thought* You Were...You're A Jew!" — provided that the definition of the word "Jew" is sufficiently traditional to encompass all those who have elected to be in God's dominion.

We may start with our pure mathematical demonstration of the undeniable relationship between the Diaspora of Jews from ancient Israel and the simultaneous appearance of Greek and Chinese philosophy, and of the Enlightenment-based religions of the Orient (see Chapter 3). Since Christianity and Islam are self-evidently Judaism-based, it follows that *all* the world's major faiths and philosophies (including modern Judaism itself) are, and always have been, derivatives of ancient Judaism.

This has always been overtly apparent with respect to the religions of the West. With respect to those of the East, this truth is also apparent, but only to those willing to look, and willing to believe the evidence of their senses. To deny this truth is as hopeless as denying that $\{2+2 = 4\}$, but, LORD knows, the stiff-necked will do this and more, if they think it will increase their wealth and power.

Therefore our World Order too shall be a derivative of ancient Judaism. It shall be so by virtue of the drawing-upon of all the faiths which ancient Judaism has given rise to. These, in total, represent a formidable well-spring of knowledge and wisdom. In this new world we will be as shepherds, each different, and each tending to different species of flocks, but all drawing from the same inexhaustible well.

But do not think that I envision a world of men in black robes and top hats, with long rabbinical beards. We seek a much more fundamental definition of "Judaism" than is embodied in any particular dress code, or contained within any one tribe or sect. For the term "Jew" is not an ethnic or racial term, and never was. In fact, most of today's Jews are *not* descendants of David or Solomon at all, but more likely the descendants of Russian and Eastern European converts[56].

Furthermore, the "Lost Tribes" of Israel were never really lost. Rather, in full view, they quietly assimilated themselves into the cultures of virtually every

---

[56] There are several virulently antisemitic "sources" of information on this subject, but the subject is not, in and of itself, antisemitic at all. If you wish to learn more, I recommend Arthur Koestler's "The Thirteenth Tribe" (Random House, New York, 1976).

nation in this world, and into the four corners of it. Our definition of "Judaism" must take into account the ways of *all* those nations, insofar as those ways may be seen to have resulted from the encounter of a people with God.

The "Line of David", from which will spring the final Messiah, is therefore virtually *everybody* now (see Chapter 4). It would, in fact, be hard to find a person who was *not*, according to the strict laws of inheritance, a legal descendent of the Line of David. This is true whether the skin is black or white, and whether the epicanthic fold of the eye slants up or down.

We found, rather, that the only durable definition of the word "Jew", in its most historically fundamental sense, was this: a member of a brotherhood of believers in God, as was defined by Jesus when his disciples interrupted him to inform him that his siblings and his mother were waiting to see him. He motioned to the people he was addressing and said:

> **...whosoever shall do the will of my Father which is in heaven, the same is my brother, and sister, and mother. (Matthew 12:50)**

This is a most worthwhile definition of the word "Jew"; one which ought to be acceptable to all, since it defines no race, or church affiliation. We have made no effort to define Jesus' Messiahship, or his relationship to God the Father, leaving that instead to the numerous Christian and Muslim sects, each of which has its own point of view, and each of which will surely want to take as much time as necessary to further refine that point of view for whatever benefit and edification can be had thereby.

Our *New* New World Order will accept, by default, whatever secular world government the people should choose in their wisdom or foolishness. But it will *not* define a world religion. Rather, our concept of world religion will be that of Micah, when he prophesied that...

> **"...in the last days it shall come to pass, that the mountain of the house of the LORD shall be established in the top of the mountains, ... and people shall flow unto it. And many nations shall come, and say, Come, and let us go up to the mountain of the LORD,...all people will walk *every one in the name of his god*, and we will walk in the name of the LORD, our God, forever and ever." (Micah 4:1-5).**

Therefore, people will practice whatever religion they choose to practice, but with the overt recognition that *God* — regardless of the Name by which He is called, or the pronoun by which He is described — is the source of the inexhaustible well-spring of knowledge and wisdom which we just spoke of.

As for the establishment of a world religious authority, to impose restraints on the evil tendencies of secular government, we shall turn to that deepest of thinkers, for whom the subject of government was a matter of constant preoccupation, and for whom no problem could be deemed solved until it had been explored to the fullest depths of its nature, and to the complete exhaustion of all possible human ability to explore those depths; such solution seeming to represent, as it were, the result of a search which seemed to be almost interminable..........like the sentence you have just read.

I refer, of course, to the great Greek thinker Socrates.

We have reviewed Socrates' concept of government (see Chapter 3), which was published in Plato's "Republic". Socrates believed in the desirability of an "aristocracy of the best". This was conceived of as a government under the reigns of a self-propagating class of "true philosophers".

He conceded that such a thing was not likely to arise in a corrupt world such as the one in which he lived, but he maintained stubbornly that it was an *attainable ideal* to be striven for.

I therefore propose that finally, after all these centuries, we give Socrates a chance. Should we study a man's ideas for over 2,000 years and *never* implement them? Let us at last have a government under the reigns of the "true philosophers". But who are they today? Where are they to be found?

Before answering this question, let us dwell further on the concept of "checks and balances". In modern times, this arose as a Masonic concept, appearing as it did among the Founding Fathers of the United States. These Fathers, recognizing the potential for corruption in an unchecked monarchy, created a *three-part* government consisting of an "executive" branch (the President), a "legislative" branch (Congress), and a "judicial" branch (the Supreme Court). These three parts were designed, quite deliberately, to be *at odds* with each other. Each one was indestructible by the other two, although individual members of any of the branches could be removed from office by a determined effort of the others.

This system worked for several centuries. It no longer does, but that is not because the concept was wrong. It is because all three branches have become subservient to the godless "New World Order" of money, influence and corruption. We are, in reality, a *one*-party system — the party of Mammon, which is rebellion against God. We therefore must create the equivalent of a second "party"; one which opposes the currently unopposed power of the bank. We must do this quickly, because it will soon become difficult or impossible to do anything at all.

To our *New* New World Order, then, we shall introduce the concept of "checks and balances". But we shall not base our system on the government of the United States. We shall base it on the government of ancient Israel under David and Solomon. Biblical scripture says that the House of David shall rise again. *If it is to be so, then **let** it be so.*

The right way to run a government

The best model I can think of for a successful state was Israel under King David. He was so effective in defeating the nations around him that his son, Solomon, was able to live a lifetime as the world's supreme monarch, without ever having to dispatch an army to fight a war.

What would the world have been like if Solomon had not defiled the Jewish religion by allowing his 900 wives and concubines to re-introduce idol worship to Israel? The removal of idolatry had been, after all, the reason for the existence of Israel in the first place. God had promised the land of Israel to the Jews, but only if they would promise, in return, to worship Him and Him only. So Solomon, with a wave of his hand, *canceled Israel* just like you, with a press of a finger on a television remote control, change a TV station.

In order to begin to find out what the world would have been like if Solomon had not ruined the nation of Israel, we need to re-create a government patterned on the government of ancient Israel before its Civil War. That ancient government had "checks and balances". The concept, therefore, was *not* invented in America, but rather *re-emerged* here 2500 years later.

Whereas the checks and balances in America consist of three branches of government, the checks and balances of Israel consisted of only two branches. Those who think that this is an insufficient number ought to bear in mind that the invisible world government which already rules today has only *one* branch. Would we not be better off, therefore, to add another?

The first branch of the government of ancient Israel was the monarchy, which combined all three of our modern branches of government into a single all-powerful King, with all the tendencies toward corruption which that entails. His power was very effectively checked, however, by the other branch of government in ancient Israel: the priesthood.

The power of the priests was immense, and it would be a serious error to underestimate it. In the Bible, when Saul, the first King of Israel, failed to wait for the High Priest Samuel to arrive to offer a sacrifice to God, burning instead his own profane offering on the altar, Samuel learned of it and was furious (I Samuel 13:13-14). Immediately upon his arrival he told Saul that the office of King would be taken away from him — and it was!.

The exact mechanics of the relationship between the High Priest and the King are never made clear in the Bible, but it is beyond a doubt that the King greatly feared the High Priest and could not proceed without his approval, except at great risk to his person and his office.

This relationship was demonstrated repeatedly during the reign of David, at which time the High Priest was Nathan. David consulted with Nathan about all matters of great importance, and when David committed the sin of adultery with Bathsheba, also murdering her husband in the process, Nathan prophesied terrible things against David. All of them came to pass.

It is important to realize that the ferocity with which Nathan attacked David would never have been permitted in the average monarchy of ancient times, or of the middle ages either. This was a system of "checks and balances" which was effective indeed. Even in the United States today, freedom of speech notwithstanding, few people would have the nerve to attack a President the way Nathan attacked David.

After Civil War split ancient Israel into two Kingdoms, the Northern Kingdom, called Samaria, turned against God and against the Priests of God. It became a crime to publicly worship according to the Jewish tradition. But the danger of challenging the authority of the Jewish High Priest was not diminished even then! This was dramatically illustrated in the interaction between Elijah[57], one of the greatest of all the Prophets, and Ahab, one of ancient Israel's most evil Kings. Elijah was a constant threat and menace to Ahab, because the King would not heed the word of the LORD.

In every encounter between Elijah and Ahab, the King was bested. God had brought drought and famine on Samaria, which the King blamed on Elijah, whom he sentenced to death. Undaunted, the prophet successfully avoided capture for three years, then boldly showed himself, openly challenging the King's 400 Priests of Baal to a contest. After defeating them, he slew them all. He prophesied terrible things against Ahab and his evil wife, Jezebel, all of which came to pass.

King Ahaziah, who succeeded Ahab at his death, sent messengers to inquire of the oracles of the pagan god Baalzebub[58] concerning his health. Elijah heard of this act of royal apostasy, and was wroth. He prophesied Ahaziah's death. In

---

[57] The exploits of Elijah are presented in I Kings chapters 17-21, and II Kings chapters 1-2.
[58] Baalzebub is a contraction of "Baal", the god of the ancient Canaanites, and "zebub", which means "fly". So Baalzebub, a name often used as if it was synonymous with "Satan", is actually a translatable phrase meaning "Lord of the flies".

retaliation, Ahaziah twice sent fifty soldiers to seize Elijah, but the prophet caused all hundred of them to be burned with fire. The third group of soldiers sent to seize Elijah fell on their knees and begged for mercy. So Elijah let them live, but Ahaziah died according to his prophecy.

Not a true theocracy; not a true monarchy

The idea of patterning a government after the government of ancient Israel may seem utterly objectionable to the modern mind. Some people are sure to find the lack of separation of church and state to be tantamount to a "theocracy". But ancient Israel was *not* a theocracy: the King was entirely in charge. He never aroused the wrath of the High Priest unless he went against the Jewish Law.

Nor did the Priest have any direct power over the King or the people. He could neither enact nor invoke any secular laws, and he had no private police or army to enforce his decrees. His power was strictly limited to the use of his moral *influence* and *good example* to try to steer the nation in the right direction.

At the same time, Israel was not a pure monarchy either. Even though the High Priest had no direct political power over the King or the nation, he had immense *indirect* power through his role as chief spokesperson for the Faith. If he prophesied in the name of God, and if his warnings were not heeded, he could "rock the whole boat" until the nation either went back on the right track, or was scuttled completely.

Ancient Israel was thus a nation which was either going to follow the ways of God, or not exist at all. During the period that it followed God's ways, it prospered and grew to be immensely powerful and prosperous. Whenever ugly personal ambitions, arrogance, and lust steered the nation toward apostasy, the High Priests and Prophets railed mightily. For several centuries, they succeeded in getting the nation back on the right track whenever it strayed. But when even *their* influence failed, the nation was destroyed and dispersed.

How can we learn by their example? That is, how can we learn to emulate those features of life in ancient Israel which made it rise up to great heights of power and prosperity, while avoiding the pitfalls which brought it down?

Obviously, no one will ever again willingly accept the rule of an absolute monarch. But, if we are to learn from the mistakes of the past, one thing we must learn is that *the government, whatever its structure, must be subservient to God.* It is not enough for our governments to be "democratically" elected. Unless all knees bow to God — by whatever Name you wish to call Him, and by whatever pronoun you wish to address Him — we will be enslaved even by rulers whom we *think* we chose.

The Council of Priests

Because the Bible promises that the house of David shall rise up again, we shall accept the word of God and pattern our World Order after ancient Israel. The modern equivalent of the all-powerful monarch, analogous to King David, has already been established. It is not, of course, a King as such, but a seemingly-democratic body of politicians, the United Nations. Will it survive? It doesn't matter. If the current U.N. goes the way of its predecessor, the League of Nations, then rest assured that the bankers will raise up another seemingly-democratic organization in its stead.

The "check and balance" against this fully-corruptible monarchy-equivalent shall be the analogue of the ancient Israeli High Priest. But it cannot be a *single* priest, because the Bible does not prophesy that there will *ever* be a single religion. Therefore, it must be a *Council* of Priests.

This, then, is the answer to the question "where are the 'true philosophers' now?", which we asked earlier when we were considering Socrates' "aristocracy of the best". They are to be found in a *Council of Priests*, to be drawn from the ranks of the world's long-established religions of God. This includes those religions which seem, on the surface, to be "atheistic", but which can be shown, on more thoughtful consideration, to have arisen as new manifestations of the Jewish religion, when it was scattered during the Diaspora of 600 BC.

The Council of Priests is therefore the manner in which the Socratic ideal of "aristocracy of the best" is to be *overlaid* on the existing concept of world government of today, as embodied in our as-yet-godless "United Nations". This Council will take no active part whatsoever in the day-to-day operations of government. It shall exist strictly as a moral watchdog, and as a supreme advisory board, to guard the world against the never-ending tendency of secular government to stray from the ways of God.

The power of the Council of Priests shall be in every way comparable to the power of ancient Israel's High Priest. Since it will be a living manifestation of the most deep-seated and ancient moral beliefs of all the people of all the countries of the world, its proclamations will carry enormous weight.

You may think that without an army, or police force, or war chest of money, the Council of Priests will be powerless, but if that's what you think, you're wrong. Every criminal denies all wrongdoing, and each one endeavors mightily to give the impression of standing on high moral ground when apprehended and put on trial. Without the illusion of "high moral ground", how can the criminal carry on his work? Only the most depraved of humanity will proceed with evil in broad daylight, and without a cloak of false righteousness, such are readily cut down. The appearance of righteousness is all-important to the perpetuation of evil.

When a Council of Priests, representing the entirety of the moral fiber of mankind, unanimously condemns a nation's actions, where is the "moral high ground" upon which that nation will stand? There is none! With the wrath of the entire world against it, that nation will go down.

On the other hand, if the Council is divided among itself, then its opinions will carry little weight. There's nothing wrong with that. If its members can't agree, than the problem at hand has not ripened to the point of being subject to a definitive solution. In that case, more time is needed.

Our "*New* New World Order", therefore, shall introduce a *Council of Priests*, the equivalent of Socrates' *philosophers*, which shall play no part whatsoever in government under normal conditions, but which shall exercise power over the governments of the world through the weight of its moral authority, which cannot be challenged.

The Council of Priests, then, shall be our "check and balance" over the power of the United Nations, or whatever new secular humanist organization rises up in its place if it fails.

Aren't "modern" governments supposed to have "separation of Church and State"?

To many westerners, the idea of imposing the will of a religious Council on the workings of a secular United Nations may seem inappropriate, or even frightening. But a moment's thought reveals that it is utterly essential that this come to pass.

God the Father shall surely not, Himself, set His holy Foot down in our defiled world, to lead us by the hand to salvation. It follows that if there is to be an ultimate worldly authority which will guide people, then the people must *choose* that authority themselves, and *accept* it once the choice has been made. *Whom*, or *what* shall it be?

A democratic popularity contest *cannot* determine whom our ultimate authority will be. If the American experience proves anything, it is that the people will vote for any candidate who promises to give them "presents". Whether or not these promises can be kept is *not* a consideration. The mere promise of worldly reward is sufficient for most people. Where will these presents come from? Ultimately, the pocket our hand is in is our *own*. We have reached the point where there's nobody left to steal from except ourselves.

Worse still, whether or not the platform on which the popular candidate is running is a *morally acceptable* platform is also *not* a consideration in American elections. Political candidates today have no binding authority imposed upon them by any Church or other moral force. Thus, if it seems pleasing to average citizens to vote for a particular program-of-the-moment, they will vote for it, even if the program boldly proposes depriving the innocent of life, liberty, and pursuit of happiness, the very bases of our Declaration of Independence.

It is self-evident to most sensible people that a *moral authority* must oversee our lives. Since there is no existing religion whose priests have the slightest power over people outside their own church, it follows that a *Council of Priests* must be this authority. Who else is *more* qualified?

Shall we place our fate in the hands of politicians entirely? How many politicians have *you* ever heard of who were incorruptible? How many politicians will steadfastly refuse to take a bribe?

Or shall we place our fate in the hands of secular, university-based philosophers? Secular philosophers careen wildly in their digressions from morality. Communism, which died in less than a century, was the work of secular humanist philosophers. Shall we labor to create a government which has an expected lifetime of less than a century? Nazism, too, came about with the full approval of certain secular philosophers. Are *these* the people who should be our "moral overseers"?

Or shall we put our fate in the hands of military leaders? Who is the "enemy" we are fighting against in a world government, that our goals should be achieved through violence? Have we not met the enemy, and is he not *us*? What wisdom, then, can guide military leaders to an "enemy", if there is no one left to subdue except ourselves?

In the Book of Isaiah and elsewhere, God says that He does not favor "sacrifice", but rather "justice and mercy". Perhaps, then, we can place our lives in the hands of secular *judges* in the name of "justice". But have *you* ever been in an American court of "justice"? I have, on altogether too many occasions. Most of our judges are utterly *corruptible*. There is no *moral authority* to which they defer, and wisdom does not necessarily spring forth spontaneously from their breasts. The highest "laws" operative in the American courtroom are the "laws" of *expedience* (since every judge's calendar is overloaded with cases) and *politics* (since judges are either elected or politically appointed). Without a doubt, there is a third "principal", *profit,* which is operative in at least some courtrooms.

Since honest judges earn less than ordinary lawyers, it is inevitable that some — pray not most — will be corrupted by money.

In the entire history of the world, no nation or empire has ever survived for very long without a moral overseer which operated independently of the political process. We are now speeding blindly and uncontrollably toward a world in which there will be essentially only *one* nation, with no moral overseer. This is a formula for sure disaster. But if we are to add an overseer, who shall it be? It cannot be the priests of any one church, because only the members of that church will listen to them. Therefore it must be a *Council of Priests*, drawn from the various churches of the world. But which churches? The world is full of churches, and we need a method to decide which ones truly represent God's plan.

That same God, in His grace and mercy, has given us that method, by showing us an infallible mathematical proof that a certain set of churches came about through His will. This, then, is our Council of Priests, and this shall be the fulfillment of the prophecy of Micah:

> "...in the last days it shall come to pass, that the mountain of the house of the LORD shall be established in the top of the mountains, ... and people shall flow unto it. And many nations shall come, and say, Come, and let us go up to the mountain of the LORD,...all people will walk *every one in the name of his god*, and we will walk in the name of the LORD, our God, forever and ever." (Micah 4:1-5).

Why isn't the United Nations, by itself, "good enough"?

There have been two attempts to create a decent and humane world government so far. The "League of Nations" died a perinatal death. After that, we were saddled with the current "United Nations".

The U.N. is a seriously flawed organization. Certainly, its health-related activities, and its activities on behalf of children in the third world, seem commendable enough, on the surface at least. But as a monitoring organization for human rights on a world-wide scale, it is truly pathetic. The "Security" Council is a tool of the superpowers, and the General Assembly is a place where blocks of corrupt nations attempt to use their voting power to deprive their "enemies" of property and freedom.

The U.N. still lacks sufficient military power to enforce its decisions, and it's a good thing, because its decisions are corrupt. What went wrong?

As Pat Robertson eloquently pointed out (in his book *The New World Order*), the words of Isaiah — *out of context* — are carved into the U.N. wall in New York:

> **"THEY SHALL BEAT THEIR SWORDS INTO PLOWSHARES, AND THEIR SPEARS INTO PRUNING HOOKS; NATION SHALL NOT LIFT UP SWORD AGAINST NATION, NEITHER SHALL THEY LEARN WAR ANYMORE."**
> **(Isaiah 2:4)**

These words were dissected out from the body of a Biblical passage whose meaning is *entirely different* than the words out of context seem to suggest. We needn't reproduce the entire passage — even a few lines suffices to show what the U.N. *left out*:

> *"FOR OUT OF ZION SHALL GO FORTH THE LAW, AND THE WORD OF THE LORD FROM JERUSALEM. HE SHALL REBUKE MANY PEOPLE;*
>
> **THEY SHALL BEAT THEIR SWORDS INTO PLOWSHARES, ... (etc.)"**

So the missing ingredient which the Founding Fathers of the U.N. left out was *God*. Evidently, the founders must have considered that to be a small thing. But when Isaiah talked about "beating swords into plowshares", he was talking about *God*, not metallurgy.

What is a Proper Structure for a New "New World Order"?

Unless the "New World Order" is an order *under God*, the future will surely be as Hollywood insists on portraying it — a miserable world in which a small super-elite class rules over a global mass of starving peasants who are without hope or substance, and utterly powerless to change anything.

How can a world order be under *God*, when every nation seems to have a different religion? The first step is to recognize that the religions which have survived in the world today emanated from the inexhaustible well-spring of knowledge and wisdom which is the God of ancient Israel. This must include the Oriental nations commonly held to be "atheistic" by Westerners. Did they really come from God? They certainly did. We have seen (Chapter 3) that this is established with absolute certainty by the coincidence of their simultaneous appearance during Israel's Diaspora of 600 BC.

The second step is to recognize that God loves no race, but respects individuals and nations alike which bow to His authority. We have seen (Chapter 10 and elsewhere), that profound faith in God has raised up many nations, both black and white, and that profound love of material wealth has likewise *destroyed* many. When God destroys a nation, He does so without prejudice based on race or ethnic origin.

Once these things are understood, and it is seen that God has dispersed His wisdom among many nations, and that His wisdom is too wide and too broad to be fully contained in any one of them, then the logic of a "Council of Priests" becomes apparent.

Our *New* New World Order, then, will add a "Council of Priests" to the current concept of a secular humanist "United Nations". The power of this Council will arise from its ability to focus the entire moral weight of world opinion against corruption in the secular government, analogous to the similar roles of the High Priest of ancient Israel, the Christian church in Europe and the Americas, and the Islamic church in Asia and Africa.

Location and Structure of The Council of Priests

There is only one conceivable location for a Council of Priests, and that is Jerusalem. But the place where its members meet should be neither on, nor immediately adjacent to the Temple Mount, which should not be defiled by secular politics.

The Council should consist of nine members, representing nine delegations. Listed in historical order, that is, the order in which their respective religions arose on earth, they are:

       1. a Jew
       2. a Hindu
       3. a Buddhist
       4. a Zoroastrian
       5. a Taoist
       6. a Confucian
       7. a Jain
       8. a Christian
       9. a Muslim

Each of these members — regardless of the size of the populations they represent — shall have a single vote. You may already suspect that there is something "undemocratic" about this. You are right. This is not a popularity contest.

First of all, if this Council was a "democratic" voting body, it would needlessly duplicate the function of the secular United Nations. Does the world really need *two* corrupt voting organizations?

Secondly, if it was a "democratic" body, its nine delegations would have to be represented *not* by a single member each, but by multiple members, in accordance with world population statistics. But then the larger delegations, some of them representing over 1 billion people, would control the fate of the world entirely, and the other inhabitants of earth would be voiceless.

Consider this: If the Council of Priests was a democratic voting organization, then there would be a strong incentive for the Christian and Muslim delegations to collaborate on any issue which did not involve the "nature of Christ". It is not at all difficult to imagine them freely abandoning the majority of their traditional principles if, by doing so, they could forge an unholy Christian-Muslim alliance; an alliance which would be a formidable voting block. The same sort of collusion would likely arise between Hindus and Buddhists. This is corruption, and it illustrates the main *danger* in a Council of Priests, which is the danger of *cooperation between the priests for political advantage.*

That is why a nine-member Council, *not* based on population, but rather with every member having the same vote as every other, is essential. These men (or women) will be required, by their delegations, to fight fanatically for the principles of their respective faiths. There is little that they will agree upon, except, perhaps, the most basic of moral precepts, as embodied in such concise sources as the Ten Commandments.

Some may object to the granting of equal power (*i.e.*, to the representatives of these traditionally-hostile religions) on the grounds that little will be accomplished at the meetings of this Council. That is good. History proves that most change is for the worse. With nine constantly-squabbling religious leaders who rarely agree on anything, we may rest assured that the world will stay on a straight course for a long time.

The Council of Priests is not the final developmental stage of human morality, but merely a stage. It will, however, be the reigning moral force in the world until the person called Messiah (by any name, and by any pronoun) arrives. The Messiah, being the voice of God in the world, speaks only truth, and requires no approval from human councils.

His arrival, however, is not something which we can plan for. If and when it happens, it will do so on a timetable which arises from outside this world. It is entirely beyond the powers of men to bring such things about.

Why these nine religions?

The nine religions listed above as constituting the Council of Priests are the complete set of long-established world religions which may be seen to have arisen from ancient Judaism either directly (as in the case of Christianity and Islam), or else as a result of extraordinary events taking place during the first Jewish Diaspora of 600 BC (see Chapter 3). This included modern Judaism itself, which, in the form into which it began to evolve after the end of the Babylonian exile, must be regarded as being itself a branch of the ancient trunk established by Noah, Moses, and the Prophets.

I, for one, therefore consider these nine to constitute the complete Word of God on earth, such Word not otherwise being fully embodied in any one of them.

Many people will object to one or another of these members, but nothing can be done about that. No system will be pleasing to everyone. The fact of the matter is that none of these religions is going to "go away". Nor would I, for one, desire that any of them do so. As already pointed out, the fact that these nine will disagree about almost *everything,* and thus move to action only very slowly, is surely for the best in a world where impulsive and thoughtless action, motivated by greed and lust, has repeatedly led nation after nation to disaster.

What about all the other religions of the world, besides these nine? And what about *new* "religions"?

The above list does *not* include such practices as the worship of nature, idols, animals, "mother earth", crystals, or anything else that is in "heaven above, or that is in the earth beneath, or that is in the water under the earth" (Exodus 20:4). Did the human race evolve to its present state so that we may sink again to the depths of depravity from which we were so painfully extricated?

Nor does it include any of the host of twentieth century psychiatrically inspired would-be religions, such as the "Church" of Scientology. Nor does it include the overt worship of Satan, which ought to be reinstated as a crime, as it once was in days gone by.

The situation may arise, however, in which a legitimate new religion may appear, or in which a fringe sect of an existing religion may wish to join itself to the main delegation. This must be left to the discretion of the main delegations themselves. Without a doubt, these will be loath to consent to the introduction of new members. If, in the eyes of the *other* delegations, such consent is being unreasonably withheld, then perhaps by a unanimous vote of the other eight, the reluctant delegation might have its hand forced.

This system will make it difficult indeed for new religions or sects to join themselves to the Council, but this is infinitely better than opening the doors to every world-worshipping group of trouble-makers who knock.

Furthermore, it's just a matter of time before the Church of Satan buys its way into the world government. Why hurry things? According to scripture, Satan will get in anyway. Let's not roll out a carpet for him.

The United Nations — the secular branch of government

It is highly *undesirable* for priests to actually get involved in the day-to-day workings of government.

It might appear that a reasonable model for a democratically-elected political deliberating body, to minister to the affairs of the world on a day-to-day basis, already exists in the current United Nations. But I have my doubts. The organization is virulently antisemitic, and the Bible says:

> Now the LORD had said unto Abram..."I will bless thee...and I will bless them that bless thee, and curse him that curseth thee...".
>
> Genesis 12:1-3

Clearly, the unrestrained Jew-hating in the U.N. General Assembly places the entire organization at risk for receiving the curse of God, and the fact that Muslims bless Abraham will not save them. They only bless him from their standpoint of being spiritual descendants of his son Ishmael, whereas the spiritual descendants of his brother Isaac (*i.e.*, Jews and Christians) they curse.

It is neither my place, nor within my power to change the U.N. But I can make a few suggestions which, if implemented, would improve the organization. These suggestions are unlikely be followed, but I make mention of them nevertheless.

Location

The *location* of the United Nations is a matter of symbolic and practical importance. Whereas it is inconceivable for a Council of Priests to be located anywhere other than Jerusalem, a secular world government ought *not* be there, but rather elsewhere.

If the religious and secular branches of government are to "check and balance" one another, then let them start to establish some distance between them by being physically located in different places.

If it doesn't matter where an organization is located, then the exact location of the site is unimportant. To the extent, however, that a particular location can affect the organization for better or worse, one should be selected which will provide whatever benefit can be had.

The current location of the U.N., at Turtle Bay in New York City, is suspiciously close to Wall Street. There is nothing whatsoever which is democratic, egalitarian, or ecumenical about this location. I was not present when New York was selected, but I suspect that either the location "selected itself" (according to such spurious logic as "where *else* but New York?"), or that it was selected by the original U.N. delegates because they wanted to carry out their deliberations in an environment of luxury and decadence. This sort of self-serving approach to government is not likely to provide a basis for a world-ministering point of view.

An excellent site for the world government would be the area adjacent to the point where Russia, China, and Mongolia meet (see Figure 13-1). This area is the geographic center of the Asian continent.

It lies within a region which has been the center of power of numerous empires of the past (Sogdiana, Transoxania, Uiger, Mongol, and the Muslim Empire of Timur). Furthermore, it is the world's religious "center of gravity". Look at Figure 13-1: The Buddhist world stretches south and east, the Muslim world south and west, and the Christian lands of Russia and Europe lie north and west.

It is a place which is sparsely populated, and considered by most people to be very remote. All the better — only those serious about the business of government will desire to be there.

It was my hope, before starting the researches for this book, that there would *already* be a city in this area where Buddhists, Muslims and Christians have lived together, side-by-side, for centuries, and that such a city would be a natural choice for the world government. But there is no such city. The cities coming closest to this ideal are the small cities of southern Siberia between Kyzyl and Lake Baykal, but they are separated from the rest of the world by the mountain ranges of northern and western Mongolia. It seems that circumstance has allowed the three faiths to *separate* themselves to an extraordinary degree, according to the "dictates" of *geography* — namely the deserts and mountain ranges at the common borders of Russia, China and Mongolia.

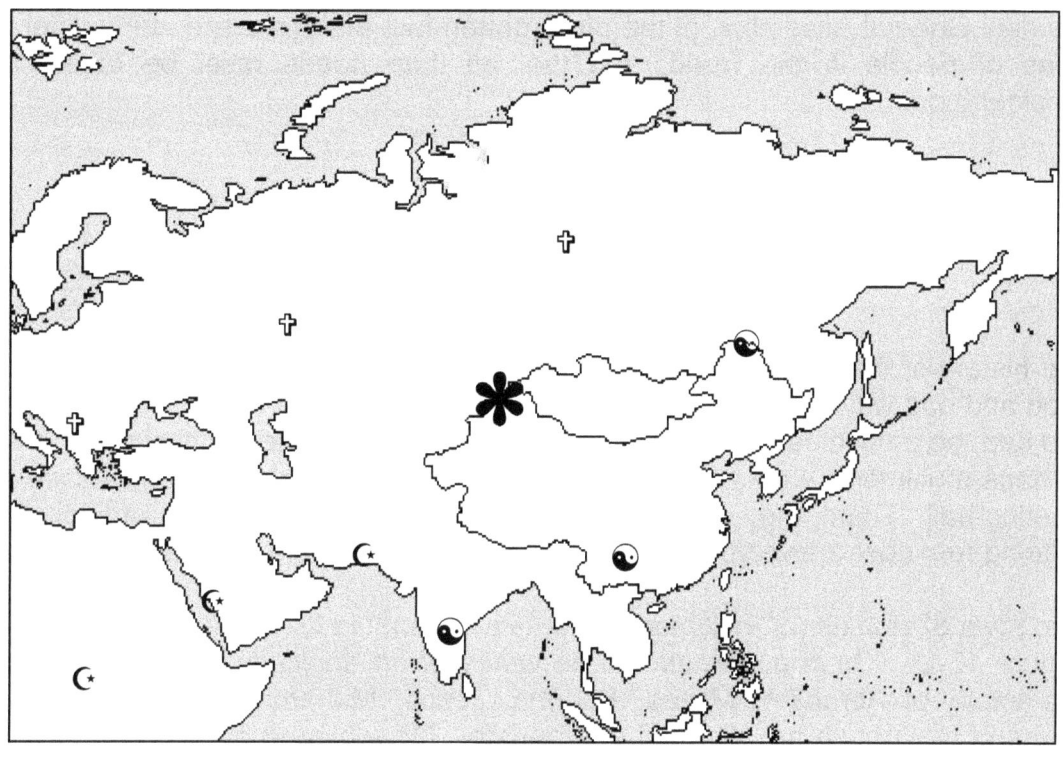

Figure 13-1. Preferred location for the secular branch of world government. The point where Russia, China and Mongolia meet (∗) is the geographic center of Asia. It has also been, in the past, the seat of many great empires.

Furthermore, this point is the "center of gravity" of the world's religions. Islam predominates to the South and West, Buddhism (and other Oriental religions) to the South and East, and the Christian lands of Russia and Europe lie to the North and West.

Perhaps it would be for the best that an entirely *new* city be built, somewhere in southern Russia or Northern China, in the area adjacent to the mountains of western Mongolia. In such a city, the imminent proximity of Christian, Muslim, and Buddhist nations would hopefully be a constant reminder, to all delegates to this new General Assembly, of the oft-forgotten fact that there are many different types of people in the world, and that all their needs must be taken into consideration.

Architecture of the meeting hall

The history of the world is long enough to have provided numerous examples of good and bad ways to live. I propose that the best of these examples, both good *and* bad, be embodied in *statues*[59] (or, for historical characters difficult to portray, perhaps multimedia works of abstract art) to be placed in the General Assembly meeting hall. There, they will constantly "watch over" the delegates, providing an ongoing reminder to everyone that certain world tactics *work*, and certain *don't*.

Two rows of statues (or multimedia alternatives) should flank the seats of the hall (Figure 13-2). On one side should be works of art depicting or suggesting the characters of Abraham, Moses, Buddha, Jesus, Muḥammad, and whichever others of like nature are deemed appropriate. On a plaque at the base of each statue should be an inscription such as:

| ABRAHAM — EMPIRE OF 4000 YEARS |

or

| MOSES — EMPIRE OF 3200 YEARS |

or

| JESUS — EMPIRE OF 2000 YEARS |

---

[59] The suggestion of statues in the meeting hall arouses the ire of some, who charge that any statue is "idolatry". See, however, Numbers 21:8-9, I Kings 7:18-25 and I Kings 10:18-20, each of which describes statues depicting living things.

Figure 13-2. Statues in the General Assembly. It is hereby proposed that the hall in which the delegates meet be flanked with statues, or alternative works of art depicting great persons of history.

On one side are to be icons symbolizing individuals who have created Empires of faith which have survived, prospered, and grown through the years. At the base of each shall be a plaque, bearing an inscription such as "Abraham — Empire of 4,000 Years", or "Muḥammad — Empire of 1,400 Years".

Opposite them, on the other side of the hall, shall be statues of individuals who have created empires by physical force. With the sole exception of the Roman Empire, none of these lasted even a century. Some, like that of Adolf Hitler, burst like bubbles after less than a decade ("Adolf Hitler — 'Empire' of 6 years").

The purpose of these works of art is to provide a constant reminder to the delegates of what *succeeds,* and what does not, from the historical standpoint. Surely, statues, by themselves, cannot "create" justice. But a proposal to deprive the weak and defenseless of their property will, just as surely, be more *difficult* to "put over", when it must be delivered under the "watchful eyes" of those who were masters of deprivation, all of whom are now on the side of the hall occupied by creators of empires which have long since vanished from the face of the earth.

Some will protest, calling this "idolatry". But the General Assembly is going to be adorned with decorations of some sort anyway, be it statues, paintings, or other works of art. That being the case, the decorations, like the works of the delegates themselves, ought to represent a diligent effort in the right direction.

Opposite, on the other side of the hall, should be statues of people like Alexander the Great, Julius Caesar, Genghis Khan, and Adolf Hitler. These should bear similar inscriptions:

> **ALEXANDER THE GREAT — EMPIRE OF 11 YEARS**

> **ADOLPH HITLER — EMPIRE OF 6 YEARS**

> **KARL MARX — EMPIRE OF 74 YEARS**

These statues are meant to be a constant reminder to all those in the hall: The empires of faith, on one side, are all thousands of years old and going strong. The empires of violence rarely lasted even a century. Some, like Hitler, burst like bubbles after six years. Let the delegates to this General Assembly look, and constantly be reminded.

Surely, statues do not bring about justice. But if a hall is to be decorated at all, then let its decorations represent a diligent effort in the right direction.

Voting rules of the General Assembly

In the absence of a Council of Priests, the veto power of the U.N. Security Council is necessary to check the virulent anti-Israel insanity which runs rampant in the third world. Someday in the future, when each nation no longer has a sword pointed at every other nation, the following voting rules would bring about a more democratic process in the General Assembly. They are based upon the principles established by the United States Constitution.

The current government of the United States of America has two houses of Congress: the "House of Representatives" and the "Senate".

This two-house structure is designed to preserve the rights of the individual states of the Union regardless of the sizes of their populations, while also giving voice to the masses of people regardless of their States of residence.

All new law must pass through the House of Representatives, where the most populous states have the most delegates. This house, then, represents the will of the *majority*.

The Founding Fathers of America, recognizing that the majority could overwhelm the rights of a small state whose citizens dissented, also therefore required that the new law pass through the *Senate*, where every state has exactly 2 votes, regardless of the state's size. This house, then, represents the will of the *states*, regardless of how large or small they may be.

This system has worked fairly well in America, and it can be the basis for a more fair voting practice in the General Assembly. In every issue of major importance, it can be required that a majority of the worlds *nations* concur, and that the majority of the worlds *people* also concur.

This can be brought about by counting the votes in each ballot *twice*. The first count can be referred to as a "national" ballot, where every country gets one vote. This gives voice to the rights of individual nations. The same ballot can then be tallied a second time, with every nation's vote being *multiplied* by a factor reflecting that nation's population. This can be referred to as a "popular" vote. Like the voting in our American House of Representatives, this would give voice to the rights of individual people, regardless of nationality.

Thus, for example, in any matter where China and India agreed, the weighted "popular" vote on the matter would be likely to pass, since there are 2 billion people in these 2 countries alone. But if the rest of the world was opposed, the measure wouldn't pass the "national" vote, where the single votes of China and India would carry no more weight than those of the tiny nations of Cyprus and Luxembourg.

Conversely, a matter which was approved by most nations could still be defeated in the weighted "popular" vote by the opposition of India and China. Thus, the rights of 2 billion people could be protected, regardless of the fact that they all live in a single small corner of the world.

Conclusions

This completes our brief discussion of a *New* New World Order. The main difference between our *New* Order and the current one is that the new imposes a religious restraint upon the world. This is a shield, guarding against the harm which will otherwise surely be done by the gold-worshipping world government which is now quickly moving toward total power.

We have also made some proposals for modifying the current secular humanist United Nations, but these proposals are only of secondary importance. The world can cope with much error on the part of its political leaders, but there will be no life worth living unless God is earnestly sought out and accepted as the true sovereign over all.

Chapter 14

Epilogue:
The Ark and the Third Temple

I. Establishment of the nation of Greater Israel

Since Israel is the spiritual center of the whole world, its boundaries, politics and religious structure matter greatly. The fate of Israel, the fate of the other nations under their "New World Order", and the events associated with the coming of Messiah are inextricably linked together.

The prophesied boundaries of Israel in the End Times encompass a substantially larger land mass than is now occupied by the Jewish nation. These boundaries are stated many times in Torah:

> Genesis 15:18
> Exodus 23:31
> Numbers 34:1-12
> Deuteronomy 1:6-8
> Deuteronomy 11:24

The most detailed description is the one from Numbers, but it is hard to comprehend, because it is stated in terms of place-names whose locations are now largely unknown. All the above references, however, are in agreement about the northern border. It is the river called, in Hebrew, "P'rath"[60], although it is sometimes referred to simply as "The River". All commentators agree that this is the Euphrates River.

The southern boundary of Greater Israel is more uncertain. Here is its description from the book of Genesis:

---

[60] Ashkenazi Jews pronounce this name "P'ras", and Sephardics "P'rat".

> **In the same day the LORD made a covenant with Abram[61], saying, Unto thy seed have I given this land, from the river of Egypt unto the great river, the river Euphrates.**
>
> Genesis 15:18

What is "the river of Egypt"? Some say it is the Wady al-Arish, which is a small seasonal stream in the Sinai Peninsula, whose mouth opens into the Mediterranean Sea about 20 miles west of the current Israeli border. This interpretation would appear to be a tribute to "political correctness", since the more likely interpretation — which is, however, far more troublesome in terms of current Arab-Israel relations — is that the "river of Egypt" is the Egyptian equivalent of the Euphrates, namely the Nile.

That, in fact, is the opinion of those rabbis who most fervently maintain belief in the imminent coming of Messiah.

If Greater Israel does, as I believe, extend from the Nile to the Euphrates, then it must contain a good many Arab Muslims. How can such a state come into existence when the region is wracked by war, as it has been since the dawn of recorded biblical history?

The answer is that it can't. Fortunately, however, it may not have to. Greater Israel, in my opinion, *already exists;* it's just not recognized.

Whether or not this is so depends entirely upon whether or not the current Nation of Israel is indeed the risen House of David, or whether, on the other hand, it is merely the latest pretender to that throne. Which is it?

That is a question whose answer is a "work in progress". Without a doubt, the current Israeli political, legal and social order is anti-biblical, which accounts almost entirely for all the bloodshed we read about day after day. Why shouldn't hundreds of thousands of displaced "Palestinians" be angry that their land has been occupied by people alleging themselves to be the "House of David", when altogether too many of these people teach their own children that the Bible is just a bunch of silly "legends"?[62]

---

[61] "Abram" was the birth name of the patriarch Abraham. God re-named him "Abraham", which is a translatable ancient Semitic phrase, said to mean "father of many nations" (or "father of a multitude").

[62] The irony and the tragedy of this is lost upon the most liberal branches of Judaism. What claim can Jews have to the land of Israel except a Bible-based claim? Yet, while teaching from one side of their mouth that Israel is "theirs" by virtue of their being the risen "House of David", with the other side they teach their children that the Bible is a heavily edited and altered document, which came not from God but from the hands of redactors. According to this absurd view, the purpose of altering the Bible was the same for Israel as for all who would re-write history, namely the advancement of wealth and military power.

It would be better for Israel to be given back to Muslims who pray five times a day to Allah, than that it be held perpetually by the unaffiliated, who revere Karl Marx and the wealth of the New World Order more than the Torah.

In order for the current Nation of Israel to survive, it must willingly put itself under the yoke of Torah Law. The Law under Qur'an is almost identical, and the teachings of Christianity change very little. But the "teachings" of the secular politicians and judges of current Israel are inadequate to rule over the Nation of God.

If Israel was under the Law — the true Law, from the Bible — then there would be no non-kosher food in the country. All males would be circumcised, according to the tradition of their religion. No store could be open on the Sabbath day. No "alternative life styles" contrary to Torah could be legal.

I should perhaps emphasize that these sorts of laws are not for the nations around Israel. How the people of the world choose to live their lives is up to them, and they will rise or fall according to their choices. But there must be *one* place in the world where the true Law prevails, and that one place is Israel.

If and when all these things come to pass, then Israel will be proven to indeed be the risen House of David. But what sort of House will it be? "Jewish"? "Christian"? Or "Muslim"?

According to the precepts recorded in the present book, when the scriptures of the three are read according to their most plain interpretations, and when their Laws are faithfully adhered to, there is no conflict. The question is not which of the three religions people belong to, but whether or not each person *obeys* the Law of their own religion, in accordance with the words of Yeshua:

> "...*whosoever* shall do the will of my Father which is in heaven, the same is my brother, and sister, and mother.
> Matthew 12:50

If you believe this in your heart, then you are *already* a citizen of Greater Israel. This nation does not come into existence through an act of any secular court, or through a military conquest, or through a U.N. resolution. It comes into existence through faith, since it has already been decreed by the LORD, and requires no further acts of men to establish. All you have to do is believe — and, of course, be prepared to act upon your beliefs, when called upon to do so.

I say that these principles are self-evident. If all who believe in God and His Law agree with me, then we ought to get together to perform the greatest spiritual exercise in 2500 years — the return of the Ark of the Covenant to the Temple in Jerusalem.

II. The Ark of the Covenant and the Third Temple

It is the most fervent hope of innumerable Jews and Christians that the Third Temple be built in our lifetimes. The Temple has a single overriding purpose: to house the Ark of the Covenant. That was the purpose of Moses' Tabernacle, and that was the purpose of both the First and Second Temples.

In the courtyard surrounding the Temple the priests are supposed to be offering daily sacrifices (animal, vegetable and liquid), and special sacrifices on the Sabbaths, New Moons and Festivals. Each and every one of these sacrifices is referred to in the Bible as "ḥaq olam", which means "eternal statute". This means they are to be offered to God forever and ever, regardless of what social changes or scientific "advances" occur in the world. Obviously, we are in default in that these sacrifices, due on a daily basis forever, have *not* been offered for 2,000 years. If it pleases you to say "Christ is my sacrifice", by all means say it, but he who said...

> **Verily I say unto you, Till heaven and earth pass, not one jot or one tittle shall pass from the law, till all be fulfilled.**
> Matthew 5:18

...is not the one who will advise you to renege on the Temple sacrifices. It is therefore absolutely certain that when the Third Temple is built, these sacrifices will resume.

Those who object to the sacrifice of a few animals to God betray their profound lack of faith in so objecting. The fast food chains have given up even trying to count the number of animals *killed* to satisfy your craving for food, throwing up their hands in despair and simply saying "billions and billions served". But a few animals sacrificed to God? "Murder", the same people say. Meanwhile the newspapers of the world report *human* murder on an unimaginable scale, day after day after day. No one seems to care[63], because each person thinks the innumerable human murders are "someone else's" crime, and "someone else's" business; certainly *not* theirs.

The prophet Hosea dealt with this absurdity 2,700 years ago, saying...

---

[63] Except, of course, when the murder strikes home. It's extraordinary how impassioned the pleas for "justice" become, when the murderers come into the homes of those who otherwise wouldn't have cared, or who, worse still, would have wasted their sympathies on the perpetrator and his "problems", often forgetting entirely about the victims.

They that kill men, kiss calves.[64]

Hosea 13:2

Do you understand what this means? The same false logic can be seen today, where animal rights are fiercely protected, but human criminal murderers are almost never executed, and rarely even kept in prison for very long. Furthermore, the abortion of human children, right up to the moment of birth, is not merely condoned, but proclaimed to be a form of "freedom". These things demonstrate, with frightening clarity, that our society has gone insane from lack of faith.

Although few would agree, I say nevertheless that the re-instituting of the Temple sacrifices would be the beginning of world peace. Peace, *shalom* in Hebrew, can only come from God, and God requires that these sacrifices be done[65]. No peace has ever come, or ever will come, from the greedy and faithless minds of men, no matter how "enlightened" by book learning.

It is therefore essential, if there is ever to be world peace, that the Third Temple be built, because biblical law forbids the Temple sacrifices from being done anywhere but the courtyard surrounding the Temple. And the Third Temple requires the Ark, because the housing of the Ark is it's sole function — no sacrifices or other religious observances take place within the Temple building itself.

How can the Third Temple be built? The spot where it will be is currently occupied by the Muslim Dome of the Rock. Many Jews and Christians eagerly desire to raze the Dome, to make way for what they perceive to be an exclusively Judeo-Christian Temple, built according to biblical specifications[66].

---

[64] This is the Masoretic reading. The ever-popular King James Bible renders this passage "Let the men that sacrifice kiss the calves", which is a sanitized but unlikely interpretation of the Hebrew. The Hebrew phrase which we have interpreted "they that kill men" is transliterated "zovḥai adam", where "adam" simply means "man" (and in fact is the very name of the first man, Adam, of Adam & Eve fame). "Zovḥai" is an adjective which means "one who kills" (where "kills" can in some cases refer to animal sacrifice). So "zovḥai adam" is a "man who kills". The additional King James words "**Let the**..." (*i.e.,* "**Let the** men that sacrifice...) are drawn out of thin air by that edition's ever-inventive translators, and are not found in the Hebrew original.

[65] Please note that the sacrifices are not a "gift" to God, who has no need of anything physical. All who have thought and written on this subject concur: The benefit of these sacrifices accrues to *us*. In defaulting on them for 2,000 years, we have merely deprived *ourselves*, not God, of these benefits.

[66] These specifications are given in their original form, *i.e.*, for Solomon's first Temple, in I Kings, Chapters 5-7, and in future form, *i.e.*, for the Third Temple, in Ezekiel, Chapters 40-47.

I cannot understand the logic behind this. The existence of the Dome has kept the Temple Mount holy, and consecrated to God, for 1,300 years[67]. If it had not been there, what profane goings-on might have taken place instead? And why, therefore, would anyone desire that it be removed?

If any additional Temple construction is to be done, it ought to be done as an addition to the Dome of the Rock, or in such a manner as to incorporate the Dome into it.

If that is architecturally impossible, then the Third Temple can still be built employing the masonry of the Dome of the Rock. It goes without saying that any such building will have to receive the approval of the Dome's Muslim landlords, who will surely not withhold their consent if the building is consistent with the principles taught by the Prophet Muḥammad.

You may say that is "impossible", *i.e.,* that the Muslims will never give such consent. If so, you are totally wrong about this. The reason you think this is because you believe that the Temple is a "private" temple for your people only, and not for them. Well, it *is* for them. It's for everyone. All the persons involved in the biblical chapters which deal with the First and Second Temples are revered figures in Islam as well as Judeo-Christianity. The Temple will not have any Names or images inscribed upon it, and therefore the answer to the question "*Whose* Temple is it?" is "No one's". It's God's Temple.

Furthermore, there are numerous biblical passages which prove that the followers of the Prophet Muḥammad (identified by passages alluding to "Ishmael", "Kedar" and "Nabioth"), *when they follow the Law,* are greatly beloved by God; even more so than Israel at certain times in history. This subject, however, is beyond the scope of this book.

III. How can the Ark be returned to Israel?

So that no stones are left unturned, we might first ask, "Can a Third Temple be built *without* the Ark?" I suppose it's not impossible, but I doubt it will ever happen. God only knows. But where is the Ark, anyway?

---

[67] Israel maintained the Temple Mount for 300 years, from Solomon to the first Diaspora of 600 BC, then about 500 years more, from the building of the Second Temple (about 500 BC) to the beginning of the Christian Era. Even in total (800 years) the record pales in comparison to the unbroken 1300 year term of the current Muslim landlords. So, although the Muslims were not scrupulous in carrying out the original Law of Moses, which has been maintained in its entirety only by Israel, they certainly have been scrupulous in maintaining the holiness of the Temple Mount. The record speaks for itself – they have done a good job, and should continue doing it.

It appears that the Ark has been in the safekeeping of Ethiopian Coptic Christians for over 2,000 years (see the end of Chapter 10). It cannot be seized by force. People *have* tried. The last person to do so was not Hitler (as the movie "Raiders of the Lost Ark" falsely suggested), but Mussolini. Obviously, he failed.

Those familiar with the Ethiopian Church inform me that their priests will not release the Ark until Christ returns. This may be a mistake on their part, since antichrist must come first. Concerning the End Times, Yeshua (Jesus) said...

> **When ye therefore shall see the abomination of desolation, spoken of by Daniel the prophet, stand in the holy place — whoso readeth, let him understand.**
>
> Matthew 24:15

Yeshua was referring to a passage from the Book of Daniel which describes a singularly evil man:

> **And he shall confirm the covenant with many for one week: and in the midst of the week he shall cause the sacrifice and the oblation to cease, and for the overspreading of abominations he shall make it desolate, even until the consummation, and that determined shall be poured upon the desolate.**
>
> Daniel 9:27

This is one of the biblical passages which defines the very concept of "antichrist", a character who is charismatic beyond all reckoning, and who sweet-talks the whole world into revering him. The Hebrew word translated "week" in the above passage is actually the word "seven", generally accepted to mean 7 years. Therefore, the antichrist will reign in apparent conformity with Law for 3½ years (*i.e.,* up to the "midst of the week"), then show his "true colors" by terminating the Temple sacrifices and rebelling against God.

The timing of Christ-antichrist is given in Daniel, Chapter 7, which teaches that *antichrist comes first.* He is described as the fourth of four beasts in Daniel's vision:

> **The fourth beast shall be the fourth kingdom upon earth, which shall be diverse from all kingdoms, and shall devour the whole earth, and shall tread it down, and break it in pieces.**
>
> Daniel 7:34

The fourth beast is given dominion for a time, but is defeated by "one like the Son of man (*i.e.,* Christ) [who] came with the clouds of heaven, and came to the Ancient of days (*i.e.,* God)" (Daniel 7:13). In sharp distinction to antichrist, the Son of man's dominion, *i.e.,* Christ's dominion, is "an everlasting dominion, which shall not pass away" (Daniel 7:14).

We thus learn that antichrist comes *before* Christ, and sits in the Temple, making himself appear to be a god. Some say that it is the antichrist who actually *builds* the Temple, although that remains in the realm of conjecture. Be that as it may, the existence of a Third Temple strongly implies that the Ark is *already there* when antichrist arrives.

Can it be otherwise? That is, might there be a Third Temple *without* the Ark? Not likely, but perhaps possible. Concerning the End Times, the prophet Jeremiah said...

> **And it shall come to pass, when ye be multiplied and increased in the land, in those days, saith the LORD, they shall say no more, The Ark of the Covenant of the LORD: neither shall it come to mind: neither shall they remember it; neither shall they visit it; neither shall that be done any more.**
> Jeremiah 3:16

This implies that we shall, some day, come to be so totally accepting of the Word of God that visible symbols such as the Ark will no longer be necessary. It also implies that the issue will be moot, because the Ark will no longer be present anyway.

But will this happen *before* the prophecies of Daniel are fulfilled? It's not for me to say, but each of us can have an opinion, and mine is "no Ark, no Temple".

Therefore, I will say that the best, and most-straightforward interpretation of scripture is that the Ark must return to Jerusalem before the other End Times prophecies can be fulfilled.

What in the world will persuade the Ethiopian high priests, who have faithfully guarded the Ark for about 2,000 years, to move it out of safekeeping to Israel, a land currently torn by war?

I can perceive two answers to this question. The first arises from a logical argument. If the Ethiopians have become so attached to the Ark that they simply cannot let go of it, then they may themselves bring about a fulfillment of the above-referenced prophecy of Jeremiah. That is, if a Third Temple is built, and the Ethiopians refuse to have anything to do with it, then people will have no choice other than to implement the teachings of Jeremiah, and permanently stop inquiring about the Ark. This could have the effect of permanently establishing the Ark as nothing more than a museum relic, with no important future role in the world.

But theirs a far better answer. According to the Bible, only a "Kohen Gadol", which means "High Priest"[68], is permitted to even see the Ark, much less touch it. The Bible teaches that only a direct hereditary descendant of Aaron, the brother of Moses, can serve as Kohen Gadol.

Now, let's talk for a moment about Jewish genealogy. Essentially all modern Jewish genealogies trace themselves back to Rashi, an esteemed French medieval Torah commentator. Rashi, in his day, claimed to be a descendent of Hillel, a towering figure in Torah commentary in the first century of the Christian Era, but this latter genealogy has been entirely lost. And Hillel, in his day, claimed to be a descendant of Solomon, which genealogy is also entirely lost. Therefore, although it's possible for a Jewish man to at least attempt to trace his roots to David and Solomon — giving him the right to proclaim himself to be of the "line of Messiah" — all such genealogies must be held to be unproven, because the well-documented family trees in no case go back more than 1,000 years.

Difficult though Davidic genealogies are to trace, that pales in comparison to the difficulty of tracing genealogies back to Aaron. First of all, it is highly probable that the majority of current Jewish Kohens are descended from converts. If, in fact, there exist a few true descendants of Aaron among today's Kohens, there would be no way to establish that with anything even approaching certainty.

The point is this: If a Third Temple were built tomorrow, the question of *who*, among today's Ashkenazi or Sephardic Jews, would be the legitimate High Priest, to minister in Aaron's stead, and to preside over the Temple sacrifices, would be an impossible question to persuasively answer.

What about the genealogy of the "Guardian of the Ark" in Ethiopia (see the end of Chapter 10)? Unlike Israel, Ethiopia, until recently, has been very stable politically. Its Falasha Jews have lived there since the dawn of biblical history (with Ethiopia receiving prominent mention from the beginning of the Book of Genesis onward), and, after the nation converted to Christianity in the 4th century of the Common era, it remained steadfastly Christian up to the present day, rejecting the Islamic conversions which rocked other African nations after the death of the Prophet Muḥammad.

A nation such as Ethiopia, then, has the stability of tradition necessary to trace genealogies back over long periods. The famed Emperor, Haile Selassie, for example, claimed to have had a reliable family tree tracing back to Solomon, and many people accepted it. So the question is, "Is the Guardian of the Ark a

---

[68] "Kohen" means "priest", and "Gadol" means "large", or "great".

Kohen?". That is, "Is the Guardian of the Ark a descendant of Aaron, brother of Moses, High Priest of Israel?"

The answer to this question is so overwhelmingly important that I shall repeat it in Amharic, the language of Ethiopia[69]:

ተቀብቶ የተሾመው የኪዳን ታቦት ጠባዊ

የሙሴ ወንድም አሮን የሲቀ ካህናት ዘር ነው ?

Why do I say this question is important? If the Guardian of the Ark has a believable genealogy tracing him back to Aaron[70], then he *is,* by default, already the High Priest of Israel! That is, in that instance, he would have the hereditary right to the post, and, having been caring for the Ark, he would also have the right of possession, which, as an old saying goes, "is nine-tenths of the law".

Because Kohen Gadol is biblically-defined as an hereditary position, only his offspring, or, in the absence of offspring, his nearest blood relative, could legally inherit his title after his death.

In other words, if the Ethiopian priests brought the Ark back to Jerusalem, the Guardian of the Ark and his descendents would reign as High Priests of Israel in perpetuity, at least until one of them voluntarily married outside his race.

Think of what this would mean. Control of the Law, the Ark, and the Temple Mount would be divided between Jews, Christians and Muslims, as well as between whites, Arabs and Negroes. This arrangement would be the very microcosm of world peace, and would symbolize the brotherhood of man in a way that could not possibly have even been conceived of in the minds of men, much less executed.

Consider the Law. The Nation of Israel would have to be under Jewish Law, which would have to remain under the control of the current Jewish leadership (*i.e.,* the Ashkenazi and Sephardic Chief Rabbis), because only the Jews have respected the entire law. The Christians have only paid lip service to most of it, and the Muslims have rejected it entirely in favor of Islamic Law, which only restates part of it.

---

[69] I wish to thank Father Gabre Silaas Tibebu Taye (ገብረ ሥላሴ ትበቡ), of St. Mary of Zion Ethiopian Orthodox Church in New York, for reviewing and correcting my fledgling Amharic grammar.
[70] As we saw, in Chapter 4, that the number of descendents of David is very large, so must be the number of descendents of Aaron. Proving that lineage persuasively, however, may not be easy.

The Temple Mount would have to remain under the control of its current Muslim landlords, because only the Muslims have proven that they can keep the Temple Mount holy to God. When it was under Jewish control, it was permitted to fall into the hands of the enemies of God, namely the Babylonians and Romans.

And the Ark would have to remain under the care of black Ethiopian Christians, because they alone have kept it for 2,000 years, and the Guardian of the Ark would be the only man with a sufficiently credible claim to the High Priesthood. Since the Priesthood is passed according to Jewish laws of inheritance, the High Priesthood would remain in Ethiopian hands for as long as they chose to hold on to it.

This solution to the building and maintenance of the Third Temple, and the performance of the mandatory rites associated with it, has an almost fairy-tale beauty and perfection to it. But it requires that the current Guardian of the Ark be a Kohen. If not, then the Ethiopians will not bring the Ark back to Jerusalem, because they will fear — and rightfully so — that as soon as it was returned, it would be seized, as they themselves seized it from Falasha Jews in the early Christian era.

Without the Ark, this plan has two major flaws. In the first place, I don't think the Temple can be built without it. Secondly, without an Ethiopian High Priesthood, there would be no obligatory role for either Christians or blacks in Greater Israel, which is an inherently unstable situation, since Greater Israel cannot exist without a total acknowledgment of Messiah, something which is not otherwise going to come from either Jews of Muslims anytime soon.

Appendix 1

Is Ishmael *really* a "wild ass"?

A rejection of the common translation of Genesis 16:12, argued from the Hebrew

For Torah-literate Jews (and Christians as well, for that matter), the introduction to Islam takes place at a very early age. This introduction, which sets the stage for all future opinions, consists of the first reading of Genesis 16:12.

This passage makes a statement about Ishmael, the son of Abraham, the brother of Isaac, and—according to Arab tradition—the co-founder (with his father, Abraham) of the religion of Islam:

וְהוּא יִהְיֶה פֶּרֶא אָדָם יָדוֹ בַכֹּל וְיַד כֹּל בּוֹ

This is "traditionally" translated:

> "And he shall be a wild ass of a man; his hand shall be against every man, and every man's hand against him..."

This is a scathing condemnation of Islam, since it portrays its founder as having the nature of a beast. There is no possibility of peace in Israel under these circumstances, since no Jew will permit an animal to have any say in the future of the nation; nor will the Muslims leave voluntarily. War is thus absolutely inevitable.

But is this *really* what it says? Let us look at the original Hebrew, which has no vowels, and reconsider this passage according to traditional Hebrew grammar:

והוא יהיה פרא אדם ידו בכל ויד כל בו

Appendix 1: Is Ishmael *really* a "wild ass"?

If this un-voweled Hebrew was given to Israeli grammar school students, how would they interpret it? First of all, let us consider the word בכל. The Hebrew preposition בּ usually means "in" or "with". Therefore, the most plausible interpretation of ידו בכל is: "his hand (shall be) *with* everyone". Not "*against* everyone"!

Langenscheidt's Hebrew Dictionary gives the following possible meanings for בּ : "In, at, to, on, among, with, towards; according to, by, because of." Can it ever mean "against"?

The answer is "yes". In certain special cases it can indeed mean "against". A perfectly representative example of a sentence in which בּ can mean "against" is found in Deuteronomy 19:15, where Moses says:

$$\text{לֹא יָקוּם עֵד אֶחָד בְּאִישׁ לְכָל עָוֹן}$$

...which is interpreted **"One witness shall not rise up *against* a man for any iniquity..."**. But the word יָקוּם is defined by Langenscheidt's Hebrew Dictionary as "to rise up *against*", and the prefix בּ in the word בְּאִישׁ does no more than define who it is *with* whom we are "rising up *against*".

The following is a list of passages in the yearly Torah-Haftorah cycle within which the Hebrew prefix בּ is properly translated "against":

> **Exodus 9:17, Exodus 14:25, Exodus 32:29, Lev 17:10, Leviticus 20:3,5,6; Leviticus 24:16,20; Leviticus 26:17, Numbers 21:7, Deuteronomy 2:15, Deuteronomy 11:17, Deuteronomy 13:10 Deuteronomy 19:15, Deuteronomy 25:18, Deuteronomy 29:19, Judges 11:12, Ezekiel 38:21, Hosea 13:9, Zechariah 3:2.**

An analysis of these passages reveals that בּ, by itself, never means "against". I shall leave it as an exercise to the interested reader to look these references up, and to persuade himself that the inseparable prefix בּ acquires this meaning only in a context where the "against-ness" is provided by another word or words in the verse.

The analogy to English is very good in this case. If we say that we are "with" someone, this almost invariably means that we are *for* him, not against him. For example, the common expression

"God be with you..."

...surely means "may God be *for* you" (not "may God be *against* you"!). But if we say:

"I shall fight *with* you..."

...then we have, in English, an example of the use of the word "with" to mean "against", for if we fight *with* someone, then we are *against* that person. But the sense of "against-ness" is provided by the word "fight", not by the word "with"!

The parallel to Hebrew is quite exact. In each of the above-cited examples, the inseparable prefix, ב, takes on the meaning "against" either because there's some other word in the passage which provides that meaning, or else because the context makes that meaning clear.

This is not so in Genesis 16:12. There are no words in the verse which suggests "against-ness", and, as we shall shortly see, the context not only fails to support that meaning, but, on the contrary, essentially rules it out.

Application of the same logic shows that the most plausible interpretation of ...

וִיד כל בו

...is: "and every man's hand (shall be) *with* him". Not "*against* him"!

Next, let us consider the word פרא. If we look back two verses, to Genesis 16:10, we see:

And the angel of the Lord said ... "I will greatly multiply thy seed, that it shall not be numbered for multitude."

Viewed in this light, the word פרא takes on an entirely different significance. The Hebrew word ...

פָּרָא

means "to bring forth, to bear fruit". Although this word is still found in modern Hebrew dictionaries, it seems that the preferred form of the verb, these days, is...

פָּרָה

...(note the different last letter), which has the same meaning. One can only speculate as to why this latter form has come to prevail.

Appendix 1: Is Ishmael *really* a "wild ass"?

Now, the participle form of פָּרָא is פּוֹרֵא. But in the Bible, the וֹ (the letter *vav*) is usually omitted from participles, so we would expect to see פרא (*i.e.,* פֵּרָא). Anyone who wishes to dispute this grammatical principle, as it applies to Genesis 16:12, will be hard-pressed to make a case, because *the very next verse*, Genesis 16:13, features the word דֹּבֵר (the participle of the Qal form of the verb דָּבַר, "to speak"). Note that there is no וֹ (vav). The participle form of the "modern" form of our key verb, *i.e.* פָּרָה, may also be seen in the Torah (see, for example, Deuteronomy 29:17). It is pointless to deny that the vav is usually omitted in participles in the Torah.

Since God says, in our passage (Genesis 16:10), that He will "greatly multiply" [Ishmael's] seed, so that it "shall not be numbered for multitude", we must ask which is the most plausible interpretation of

פרא אדם

Does it mean "a wild ass of a man", or does it mean "a fruitful man"? In the context of the passage, it can have only one plausible interpretation:

"...a fruitful man..."

Our suspicions are further aroused when we consult the Brown, Driver and Briggs lexicon (BDB), to find out where in the Bible — other than Genesis 16:12 — פֶּרֶא occurs in a setting in which it really *does* mean "wild ass". BDB gives the following:

> **Psalm 104:11, Isaiah 32:14, Jeremiah 2:24, Jeremiah 14:6+, Hosea 8:9+, Job 6:5, Job 11:12, Job 24:5, Job 39:5.**

So the word occurs in the Psalms, the Prophets and Job. Note that there is *no use of the word anywhere in the Torah!* (Unless Genesis 16:12 is considered to be such a use). In general then, it can be said that the word פֶּרֶא , meaning "wild ass", *does not appear in Hebrew literature until a thousand years after the death of Ishmael!*

What other contextual evidence is there which confirms that correct vowel points would render the word פָּרָה ("fruitful")? We have already seen that two verses above, in Genesis 16:10, God says to Hagar, **"I will greatly multiply thy seed, that it shall not be numbered for multitude"**. Is this not synonymous with "fruitful"? If we now look ahead slightly, to Genesis 17:6, we see God blessing Abraham with the following words:

וְהִפְרֵתִי אֹתְךָ בִּמְאֹד מְאֹד

Here we see the Hifil form of the same verb, פָּרָא (= פָּרָה) to inform us that God will make Abraham "fruitful". *Fruitful,* not "ass-like"!! Again, a few verses down (Genesis 17:20), God addresses Ishmael in the same manner, promising to make him "fruitful" also, according to the words:

... וְהִפְרֵתִי אֹתוֹ

This again is the Hifil form of the verb פָּרָא (= פָּרָה) to reiterate the message of Genesis 16:10, where God told Hagar "I will greatly multiply thy seed, that it shall not be numbered for multitude".

The equivalence of פָּרָא and פָּרָה is further evidenced in Hosea 13:15 (Haftorah Vayyetze for Ashkenazim), where we see the word יַפְרִיא , which BDB identifies as the Hifil form of פָּרָה, imperfect, 3rd person masculine, **"as if from** פרא**"** (!).

If we now employ the most plausible interpretation of the word פרא, and utilize the standard grammar of the preposition ב , we arrive at the following new interpretation of Genesis 16:12:

וְהוּא יִהְיֶה פֶּרֶא אָדָם יָדוֹ בַכֹּל וְיַד כֹּל בּוֹ

...which means that what our Bible *really* says about Ishmael is:

"... he will be a *fruitful* man: his hand shall be *with* everyone, and every man's hand shall be *with* him..." (!!)

Appendix 1: Is Ishmael *really* a "wild ass"?

This is a markedly different interpretation than the one which invariably appears in translated editions of the Bible. Why have the translators beguiled us?

In the case of translated editions of the Hebrew Old Testament, the explanation is simple. The ideological descendants of Isaac and Ishmael have been arguing for millennia over the question of exactly with *whom* God made His Covenant. It pleases the Jews to believe that the Covenant was made *exclusively* with Isaac, and calling Ishmael—the founder of Islam—a "wild ass" helps them psychologically to maintain that tenuous belief.

The translators of the various Christian Bibles—even the *Arabic* version—also like "wild ass". If it was possible to do so, the Christians might hate Islam even more than the Jews do, because the Muslims say that Jesus was "only a prophet", and the Christians say that Jesus was God. Since the Crusades, if not earlier, Christianity and Islam have been physically at war. What better way to insult your enemy than to teach your children that God Himself declared him to be a "wild ass"?

Why, however, do the *Muslims* put up with the "wild ass" subterfuge? One would think that Islamic scholars, many of whom would have no difficulty at all with the simple Semitic points of grammar we raise here, would have long since come to the rescue of Ishmael's tarnished reputation. But they don't. I can only guess why, but it's an educated guess.

The leaders of Islam have greatly prospered by vigorously maintaining a complete separation of their flocks from those of Judaism and Christianity. The official basis for this separation is the [false] teaching that Islam has *replaced* the former religions, and is the only valid Word of God remaining in the world. The essential core of this teaching is that the earlier scriptures have been *corrupted by man,* and that it was therefore necessary for Allah (God) to reveal His truths to another messenger—Muḥammad—so that a pure, unspoiled testament could exist in the world.

With respect to Islamic tolerance for the "wild ass" misinterpretation of Genesis 16:12, there are two points of view which may pertain. First of all, the misinterpretation itself may be one of the very corruptions which caused Muslims to reject the Bible. Secondly, if Muslim scholars were to now start a fight over Genesis 16:12, this might give their flocks the impression that they consider the Bible to be worth fighting over—an impression they surely wish to avoid.

Therefore, even the Muslims put up with the "wild ass". Incredible!

The House of David has thus relied, in part, on falsehood to maintain an image of moral superiority through the millennia. If this House is to rise up again—and scripture assures us that it shall so do—then it can do so only through truth. There is absolutely no room for falsehood, libel, or gratuitous insult in the restoration of the House of David.

Note that the Jewish Bible does not predict a "Jewish" world. On the contrary, Micah said:

> "...in the last days it shall come to pass, that the mountain of the house of the LORD shall be established in the top of the mountains, ... and people shall flow unto it. And many nations shall come, and say, Come, and let us go up to the mountain of the LORD, ... <u>all people will walk every one in the name of *his* god</u>, and we will walk in the name of the LORD, our God, forever and ever."
>
> Micah 4:1-5

Therefore, the Messianic Era called for by all the Prophets of the Hebrew Old Testament is not an era in which everyone "converts to Judaism", but one in which everyone focuses his attention upon Jerusalem; walking, however, in the name of *"his god"*. Exactly how this might come about is not as much of a mystery as it might seem, and will certainly not be to those who have read the present book.

How the Messianic Era will *not* come about, however, is quite evident. It will *not* come about by further libelous attacks upon Ishmael and his descendants. The Bible teaches that Ishmael and Isaac joined forces and buried father Abraham together. It would appear that the founders of Judaism and Islam hated each other far less than their descendants do. It's clear enough that the hatred is largely based upon falsehood, and it's time for it to come to a halt.

The consequences of it *not* coming to a halt will be horrible indeed. It is my fond hope that these consequences will never need to be seen, or even spelled out.

Appendix 2

The Covenant between God and Abraham: with *whom* was it made?

> "In the same day the LORD made a covenant with Abram, saying, Unto thy seed have I given this land, from the river of Egypt unto the great river, the river Euphrates."
>
> Genesis 15:18

This appendix is intended primarily for readers with at least basic training in Hebrew. It is designed, however, to be understandable to any reader who is sufficiently motivated to read the transliterations provided, and to associate them with their English translations.

Let us begin. The quote at the top of this page refers to a rather *large* chunk of land!

It has also been a bitterly disputed chunk of land. Throughout human history, countless lives have been lost in the pursuit of it. *Whose is it?*

Jews and Christians, who rarely agree about anything, are often very much in agreement about one thing: **Arabs have no place in Israel!** In spite of the obvious historical fact of continuous occupation of the above-mentioned land by Palestinian Arab Muslims (and their pre-Muhammadan predecessors) -- at least since the days of the Assyrian conquest of Israel around 700 BC -- these Jews and Christians have concluded that Israel is spiritually "theirs". Sure, a few Arabs can *live* there, but they have no *spiritual* claim to the land.

As the Jews and Christians correctly point out, Muslims trace their descent from Ishmael. Didn't God "give" the land to the descendants of his brother *Isaac?* And isn't Isaac *"them"?*

Setting aside the racial questions which arise from the fact that the ancestors of many of today's Jews, especially the Ashkenazi Jews, were probably *converts* to

Judaism in the Middle Ages, we need to ask ourselves whether the Bible *really* contains an **exclusive** covenant with Isaac in the first place.

And I can tell you already, the answer is "maybe". Or "maybe not". You'll have to decide for yourself. Let's look directly at the relevant passage. Those of you who haven't read the 17th chapter of Genesis ought to read the whole thing. It's short, and it's reproduced here:

Genesis Chapter 17

1. And when Abram was ninety-nine years old, the LORD appeared to Abram, and said unto him, I am God Almighty; walk before me, and be thou perfect.
2. And I will make my covenant between me and thee, and will multiply thee exceedingly.
3. And Abram fell on his face: and God talked with him, saying,
4. As for me, behold, my covenant is with thee, and thou shalt be a father of many nations.
5. Neither shall thy name any more be called Abram, but thy name shall be Abraham; for a father of many nations have I made thee.
6. And I will make thee exceeding fruitful, and I will make nations of thee, and kings shall come out of thee.
7. And I will establish my covenant between me and thee and thy seed after thee in their generations for an everlasting covenant, to be a God unto thee, and to thy seed after thee.
8. And I will give unto thee, and to thy seed after thee, the land wherein thou art a stranger, all the land of Canaan, for an everlasting possession; and I will be their God.
9. And God said unto Abraham, Thou shalt keep my covenant therefore, thou, and thy seed after thee in their generations.
10. **<u>This is my covenant, which ye shall keep, between me and you and thy seed after thee: Every man child among you shall be circumcised</u>**.
11. And ye shall circumcise the flesh of your foreskin; and it shall be a token of the covenant betwixt me and you.
12. And he that is **<u>eight days old</u>** shall be circumcised among you, every man child in your generations, he that is born in the house, or bought with money of any stranger, which is not of thy seed.
13. He that is born in thy house, and he that is bought with thy money, must needs be circumcised: and my covenant shall be in your flesh for an everlasting covenant.
14. And the uncircumcised man child whose flesh of his foreskin is not circumcised, that soul shall be cut off from his people; he hath broken my covenant.
15. And God said unto Abraham, As for Sarai thy wife, thou shalt not call her name Sarai, but Sarah [which means "princess"] shall her name be.

Appendix 2: The Covenant between God and Abraham

16. And I will bless her, and give thee a son also of her: yea, I will bless her, and she shall be a mother of nations; kings of people shall be of her.
17. Then Abraham fell upon his face, and laughed, and said in his heart, Shall a child be born unto him that is an hundred years old? and shall Sarah, that is ninety years old, bear?
18. And Abraham said unto God, O that Ishmael might live before thee!
19. And God said, Sarah thy wife shall bear thee a son indeed; and thou shalt call his name Isaac: **and** I will establish my covenant with him for an everlasting covenant, and with his seed after him.
20. And as for Ishmael, I have heard thee: Behold, I have blessed him, and will make him fruitful, and will multiply him exceedingly; twelve princes shall he beget, and I will make him a great nation.
21. ***But my covenant will I establish with Isaac,*** which Sarah shall bear unto thee at this set time in the next year.
22. And he left off talking with him, and God went up from Abraham.
23. **And Abraham took Ishmael** his son, and all that were born in his house, and all that were bought with his money, every male among the men of Abraham's house; **and circumcised the flesh of their foreskin in the selfsame day,** as God had said unto him.
24. And Abraham was ninety-nine years old, when he was circumcised in the flesh of his foreskin.
25. And Ishmael his son was thirteen years old, when he was circumcised in the flesh of his foreskin.
26. **In the selfsame day was Abraham circumcised, and Ishmael his son**.
27. And all the men of his house, born in the house, and bought with money of the stranger, were circumcised with him.

Discussion

I must direct your attention to verse 10 above, where God says "this *is* my covenant ... every man child among you shall be circumcised". In verse 23 we learn that Ishmael, who was 13 years old at that time, was immediately circumcised (ouch!). Therefore, the Bible says -- in plain Hebrew -- that God has a covenant with Ishmael.

If you are an ill-willed and argumentative sort of person, you could claim that circumcision must be performed on the 8th day of life to be "valid" (see verse 12 above), suggesting the possibility that Ishmael's circumcision, done at age 13 *years* of age, was "untimely". Look, however, at verses 24-26. Abraham was 99 years old the day he and his son Ishmael were circumcised. Would anyone allege that God made *no covenant* with Abraham himself?

Note that Isaac was not yet born!

Although it is therefore certain that a covenant was made with Ishmael, one can still belligerently argue that there's "more than one covenant", *i.e.,* that there exists a "covenant of circumcision", a "covenant of land", a "covenant of dietary laws", etc., etc. Then one can claim that Ishmael was granted the right to have flesh cut away from the tip of his penis at the age of 13, but that he was given no land! Talk about a "raw deal"!

But wait a minute. A complication enters into the picture in verse 21. Here, God says **"*But* my covenant will I establish with Isaac".**

That word *"But..."* disturbs me. It has an *exclusive* ring to it, does it not? Maybe the land really does belong to the descendants of Isaac exclusively. If so, then every Muslim is, at best, a guest, and at worst, an out-and-out invader.

Furthermore, the territorial boundaries given at the head of this appendix (**"from the river of Egypt unto the great river, the river Euphrates..."**) are repeated by Moses centuries later, and are taken deadly seriously by Orthodox Jews, not to mention Evangelical Christians. Now, there are tens of millions of Arab Muslims living in this area today. What's to become of them?

How about a neutron bomb? That will only kill the people, sparing the buildings.

Morally unacceptable? Then what? I think you can see that it would be very desirable to find a Biblically-acceptable formula to mediate the territorial dispute.

Therefore, it would be expedient, to say the least, to find evidence that Muslims have a territorial claim in the Promised Land, so that Jews and Christians don't have to feel obligated to kill them -- because, I can tell you right now -- *they're not moving!*

Let's also not forget that *they* may kill us first. Remember the old saying, "when you go out to seek revenge, dig *two* graves"? Likewise, in the matter of *land-grab* as well, the outcome cannot be guaranteed to be the way *you* want it to be. *Unless*, that is, God Himself *really did* predetermine the outcome.

Did He?

The only way to be sure is to look at the original Biblical text, which means to read it in Hebrew. The vast majority of Jews and Christians, who are non-Hebrew-reading, derive their information about Genesis 17 from translations. We have already seen, in other parts of this book, that translators may lie with impunity when they reach a passage which is politically charged. You can't count on a Jewish or Christian translator to tell the truth about Ishmael, when the translator was taught, from his youth, that Ishmael was a deadly enemy.

So, without further ado, here's Genesis 17:21 in Hebrew:

Appendix 2: The Covenant between God and Abraham

Those of you who don't read Hebrew, be aware that Hebrew is read in the direction *opposite* English, namely right-to-left. There are *five* word here. Let's start by transliterating them into the English alphabet (the hyphens are added to show the syllables):

V'et b'ree-tee a-keem et Yitz<u>ch</u>ak...

(The <u>ch</u> sound is the guttural, like the clearing of the throat, not found in the English language).

Now, let's put these five words into a table for easy reference:

1	2	3	4	5
V'et	b'ree-tee	a-keem	et	Yitzchak
(Direct object marker)	"my covenant"	"I will establish"	(Direct object marker)	"Isaac"

These are the five words, in tabular array. Now bear with me, and let us start not with the 1st, but with the *2nd* word. The 2nd word, "b'ree-tee", means "my covenant".

The 3rd word, "a-keem", means "I will raise up" or "I will establish".

The 5th word, "Yitzchak", is the correct English spelling of the real Hebrew name we Americans (mistakenly) pronounce "Isaac".

Thus, so far, before considering the 1st and 4th words, we have "My covenant—I will establish—Isaac".

The 1st and 4th words, "et", are essentially the same (the 1st "et" has a "V" prefix, which we shall be getting to shortly).

Now "et" is what is called, in Hebrew, the "direct object marker", and it is not literally translated into English. It indicates to the Hebrew reader what word receives the action of the verb. The only verb in the sentence is word #3, "a-keem" ("I will establish"). So, both "b'ree-tee" ("my covenant") and "Yitzchak" ("Isaac") are the direct objects of God's "establishment".

Put it all together and you get something very much like the King James translation:

"*But* my covenant will I establish with Isaac"...

Notice, however, that the word "*But...*" doesn't appear in our Table. Where does it come from?

It comes from that first letter "V-". It is a prefix, consisting of a single Hebrew letter. The letter, in modern Hebrew, is called "vav", and it's written "ו". (Even if you're a non-Hebrew reader, you should have no trouble discerning that the letter "vav", or "ו", is the first Hebrew letter -- on the *right* -- in the all-Hebrew translation above).

The Hebrew letter "vav" ("ו") is equivalent to the English letter "V", and that is how we've transliterated it in the table above. "Vav" is defined by Langenscheidt's Hebrew Dictionary as a conjunction, meaning **"and, and therefore, also, then, yet"**.

Amongst you readers who actually read Hebrew, I trust that none of you will take serious issue with me when I calmly and matter-of-factly state that the usual meaning of "V-" is the first of the dictionary definitions given above, namely **"and"**.

In Hebrew elementary school, when "vav" ("ו") is first introduced to beginning Hebrew students, they are taught that it means **"and"**.

How does that affect our convenant? A lot! If we employ **"and"** instead of **"but"**, then the apparent exclusivity of our verse is lost. Here's what we get:

(V'et b'ree-tee a-keem et Yitzchak) =
"*And* my covenant will I establish with Isaac"...

... which has a vastly different meaning than:

"*But* my covenant will I establish with Isaac"...

The former translation implies that there *is* a covenant -- perhaps even *of land* -- with Ishmael, AND there is also such a covenant with Isaac.

The latter translation implies that there is a covenant -- of some poorly-defined sort -- with Ishmael, BUT the "real" covenant -- *especially* that part involving the land -- is exclusively with Isaac!

Appendix 2: The Covenant between God and Abraham

Langenscheidt's dictionary does not even include "but" as a definition of "vav" ("ו"). In the Bible, however, "vav" ("ו") *is* in fact sometimes rendered "but" by the English translators. However, the contexts in which this is done are unlikely to be contexts in which a life-threateningly important *exclusivity* is being established.

For the critically-exclusive "but", Hebrew has other words. First of all, there's "aval", which in Hebrew is spelled

$$אֲבָל$$

... which means "but, yet". If the Bible had said "**Aval** et b'ree-tee a-keem et Yitzchak", then the correct English translation of the verse would be as King James' agents reported, namely

"*But* my covenant will I establish with Isaac"...

... in the totally exclusive sense of the word "but". That would mean that Ishmael is decidedly *"out"!*

There's an even *stronger* exclusive expression in Hebrew, when one wants to really draw a line. It's transliterated **" kee im "**, and it looks like this in Hebrew:

$$כִּי אִם$$

Among other definitions -- all *exclusive* -- " kee im ", in English, means **"but"** and **"nay but"**. If Genesis 17:21 had been written with " kee im ", then the correct sense of the translation might have been something like this heavily-annotated version:

- 20. "And as for Ishmael, I have heard thee: Behold, I have blessed him ...(etc.) ... and I will make him a great nation" (*only*, however, in 'Arab' territory, not in Israel). (The following is not explicitly stated, but must be assumed to be implied by what follows in the next verse): "Shall I physically bar his descendants from the Holy Land of Israel?"

- 21. "***Nay*** ... (*i.e.*, they will be permitted to dwell there physically on a day-by-day basis, only without "divine" property rights) ... ***but my covenant*** (*i.e.*, territorial covenant) ***will I establish with Isaac*** (only!), which Sarah shall bear unto thee at this set time in the next year."

If the Bible actually had said that, then I would go down myself with a pitchfork and [try to] drive Ishmael out -- *not* because I have anything against Ishmael, but because I have something *for* God.

But the Bible doesn't say that! If we humble ourselves, and deign to employ the most common definition of "vav" ("ו"), we see that the correct translation of the passage is most likely to be:

> 20. And as for Ishmael, I have heard thee: Behold, I have blessed him, and will make him fruitful, and will multiply him exceedingly; twelve princes shall he beget, and I will make him a great nation.
>
> 21. **_And_** my covenant will I establish with Isaac, which Sarah shall bear unto thee at this set time in the next year.

This implies that a covenant already exists with Ishmael, and now an additional one shall be added for Isaac.

As a final logical argument, please return to our translation of Genesis chapter 17 above, and look at verse 19, just two verses above the verse we have been studying:

> And God said, Sarah thy wife shall bear thee a son indeed; and thou shalt call his name Isaac: **and** I will establish my covenant with him for an everlasting covenant, and with his seed after him.

Here the self-same prefix "vav" ("ו") is indeed translated "**and**". Why not "**but**" here also? I guess the reason is that verse 19 does not speak of a covenant with Ishmael, and so there's no need to adopt an unlikely interpretation of the prefix.

Every man must decide this matter for himself. For my part, in consideration of the foregoing facts, I have concluded that the existence of a covenant between God and Isaac is an established fact, and that the existence of a covenant between God and Ishmael is also an established fact. Whether these two covenants are exactly the same, is surely not for me to say. But God's promise will be fulfilled through the children of Abraham, and both Isaac and Ishmael are children of Abraham.

Moreover, the covenant is specifically said to be in the flesh, namely circumcision, and both were circumcised immediately that the opportunity arose to do so. Ishmael was circumcised at 13, because that was his age when God established his covenant with Abraham, and Isaac was circumcised at 8 days, because after Ishmael, all male children were to be circumcised thusly, in their infancy.

It is fitting and proper that Jews and Christians should be in Israel at this time. But anyone who says that Muslim Arabs have no part is seriously mistaken. Attempting to magnify that mistake by military action is a sure recipe for disaster. Don't forget what the LORD said of Abraham in Genesis 12:1:

Appendix 2: The Covenant between God and Abraham

"...I will make of thee a great nation, and I will bless thee, and make thy name great; and thou shalt be a blessing. And I will bless them that bless thee, and curse him that curseth thee: and in thee shall <u>all the families of the earth</u> be blessed."

About the book, and about the author

Ken Biegeleisen, M.D. Ph.D.

"Whoever You *Thought* You Were…You're A Jew!" has been called the "Star of Hope for all Humankind". Although the first edition, written in 1994, attracted little notice in the English-speaking world, it caught the attention of Nobel Prize Nominee Dr. Prof. Hisatoki Komaki, founder of the Komaki Peace Foundation in Tokyo.

Prof. Komaki read the 576-page book in one night, and immediately offered Dr. Biegeleisen the position of American representative for the Foundation; a position formerly occupied by the late double-Nobel Prize laureate Linus Pauling. Komaki also called upon the services of his colleague and distinguished linguist, Prof. Junichi Nakayama, to translate the book into Japanese. This was a labor of love, for which Nakayama received no financial remuneration.

Prof. Nakayama passed away only a few weeks after completing the translation. Upon his death, he was granted a posthumous award by Japan's Emperor Akahito for his lifetime scholarly achievements, of which this translation was one of the last.

Prof. Komaki used Dr. Biegeleisen's book, in Japanese translation, as a text in his post-graduate courses in subjects relating to world peace. It was one of his Komaki Peace Foundation members, Prof. Toru Matsufuji, who wrote that the teachings of that first edition were the "Star of Hope for all Humankind".

Dr. Biegeleisen, has achieved distinction in several fields besides religion, including medicine, molecular biology and music.

In medicine he is known as a practitioner of *Phlebology*, the art and science of treating diseases of the veins. His family has occupied a prominent position in this field for nearly a century. In his youth, he had no attraction to medicine other than family pressure, and he entered the field with great reluctance. He nevertheless managed to achieve significant advances. He organized the nation's Phlebologists into a medical society, which has now evolved into the American College of Phlebology, the primary certifying board for venous diseases. He also pioneered the treatment of vein diseases by fiberoptic catheter-based instruments, now considered the treatment of choice, and used in virtually every hospital in the United States.

Dr. Biegeleisen attended Cornell University and the New York University School of Medicine, where he graduated from the MD-PhD program in 1978. His PhD is in Molecular Biology, and he has been involved in DNA research for many decades. His recent publication of the structure of the Protamine-DNA complex[71] has proven that the world-famous DNA "double helix" is not necessarily the structure of DNA in all living systems. In fact, it may turn out that most DNA inside cells has a non-helical structure.

In addition to having written several other books, and quite a bit of music in various styles, Dr. Biegeleisen has served as a Baal Koree (Torah reader) in synagogues for many years, and has become proficient in reading all three extant Semitic languages: Hebrew, Arabic and Amharic (the language of Ethiopia). He is thus able to read the Bible and Qur'an in the original tongues, freeing himself from the occasionally misleading antics of translators.

---

[71] "The probable structure of the protamine-DNA complex", *Journal of Theoretical Biology*, Vol. 241, August 7, 2006, pp. 533-540.

Index

Abraham, 11 *ff*, 90, 118 *ff*, 146
Ahura Mazda, 41
Al-Ghazali, 208
Al-Haram Mosque, 121
Al-ḥudaybiyah, 162
Alexander the Great, 85
Alfonso VI (Spanish Christian King), 173
Ali, Sonni (King of Songhay), 180
Allah, (comparison with "El"), 134
Al-Mansur (Muslim conquerer), 175
Almohads, 175
Almoravids, 173
American Revolution, 21
Amon, evil King of Judah, 182
Amraphel, 119
Analects, see *Confucius*
Anthony, Saint, of Korma, 207
Antichrist, 240
Antiochus Epiphanes, 85
Archaemenian Empire, 40
Arian Christians, 171
Arius, 129
Arjuna, 46
Ark of the Covenant, 23, 25, 182 *ff*, 237 *ff*7
Aryan, 39
Askia, Muḥammad, 180
Assyrians, 26
Axum, capital of ancient Ethiopia, 183
Babylon, Babylonians, 28, 37, 119
Babylonian Captivity, 28
Batuta, Ibn, 181
Bhagavad-Gita, 46, 111, 190
Bathsheba, 25, 67
Bene-Israel (Indian Jews), 42
Ben Yohai, Simeon, 206
Black Rock, 134
Bombay, 42
Brahman-Atman, 46
Buddha's race, speculation concerning, 43

Canaan, son of Noah, 168
China, 47
Christ, see *Messiah*
Christian Councils, 123 *ff*
Circumcision, 12, 126
Cochin, 42
Comforter, the, 138
Confucius, 49, 51
Covenant (God and man), 117 *ff*, 126, 146, 252 *ff*
Cyrus the Great, 40
Daniel, 40 *ff*, 80, 90, 199 *ff*, 240-1
Dark Ages, see *Middle Ages*
David, King of Israel, 25, 66 *ff*, 99
De León, Moses, 207
Diaspora, Jewish, 28, 70
Divorce, 93
Dome of the Rock, 111, 133, 238-9
Dravidians, 39
Eightfold Noble Path, 195
El Cid, 174
Eldad the Danite, 178
Elephantine Island, 183
Elijah, 26, 86, 135, 216
Enlightenment, 9, 187 *ff*
Ethiopia, 39, 131, 136, 178, 183-4, 242, 243
Ethiopian Church, 183, 240 *ff*
Exodus from Egypt, 23
Fourfold Noble Truth About Suffering, 44, 187 *ff*
Gabriel, 100, 135
Garden of Eden, 7
Ghana, medieval Kingdom of, 178
Gibraltar, 171
Goliath, 25
Golden calf, 23
Golden Rule, 49, 152
Goths, 171
Guardian of the Ark, 183, 242 *ff*
Hagar, 13, 120
Ham, son of Noah, 167
Hammurabi, see *Amraphel*

Index

Hanukkah, 85
Hebrew language, 13
Herod, 90
Hezekiah, 28
Hijrah, 136
Hillel, 50, 93, 242
Hindu religion, 46
Holy war, see *Jihad*
Hosea, 237
Hunafa, 138
Hypocrites, 157, 159 *ff*
India, 39, 42 *ff*
India, ancient gods of, 39
Iran, 39
Irving, Washington, 176
Isaac, 12, 90
Isaiah, 28, 36, 89, 105
Isaiah Chapter 11, 102
Isaiah Chapter 53, 77
Ishmael, 12, 134
Israel, boundaries, End Times, 234
Jain religion, 45
Jeremiah, 36, 137, 203
Jericho, Battle of, 150
Jewish genealogy, 242
Jesuits, 47
Jesus, see *Yeshua*
Jihad ("holy war"), 146 *ff*
Joseph of Arimathaea, 96
Joseph (father of Yeshua), 89
Joseph (son of Patriarch Jacob), 105
Joshua, 150
Josiah, 28, 182
Judah, Tribe of, 26
Judah, Kingdom, see *Southern Kingdom*
Judas (Maccabee), see *Maccabee*
Ka'bah, 121, 134
Kabbalah, 206
Kankan Musa (King of medieval Mali), 180
Karma, 188
Khadijah, 134
Kaifeng Jews (China), 47
Karaite sect, 82
Kedar (son of Ishmael), 137
Knights Templar, see *Templars*
Koran, see *Qur'an*
Krishna, 46, 111
Lao-tsu, 48
Lost tribes of Israel, 26
Love thy neighbor, 50
Maccabees, 84
Mahabharata, 46
Mahavira, 45, 195
Mahdi (Muslim Messiah), 66
Maimonides, 172
Malabar Coast Jews, 42
Mali, medieval Kingdom of, 179
Manasseh, evil King of Judah 26, 182
Mary (mother of Yeshua), 89
Masoretes, 14
Medes, 40
Medieval times, see *Middle Ages*
Medina, 136
Messiah, 73 *ff*, 98 *ff*
Messiah, son of David, 102 *ff*
Messiah, son of Joseph, 105 *ff*
Middle Ages, 170 *ff*
Monasteries, 207
Moors, 170 *ff*
Mormons, 34
Moses, 21, 23 *ff*, 74, 112, 115, 146
Muhammad, 134 *ff*
Nebuchadnezzar, 28
Nestorius, 129
New Covenant, 203
New World Order, 1, 21, 64, 210, 211 *ff*
Noah, 167
Noble Truth, see *Fourfold Noble Truth*
Obadiah, 106
Oriental religion, appearance, 28
Pachomius, Saint, 207
Paracletos, see *Comforter*
Paul, 123 *ff*
People of the Book, 111, 157
Persia, 39
Pharisees, 88

Pillars of Hercules, 171
Pontius Pilate, 97
Protamine-DNA complex, 262
Qur'an, 140 *ff*
Rachael, 105
Rashi, 242
Rebekah, 90
Rebellion, against God, 7
Reincarnation, 188
Rome, 87
Roosevelt, Franklin, 194
Sadducees, 88
Sarah, 13, 120
Samaria, 26
Samuel, 24
Sanhedrin, 95
Saul, 24, 99
Sennacherib, 28
Six hundred year cycles of religious history, 20
Socrates, 34, 54 *ff*, 152, 214, 218
Solomon, 25, 67
Songhay, medieval Kingdom of, 180
Southern Kingdom (Judah), 26, 28, 36, 53, 182
Spain, Muslim (Middle Ages), 171 *ff*
Spirit of Truth, see *Comforter*
Stephen (Christian martyr), 114
Strabo, 38
Sufi (sect of Islam), 207
Tao, 48
Tao Tê Ching, 48
Talmud, 40, 47, 75, 82, 97, 105, 107
Tariq ibn Ziyad, 171
Tchiang (Indian Jews), 42
Templars, 183
Temple (in Jerusalem), 34, 26, 28, 37, 41, 86, 87, 91, 100-101, 182 *ff*, 237 *ff*
Third Temple, see *Temple*
Timbuktu, 34, 170, 175, 177 *ff*
Time line of religious history, 20
Transmigration of the soul, see *reincarnation*
Tree of Knowledge of Good and Evil, 8, 198

Twelve Tribes of Israel, 22
Tzion, (Zion), 25
Umayyad world Islamic government, 173
University of Sankore, 180
Upanishads, 46
Virgin, Hebrew word for, 89
Wild ass, 14 *ff*, 245 *ff*
Wise men, 90
Yaḥya (Muslim conquerer), 173
Yeshua, 73 *ff*, 141 *ff*
Yusuf ibn Tashfin (Muslim conquerer), 174
Za Dynasty, 178
Zalacca, Battle of, 174
Zamzam, well of, 121
Zion...see *Tzion*
Zohar, 207
Zoroaster, 41, 91
Zoroastrianism, rise of, 41

www.ingramcontent.com/pod-product-compliance
Lightning Source LLC
Chambersburg PA
CBHW080534170426
43195CB00016B/2563